T0062984

Karmath Jeevan

Karmath Jeevan
(कर्मठ जीवन)

Passionate About Karma

THE AUTOBIOGRAPHY OF

KRISHAN ANEJA

PARTRIDGE
A Penguin Random House Company

To order additional copies of this book, contact
Partridge India
000 800 10062 62
orders.india@partridgepublishing.com

www.partridgepublishing.com/india

Welcome, my esteemed readers!

I am not a celebrity. I am an unknown person and an old timer, so to say; yet keen to present my story for an impartial evaluation at your hands. I dare to say it is different; a lot educative and enjoyable both.

Please give me the benefit of your patience.

Your frank views are welcome.

Email: aneja.krishanlal@gmail.com

Dedicated to,

My Mother, Amrit Devi,
Always an inspiration to me during her life time and after it.
And,
My beautiful life-partner, Krishna,
Exuberant, untiring and highly self-motivated.

Contents

सदस्य उत्तराखण्ड विधानसभा

हरबंस कपूर
विधायक
पूर्व अध्यक्ष, विधानसभा

230, इन्दिरा नगर कालोनी,
देहरादून–248006
टेलीफैक्सः 91–135–2761622
मोबाईल : 91 9719233999

FOREWORD

I have known Shri. Aneja for quite some time. However, after reading "Karmath Jeevan", I feel happy that I agreed to his request to write a Foreword, "Do Shabd" as they say it in Hindi.

2 I find that the flow of information about his journey is lucid, the script is in simple language, makes an interesting reading and one feels like continuing to read it till end.

3. The book is a tell-tale narrative of how a determined mind can overcome multiple challenges, make a mark in life and achieve what appears to be a big challenge. How a challenge can be met with challenge is the moral of Shri Aneja's success story. How an orphan child, an adolescent refugee keeps pushing ahead and scales great heights is an inspiration for others to follow.

4.The autobiography of Shri Aneja is a shining example of what an individual with focus on sincere hard work, open mind and honesty of purpose pursued with determination can fulfill his/her dreams. In his words; "The basic salt for an individual to be successful is to have a strong will to perform come what may, have patience to neglect/ignore one's own comforts, be able to work out and pursue a grudging routine of hard work every day."

5. A bigger take-away from the book is how a mother can lay a sound foundation for her child's balanced growth which Shri Aneja's mother aptly did. She was his idol, his confidant and helped him in picking up strong values (Sanskars) for an honest life with a determined mind. It epitomizes what an anxious loving mother can do for her children's over-all growth and welfare.

6. What is responsible parenting? The answer lies in few pages in the book. How it blossoms into success is the learning for those aspiring to make a difference in their child's life.

7. The most tragic event in India's recent history was partition of the country in 1947. Millions were uprooted from their hearth and homes and made to run for safety and shelter on the other side of the border. In the midst of holocaust that followed, millions of innocents were butchered. My family also was one of those affected and I had heard a lot about the ghastly events from my elders. But the chapter on partition in "Karmath Jeevan" being an eye-witness account of what the author saw and lived through is a revealing commentary. It captures vividly the sufferings and emotional break-down of the affected people who lost their identity, became refugees overnight in their own country and were forced to live on alms and govt. support in camps.

8. The script rightly mentions that these un-fortunate but brave souls did not cave in and felt a strong urge in their hearts to fend for themselves and start living an honorable self-supporting life, once again as quickly as possible. They called themselves "Pursharthi" (believers in self and hard work) and hated to be addressed as "Sharnarthi"

9."Karmath Jeevan" is not just memoirs of a senior citizen. It is a repository of values that make life meaningful and worth living.

दिनेश कुमार शर्राफ
Dinesh K. Sarraf

अध्यक्षएवं प्रबन्ध निदेशक
Chairman & Managing Director

ऑयलएण्ड नेचुरल गैस कॉर्पोरेशन
Oil and Natural Gas Corporation Ltd.

PREFACE

The navigation of Karmath Jeevan, offers gripping tales of the author's experience during the tragic part of Indian history- the partition of India, and how a peaceful life suddenly transforms itself, when millions are displaced during such appalling period of Indian freedom struggle.

*Krishan's **"Karmath Jeevan"** is an eloquent tribute to his parents especially his mother, who moulds him and other siblings, and inculcates in them strong values at the early age, to face life with a willingness to commit themselves to face any challenges and continue to persist in the face of such difficulties.*

Such a tribute to the long–reaching effects of parent–child relationship captured all through this book will be of immense help for parents and children to strengthen and restore their relationships to build a solid foundation in today's modern day living.

*The narration by Krishan from pre-independence era to the present day life and how his loyalty towards work and engagement with challenges while working for different Companies resulted in shared goals, commitments and achievements. This reaffirms my strong belief that **"Its never what you are, but what you do".***

One of the most powerful messages of 'Karmath Jeevan' is "to have a strong will–power to perform come what may, have patience to neglect one's own comfort" which is the essence of human understanding *"to perform your best and leave the outcome to me"* from the timeless Shrimad Bhagwad Geeta.

Overall, I agree and hope that a disciplined life and principled contributions by the author all throughout his life, brought out in this well written memoir will inspire all the readers and redirect them to remain focused and selflessly contribute in building this society.

(Dinesh K. Sarraf)

Thanks and Gratitude

My wife, Krishna's feelings that my tales of pre-marital and post-marital endeavours/struggles to make it big in life are worth being brought to light was the trigger that encouraged me to lift the pen. And her well-considered affirmation in finally choosing "Karmath Jeevan" as the title of the book out of many others thought off by me set the agenda of the script.

In the first few weeks, when I seriously needed meaningful encouragement to keep pushing ahead, her occasional appreciative comments helped maintain the tempo. Whenever possible, she would spend her free time with me in the evenings and listen to the day's output. This proved to be the booster dose of unmitigated support I sorely needed.

All along in my life, I have been busy reading and interpreting Govt. Rules & Regulations and scripting notes and offering comments in official language. This being my first-ever attempt at writing something of a different genre boosted my morale when my sons, Sandeep and Ashish after going through some initial chapters conveyed; "You have a language & style of your own. It is good." Another significant fall-out during the course of this endeavour has been Sandeep's comments; "Dad, I understand you better now." Ashish, who is away in USA boosted my confidence conveying; "Your initiative is well-appreciated and is meaningful. I am sure; posterity will benefit in many ways." I knew; Sandeep and Ashish who are mature and balanced individuals would not make comments of appreciation just to please me. I felt genuinely happy to receive their well-thought-out responses.

The silent support and huge expectations of success of the book by Sunita, my illustrious daughter is not only a big source of satisfaction for me but also an ominous responsibility too. If I am not wrong, her Dad is her hero and not surprisingly, she is eagerly looking forward to the D-day. I pray; I don't belie her expectations!

I am conscious many book lover acquaintances, friends and relatives are keen to see the final output soon. I am grateful to all of them and hope to present the hard copies to them soon.

Krishan Aneja

Sanjay, my young friend, has been a solid support for me throughout this effort. He is into book-publishing business and is a computer wizard in his own right. His first affirmative nod for the title of the book "Karmath Jeevan" strengthened my resolve not to deviate from it. He says the title aptly sums up my tale of struggles and resultant success. His self-less support is a genuine morale-booster for me. But for his help, I would have given up in desperation and alas, that would have been the sad end of story writing! I owe it to him for helping me for successfully completing the act of writing. And giving the manuscript a final shape by Sanjay is the thought that invigorates my nerve-center and makes me hopeful of bright future for the book.

Yet another brilliant contribution during my days of struggles by Sanjay has been his suggestion that I meet Ms. Ruby Gupta, Head of English Dept. of D.I.T University and seek her guidance. Honestly I am too happy I followed his advice and met this illustrious lady, a renowned author. Her patient listening of my story and giving me valuable tips on dos & don'ts sharpened my vision and boosted my confidence level. I am grateful to Manisha, an Asstt Professor in DIT University and my co-brother's daughter who happily came forward and arranged the meeting with Ms. Ruby Gupta.

My weakness in handling properly the various facilities available in MS Word system could have proved a stumbling block but for the help extended from time to time by Mr. Tribhuvan Mall & Jagjit Singh, my old friends. Both of them would spare time for me out of their busy schedules and relieve me of the tension.

The keen interest shown by my old friends of AG, Punjab Office, Shimla, now in Chandigarh, added to my enthusiasm. In particular, VC Jauhri, stands out as my icon. He is un-happy on the delay and demands that the book should be in his hands sooner the better. I am sorry and have promised him 'no delay' now.

Sincerely,
Krishan Aneja

xvi

INTRODUCTION

My life's journey spanning from childhood on the banks of mighty Indus River in Isa Khel, a town bordering Waziristan, the notorious terror-infested region in Pakistan to Dehra Dun near the holy waves of the Ganges, is a tell-tale description of 'determination winning over adversities.'

Millions were affected by the partition of India and my family was one of those directly hit. We were uprooted, left behind our hearth and home and were lucky to have escaped from the murderous assaults on our lives. All of this had a severe crippling impact on our lives resulting in untold misery and deprivation. Providence had saved us no doubt but survival was a bigger challenge now. Not deterred by the grim situation and big challenges, our elders decided to put us in school in the Refugee camp itself rather than pushing us into streets as petty hawkers. I was eleven then and had passed 5th class in Pakistan. This extraordinary long-term vision of my elders molded my future. The refrain was, "Enable him to pass the High School exam to be eligible for the post of a clerk." This milestone decision shaped my future. This God-sent opportunity made me eligible to make a reasonable beginning in life. Not surprisingly their inspirational lead continued to motivate me all my life.

My journey is the saga of survival and hard-earned progress of a child who lost his father when he was just about 4 years, migrated to India as a hapless and destitute refugee in 1947 yet remained unfazed by challenges, dedicated his life to hard work, picked up odd jobs and continued to pursue higher studies as a private candidate; the aim being survival in the first place and simultaneously pushing ahead for further growth. Starting as a petty rent-collector on commission basis at the young age of 17, I was able to secure first regular job of a Goods Clerk in Railways on merit in the open selection process in the year 1956. That was a reasonable beginning which brought about a sort of stability after arduous struggles of about 10 years. Thus having taken care of two square meals a day one could think of feeling settled. But it was not so for me. I kept pursuing higher studies as a private candidate with a view to achieve more and earn a place of distinction in society. That I was burning with big ambitions was un-known to me but surely I was conscious that higher growth could be achieved only through sincere hard work. "Innovate, look out for and explore various options of growth available in the horizon, deliver more than what is expected" was the Mantra I continued to follow throughout my work-life. And this realization kept pushing me all along. Well, it is not surprising that I achieved what could be the dream of many; rising to the position of General Manager in the prestigious national oil Co of India, ONGC.

My journey is a proof that no matter where you start from, you can go where you want to go. Regardless of some failures on the way, you can achieve the goal for failure is just an event. My journey enforces the belief, "Persist on the chosen path with clarity of purpose and purity of action and thought. Success will be yours."

This book is the result of a call from my inner-self. Its genesis is the conviction that despite extremely difficult conditions faced as a refugee in the first few years after migration to India, I did have the gumption to push ahead continuously to carve out a position of respect for myself in work-place(s) and for my family in society. Quite expectedly, the excitement is palpable down the memory-lane while I am attempting to recall and narrate the sweet and enchanting memories of eventful span of over seven decades of my journey.

I owe it to myself to place on record my respects and deep gratitude to my mother in the first place followed by wise seniors in the family and my beautiful life partner, Krishna, without whose support all what I am boasting of today would not have been possible.

Shall I conclude saying that my journey is not a usual rag to riches story; riches and position acquired through unscrupulous and questionable means. It is different in substance. The journey got enriched /influenced and shaped by my meaningful observational and sifting attitude; pick up and internalize what is of substance. Have faith in self and apply the learning in real life situations.

Clean and open mind is a vital key to success.

PART - I

෪ා ൬

Chapter 1
My Parents; my pride

My Father

My father passed away at the young age of 39/40. He struggled for life after being afflicted with TB, a dreadful disease then. I still remember having seen him lying straight on his clean bed in the front room of the house, always in pensive and peaceful mood and when awake, looking with blank and emotion-less face the happenings around him. Probably he was mindful of the certainty of the inevitable; an end of the long journey of struggle for survival. He had been taken ill at the young age of about 30 years and even after proper care/treatment/struggle of nearly a decade, there was no hope of full recovery. The medical science had not invented till then any sure cure for it. One's life span could possibly be lengthened and living made less painful by living in Sanatoriums in hill stations and eating nutritious and rich diet apart from taking care of hygiene and sanitation. I remember; my mother telling me that all that was necessary and possible was done for his treatment etc. and he could survive for 8-10 years probably because of care and attention given by the family.

I was not fortunate enough to have been close to my father. Knowing little about the nature of his illness, we both (myself and my younger brother) would come closer to him but the seniors would prohibit us from doing so, which surely would have been very painful to him. I was about $3\frac{1}{2}$ yrs. old when he passed away. I don't know exactly how the end came and how the seniors in the family, especially our mother, faced it. We, the young boys, were kept away from all the mourning sessions, though I can recall having seen the gatherings of persons in white attire joining in prayers and listening to scriptures and hymns being rendered by some "Pundit ji". Unlike now, these rituals used to continue for many days and the last prayer/condolence meeting was held on 10th day of expiry.

It is believed in our society that mass community prayers and recitation of scriptures, apart from one's own "Karma" earns for the departed soul a peaceful end and entitles it to enter the heavens, the abode of Gods.

His Persona

I cannot describe him in details because of the lack of proper information. However, from the sketchy details heard from seniors, especially my mother, I believe, he was a man of great principles, an upright person, fearless, sincere and helpful. He was always full of zest for life including during his prolonged illness. He was manliness personified. This attribute was considered to be critical in males and separated men of action, courage and strong determination from the normal males of those times. Such persons occupied high pedestals in society and commanded lot of respect for themselves. Folklore was all praise for manlike behavior which was expected to be a must for persons of high origin.

No temptation, howsoever big, could lure him to the path of greed or unscrupulous business dealings. He was tall in personal conduct and stature like his height. He practiced and lived a life full of virtues.

He was the only son of his parents who were wealthy landlords and chieftain of the village. My grand-father and great grand-father were known as "Pansarees" suggesting they were in the business of herbs and my grand-father was a known practitioner of "Ayurveda". My mother told me that getting married in this high class family of "Pansarees" was a great privilege and she thought herself lucky being a proud member of this famous house-hold. The "Pansarees" owned lot of landed property apart from flourishing business of herbs and owned camels, horses and other useful animals.

4

My father was fond of horse riding and playing a local version of Polo. He did his Matriculation (10th standard) in early twenties; may be between the years 1920-22 at about the age of 20/21 and had a daughter (our eldest sister) by then. He would travel to Mianwali (Dist. HQ) and also to Lahore (State capital) for pursuing his studies. During those days, this academic qualification entitled him to civil service and in fact, he was offered 'Naib Tehsildar's post, which he did not join, for he wanted to be his own master. I remember having heard some senior member of our family (I am not able to recall who) saying that our father refused to work for a billionaire widow's family of Kalabagh, though the family was our distant relation also, for fear of losing his independence. He also didn't like the idea of working for a widow, which could give rise to concocted gossip also. My mother explained that though the acceptance of this assignment could have meant easy money for him because the family had lot of property, were a leading govt. contractors, had lot of influence in society and this association could have opened up for him the avenues of growth and a respectable place in the higher echelons of society yet he refused it saying it was against his inner-call. It didn't click with him. His belief was that this assignment was too good to be lured into it. Mother told me that later some controversies cropped up with regard to this family and our father's position was vindicated.

He was a man of principles, would stand by his words and would not yield to temptations for the sake of making a quick buck. A promise made or a word given must be honored.

He was quite generous and helpful while dealing with the team of his workers. The laborers who were hired on daily basis at the time of harvesting crops had to be fed 'halwa' a pudding made of pure ghee (clarified butter) to their satisfaction at the end of day's work apart from wages in cash even though it was not a norm to do so. All this meant a lot of hard work and fatigue for the ladies of the house. He won't accept any resistance to this idea since in his views, the laborers deserved this nourishment after all day's hard-work. He was straight-forward in his business and personal dealings and would not tolerate arrogance, ill-behavior and other unfair similar actions.

Listening to all such and other similar events from our mother made me proud of him even as a child. I believe, apart from the concept of genetics, which does have an important influence on one's value-system and ethos, listening to such tales reinforces the concept in one's mind.

Well, this is my inheritance and I am proud of it. I cherish it. I love it. I am lucky to have been born to such illustrious parents; who may not have been stinking rich financially but really rich in principles worthy of emulation. This is the real treasure trove if one understands what the intrinsic value of treasure is.

Impact on family with his untimely demise

An arduous journey of struggle for survival started for the family with his departure. We were seven in the family; our mother, two sisters, and four brothers to be taken care of. The eldest male member (my brother Manohar Lal) was about 13/14 years and had just completed his 8th standard; when the burden of winding up the business of our father fell on his shoulders. Hardly had he started knowing the set-up of the business, the whole-sale merchants (Suppliers) from Lahore and Amritsar, the two main distribution centers of north India landed in our city and forcibly carried the merchandise and the shop was empty. Nobody in the family could stop this plundering. On the other hand, the debtors (petty shop-keepers of nearby villages and hawkers) virtually vanished from the scene and even those who could be contacted did not own up any dues against supplies made to them though some details were written in our father's accounts books. There was yet another class of our father's debtors (the borrowers of money whom our father had lent it) most of them denied any such dues.

The poor widow, our mother, was now face to face with serious challenge of survival of the family. It was then that our eldest sister's husband stepped in. He quit his secure job in Bannu and shifted to our town to lend support to the embattled family. His presence at this critical stage provided security and stability to our life.

6

A Mother

"The Mother is held as the object of affectionate reverence in Indian culture. The mother's lap is the first school for every child. It is his/her first temple; mother is the foremost God. Mother is every one's primary wealth. It is the duty of every person to recognize this truth. Everyone must cherish their parents as embodiment of the Divine."

Sri Sathya Sai Baba.

Our mother; courage personified

A true practitioner of Karma, courageous, wise, pillar of strength, savior of her family in distress, never tiring in her efforts to protect her kids, an embodiment of sacrifice and above all, a truly loving and benevolent 'Maa'. Try hard as I may, I fail to comprehend where to begin and where to end while attempting to profile her. I am not sure if my attempt will do justice to the lady as inspiring as her. God-fearing and religious minded, conscious that she was doing doubles in the absence of our father and determined in her resolve to meet the challenges before her, is how I think, would partly describe her personality. Even during our father's life time this lady was in the fore-front (because of his illness) and would handle difficult situations with poise and confidence. She honestly believed he would recover soon and then she would happily retire to her natural abode in the house; the house-hold and the kitchen. Meeting the challenges associated with bread-earner's illness could not deflect her from protecting family's honor. And the real challenge was not to let others know that she was mentally and physically fatigued and really needed some respite. Handling family's affairs single-handedly was no easy job but not for her.

Above all, she was an ideal Indian mother lovingly idolized as 'Mamta ki Moorat' in ancient scriptures and in vast domain of literature; lyrics, poetry and prose, modern and ancient both.

Be my 'Maa' in my next birth if and when I get it. Let me cry on your feet. Enable me to do my part of duty which I missed in this life.

We humbly pray and seek thy blessings!

7

Shri Milawa Ram,
My Father

Shrimati Amrit Devi,
My Mother

Our mother; family's pillar of strength

Due to our father's prolonged illness, the family was already facing severe cash crunch resulting from neglect of his business and very heavy on-going expenditure on his treatment etc. Gradually, all the family reserves were getting depleted in his life time itself. And now his departure was the proverbial last death-knell for the family; the end of all hope. The business creditors suddenly became vocal demanding immediate settlement of their dues while the debtors were nowhere to be seen. There was nobody in the family who could take charge and make attempts to run the business.

A widow with six children, grown up adolescents and kids, without any regular or steady source of income available in hand, was face to face with crisis after crisis every day. The kitchen store was virtually empty each day. To me, the youngest but one amongst her children, it was a mystery as to how she was managing to feed us somehow though it was not exactly what she would want to serve. It was indeed painful for her to be not able to provide us nutritious food items like ghee, eggs, milk and its products like curd, 'Paneer' or other delicacies made of milk. In fact, to keep us warm and protected in harsh winters, we were given tea instead of milk much against her wishes. Common house-hold delicacies like 'Parathas', 'milk-rice pudding etc. was beyond her means, and many a times she regretted it profusely. She had seen very good times and the pain of scarcity being faced now got occasionally reflected in her wails and tears. But the brave woman didn't give up and squarely faced the endless stream of odds and problems with skill and patience. Many a times she would lose her calm and start cribbing but only for a while and soon she would put up a brave face turning her attention to an appropriate proverb. Protecting her children, making attempts to feed them somehow with little resources that she could manage, facing the greedy eyes of creditors and handling them with tact and not revealing any distress in her attitude was her routine now.

Even in such a difficult situation she didn't withdraw us from school. She knew education of her children was their future strength. Truly, she was a visionary. As a kid I didn't realize all this but now that I am trying to figure out the mammoth problems that she faced then, my head bows in reverence to salute her; a homage of a grateful beneficiary.

She had had no formal education herself but surely she knew that proper education was the only option for us. Her reservoir of knowledge was practical wisdom which she utilized adroitly when face to face with some difficult situation. She would handle the difficult situations and inter-personal wrangling etc. between members of the family as also in the neighborhood with ease by quoting from scriptures and proverbs relevant to the issue and thus calm down the tension. Mind it, her proverbs were in colloquial language and I was always enamored of her ability and capacity to rise to the occasion and make it easy for us to accept and appreciate the sayings and bits of practical wisdom.

Her approach to healthy and responsible parenting

Time permitting; she would take us to a world of fantasies and dreams. This used to happen mostly at bed time. The illiterate lady knew how to make her kids comfortable. Often, overlooking the burden of mountains of pending jobs she would sit down with us at bed time, would hug us, kiss us on foreheads, massage our legs, arms and head and also tell some story/tale and this would have the desired effect; children going to sleep happily and peacefully.

The cozy and comfortable relations between the two generations in our times was simply attributable to parents; mostly mothers spending quality time with kids and being at ease in communication with them. During those days the fathers or leading male members were thought to be responsible mainly for earning and creating wealth for the family and coming generations. The kids used to be at ease more with females; mothers, sisters and aunts etc. I am happy to recall that our elders used to be close-confidants and a bond of friendship existed between kids and mothers/sisters/aunties in the household. This generated trust and helped in sharing of personal information and dilemmas of difficult situation, if any, faced by the kids. The relationship, thus nurtured, was generally smooth and satisfying.

Mothers; a cradle of love

I have a firm belief that a mother is better placed, being soft natured, and being, generally, gifted with an amiable and kind temperament by God, has a most critical role in shaping the future of the kids. Our mother used to emphasize the difference in a man's temperament and a women's temperament like this; a woman would put her child under a shaded tree after rebuking/thrashing her child as a punishment for child's misdemeanor, whereas the males wouldn't care about any such details and soon get busy in their affairs.

A mother is at ease in getting close to the kids, more so with girls. God has bestowed the ladies with a kind heart and an instinct of emotions. They don't have to work hard to acquire it. Probably, nature keeps a balance in this universe in this manner. On the contrary, most of us, the male members are difficult to please, have their attitudes, are the ones to face first-hand the harsh realities of life to protect the family and that probably makes the males down to earth practical.

Her efforts at building values in kids

She would find time to visit Hindu and Sikh temples on festival days or holidays etc. when possible for her and take us along. On the way, she would explain the importance of festivals in our life and also narrate anecdotes and stories related to the deity we were going to visit.

Her favorite deity was Lord Hanuman. She was fascinated by the heroic deeds Lord Hanuman is said to have performed as a child and later in the service of Lord Rama. She would tell, "He is a great protector especially of children who regularly pray to him. Seek Him silently in your heart when in trouble and surely the Lord will come to your rescue. Therefore, chant 'Hanuman Chalisa' every day."

She had deep faith in 'Gayatri Mantra'. She used to tell, "Chant it in the mornings after bath and on the way to school, you will become free of fear and tension."

The underlying idea behind these steps was to initiate us on the path of religion. Her personal unflinching faith in religion got reflected in prayers and singing of hymns early in the morning when the environment was peaceful and calm. She sincerely believed in the correctness of what she told us and believed that this would lead to deeper knowledge of religion when we grow up and are exposed to the scriptures. I acknowledge; this simple advice was easier to accept and follow, it proved to be more effective than big sermons in temples and helped me in not paying much attention to rituals. In hindsight, it is obvious that she succeeded in her attempts.

Another important objective for the visits seemed to be a poor mother's attempt to provide her children with an opportunity to enjoy the sweets and meals offered after the congregation.

Her relentless struggle/efforts for meeting her obligations as head of family

Without narrating the heroic efforts of our mother, the picture of how the family survived despite the adversities and severe scarcity of financial resources, will be incomplete.

She was always alert and vigilant about attending to every member's needs. She would be up in the morning very early, attend to the cattle, milch the cows, clean and sweep the rooms, kitchen and courtyard and be ready after bath to wake us up, give us bath and get us ready for going to school and give us our break-fast and some tiffin for the school. Of course, in all these activities, the two sisters would give her support when possible for them.

I never saw her sleeping in the bed. She was always up, working, whether in the night before we were made comfortable in the beds or in the morning, when we got up. On many occasions when I felt, it was mid-night, I saw her working; either spinning cotton/raw-wool on the wheel or working with hands on stone-grinder and making wheat flour etc. All these activities would be accompanied by singing in low tones some religious hymns in her extremely sweet and amazingly melodious voice. It was a heavenly soul-stirring serene scene even for a kid like me. When I recall all this even now, my head bows in reverence to her. Many a times, I pretended I was not awake, for I did not want to distract her attention and disrupt the melody and let go the pure and simple bliss. I believe, in these moments, she was nearer to God, oblivious of routine earthly concerns. Possibly, she was in silent communication with HIM, opening up her heart, keeping her problems before HIM and seeking His Guidance. Obviously, she drew her undiminishing strength (emotional as well as physical) from unflinching faith in Him.

Whenever in difficult situation, she would say, "It is His Will, we are bound to accept it. It is no use complaining about adversities. Don't complain if it is dark night for it will be followed by bright sun in the morning." It is not that she never lost her temper or conveyed her anguish but this was always momentary. Soon she would be her normal self and get busy in routine.

To sum up, if appropriate for me to attempt it for a person like her, I would say she was an angel. She would say, many a times, she would get in touch with HIM when not being able to find answers to our difficult queries. Even now when I attempt to visualize an insight of what it was, I get carried away by those sweet lingering memories. I silently cry for her, without letting the others to know it. I am unable to give words to my feelings/emotions of respect and regards for her.

A popular saying in Punjabi language, "Manwan thandiyan chhawan', meaning mothers are a never ending source of cool breeze, very aptly brings out my deep sentiments of what she was to me. When in trouble or hurt, go to her and you feel cool.

My humble respects to the angel that she was, "Maa tujhe salam. Shower your blessings on all of us from heavens."

"Oh God, give me the wisdom to live according to norms/teachings told by her."

Her unwavering commitment to her family

I was always fascinated by her never-tiring attitude of commitment to family. She took it as her pious duty to take full care of all of us realizing zealously that God had decided in His own Wisdom to give this onerous responsibility to her. When frustrated and annoyed with our pranks, she would threaten, "I would leave you alone and join your father in heaven." And this would have the desired effect. We would calm down and seriously promise, out of fear, not to do it again. Seeing us terrified, the poor lady would hug us and assure she would never leave us alone. On such occasions, which were many, she would tell us that during the first few days, she had an encounter during sleep with our deceased father when he is stated to have told her to continue to shoulder this responsibility. He had commanded, "Do not follow me, stay back and take care of the kids."

I do realize now, how a sincere and committed leading member of the family can reduce, if not eliminate the sufferings and misery. In fact, all the family members except me and my younger brother, contributed to making less painful the struggle for survival, by taking up petty jobs to earn few coins, whenever possible. The elder brother, V.P., picked up for himself the role of senior male member and provided support to mother and brother-in-law, apart from pursuing his studies. In the process, he lost his adolescence and started behaving like adults; always watchful and reprimanding us all including the elder sisters, whenever, he felt, there was need for it. Not only that, he would be asked to join the elders in serious consultations regarding the affairs of the household. In the process, he developed impatience and became short-tempered. To the extent possible, we would avoid him. Alas I realize now, it was very harsh and unfair to him.

Mother's unique sense of rationality

Talking about God's statues, our mother would emphasize, "In His Statues, which we Hindus worship, is God incarnate Himself if one looks at it with 'Shradha' (unflinching & total faith full of devotion); otherwise,

14

it is stone". True Faith gives us the vision to think rationally, provides support and strength to one's character. Absolute faith in Absolute Divine is the first step on the path of 'Bhakti' (complete devotion in absolute surrender before Him) a harbinger of peace of mind and which provides a sense of fulfillment. Penance and regular practice help generate faith and encourage us to meditate peacefully and positively to make life meaningful. It transcends the barriers of falsehood and ego.

Her pearls of wisdom:-
"Be satisfied with what you have and aspire for better days ahead."

She did not have resources to satisfy even small needs and petty demands of us, kids, but she would satisfy us, somehow with love and promise of betterment in days to come. She would advise us to be patient saying if we are facing bad days now, can the better days be far behind? It was like a well-known quote; "If it is winter now can the spring be far behind?" To pacify us, she would often narrate two tales; one of Sudama, the legendary poor Brahmin friend of Lord Krishna who could not afford to buy any costly gifts for Krishna, his old mate, when he went to meet Him. The poor Brahmin had carried with him some Sattu (chick-pea flour) wrapped up in a sack of old cloth. Ostensibly it was a courtesy call, but was actually motivated by an expectation of generous help and support from the king Krishna. And the Wise and Kind Lord did provide him with riches beyond his expectations.

And two, the tale of Shabri, the poor woman of Ramayana. As the story goes, Shabri (Bhilni) was a destitute and couldn't manage to offer to Lord Rama anything other than berries which she had been collecting from jungle and storing them in her hut. She would bite each berry before offering it to Him to make sure that it was sweet forgetting that her bite would spoil it. And Lord Rama graciously ate them without letting the poor lady realize her mistake.

Our mother would seek consolation at her inability to offer her kids a variety of dishes justifying it like what happened to Bhilni in her similar circumstances. She would say I am no better than Shabri (Bhilni), my boys. Be happy with what I can offer you now and wait for golden days to come.

She did not have the opportunity to read the scriptures like Gita, Mahabharata or Ramayana or other holy texts of Hindu mythology but she was very well aware of teachings contained therein as though she had read them. When required, she would present them in her simple language and bring out lucidly the underlying messages contained therein. Obviously, she remembered precisely what she had heard in religious concerts in temples or gurdwaras earlier in childhood and young age. To pacify us when unable to meet our demands she would narrate some story from holy texts with a message relevant to the occasion. And children would nod in affirmation as if they had understood message's significance and were satisfied with it.

"Prevention is better than cure."

Organized Medical care being what it was then, the elders believed in and practiced, "prevention is better than cure." She would keep a close watch on our health parameters and give due attention to our physical wellbeing not only by feeding us well but also by administering herbal preventive medicines especially at the time of change of weather. She thought that sometimes in October/November i.e. before the onset of winters and again in March/April i.e. before the arrival of summers, the human body required to be toned up by eliminating impurities in the blood. Colloquially, she used to call it change of blood necessitated by change of weather. For this she would administer some anti-infection blood-purifying herbs which were available locally and had very bitter taste. We the children would resist taking these drugs. The dose of most of these essential drugs was small pills. Swallowing these pills with water would leave an extremely bitter taste in mouth. The way out was, "wrap them up in a lump of home-made fresh butter and let the children swallow the lump." Of course, for this so-called brave act, we were offered some sweet goodies as bait.

Even for day to day illnesses like fever, cough and cold, body ache/ headache etc. the remedial medicines were made at home out of herbs. Ayurveda (Indigenous System of Medicine, as we call it now or Alternate System as West describes it) was the most common and practiced system. It was thought that such medicines do not have any residues and side-effects. I believe; modern research has corroborated it. These small steps mostly preventive in nature, helped in abating and reducing the challenges of illness even if they occurred.

The moral of the story, "Prevention is better than cure."

"Persuade and win."

Her real strength was persuasion and patience while dealing with us. Finding some day that we were still sleeping and would get late for school, she would not shout at us. Instead, she would sing first few lines of a popular early morning song "Uth jag musafir bhor bhayee, ab rain kahan jo sowat hai" (which means get up thee, the night has given way to morning and the sun is up in the horizon") and punctuate it with her request. And this used to work; ourselves getting up without cribbing or murmuring. I remember; this song was close to the heart of Mahatma Gandhi, our Father of Nation.

"Men of substance don't ever cry."

"Face the challenges head on; let not obstacles deter or cross your path. Come what may, whatever difficulties and hardships you may face, meet them resolutely and face them with courage head on. Don't ever cry. Men never do this cowardly act. They face the adversities and difficult situations determinedly. Her golden words, "Tears lie deep down in the bottom of men-folks' heals" conveyed it all. Even when I was a small child she would make a sarcastic comment, "Look here, a man is crying." Crying in pain is the preserve of women-folk. Let them be blessed with it. Probably, that is why I do not let my difficulties, pains or agony to pour out as tears in my eyes even now.

I do sob silently sometimes either when reminiscing about a tragic/cruel situation faced earlier by my dear and near ones or as a gratitude to someone for his/her kind acts or as a fall out of deep emotional, pathetic and scenes of barbaric cruelty witnessed on TV/Movie screen or when trying to inter-act with the Lord Almighty at times of pensive mood. This outburst of emotions happens mostly at the time of prayers when I attempt to seek His Blessings for those whom I love. Seeking personal favors from Him is too difficult for me. Mother used to say it belittles you when you do so. Have faith in Him and His all-pervasive Hands of Krupa. You will be blessed if you deserve so.

"Practice thrift and remember the phrase, 'value for money'.

Instead of big hard hitting sermons, she would use adage, sayings and quotes in folk language to convey the message and the practical meaning inherent in them. A few learning which have had a lasting impact on me as a child/an adolescent are; 'Jitni chadar utne paer pasaro' which means 'cut your coat according to your cloth', and 'mangan gaya so mar gaya, mangan mool na ja' which means 'seeking alms and asking for favors amounts to being dead. Refrain from it to live a life of honor.' According to her, even borrowing meant spreading your hands before others which, she believed was below human dignity. Of-course, loans from banks were unheard of in those days. She would often convey that easy money leads to lethargy and is anti-progress and seeking favors from others deprives you of a dignified living and a respectable place in society. Manage your needs within your resources and learn how wonderfully it helps you to live and grow with dignity. The essence of this practical wisdom was, "Don't ever splurge or practice unscrupulous indulgence." These messages were significant and well-served their purpose considering over-all environment of austerity prevalent in society then. It shaped approach to life and enriched our value-system. It not only allowed us to be happy and satisfied with our present lot but also made us aware of the need to augment family's income through extra efforts.

"Learn to live within your means"

"One should not stretch his/her needs beyond affordable limits failing which it may lead to employing of unfair means. Earn more and augment resources by all means but only by employing fair means for the purpose. No compromise is worth considering."

It was thanks to these learning that I never borrowed money or to seek loans for meeting my family's monthly budget and never indulged in making purchases on credit. I lived on these principles all my life and we were happy to manage our finances well. I did take loans but only from banks etc. and that too for some capital investments like buying a plot of land or buying a car. These principles of thrift helped me to lead an austere and modest life. It also rescued me from the temptation of indulging in unfair means and corrupt practices in work life. Of course, my better-half played a genuine supporting role in helping me to adhere to these jewels of principles. She never pestered me to buy for her something which was beyond our means. Rather, it usually used be the other way round. She would stop me from going in for something which, in her opinion, was not necessary. I will come to this later with lot more on her role in shaping the destiny of all of us.

It is true; "Not going beyond means is a virtue par-excellence. It bestows you with that priceless gift in life; Contentment and peace of mind."

"Be not self-centred. Share and be happy."

Another very important quote she was narrating regularly was; do not ever ask for a boon from God for yourself alone. Always put forth request to Him to shower His blessings on 'all' and surely such a prayer has more chances of being accepted. Remember, you are also a part of 'all'. She would explain that you are being selfish when you seek blessings from Him for yourself alone and the boon you are seeking may not be granted for you may not deserve it. But when you are a part of the group, the boon may be granted thanks to others' good track record.

She would often also tell, "Don't be petty minded or jealous, be generous to others, ultimately it comes back to you as a reward by HIM in many ways. Such an approach rewards you with a large heart, an open and benevolent mind and makes you considerate to others."

"vand khao- khand khao" was another rustic but deeply significant phrase which she was regularly telling us. To her this actually meant, "Share and be happy. Being generous and big-hearted makes life sweet like sugar." This message helped the kids to avoid conflicts over petty things and made her life easier too.

"Adjust, be practical and yield when necessary."

Children especially boys in same age-group in a family fighting over petty things is quite common. Seeing me and my elder brother squabbling or shouting at each other over some matter or fighting for an item, she would tell me, "you are younger, he loves you so much but is in some rash mood now. Yield and let the matter subside. Be three quarters and let him be whole one." Finding me obstinate or in no mood to yield she would threaten, "I am going and will not come back till you both settle the matter. Beware, it could mean denial of food or some other goodie." Also, she would whisper in my ears, "give in at the moment and I will settle the matter later with him to your satisfaction." Some similar message would be aired in his ears also and see the confrontation is gone and soon the tussle ends. I remember, many of such occasions I would really follow her advice and get relieved of the tension.

Like many of her other similar useful messages/tips, this particular advice always came to my rescue whether in personal life or work-life.

"Cleanliness is next to Godliness"

She would regularly emphasize the importance of hygiene and cleanliness for being healthy and being a step closer to HIM, quoting the famous saying; "Cleanliness is next to Godliness". Her rustic and easily understandable quote was, "Even the dog wipes the place with its tail before sitting on it". You are human beings, have brains. Make cleanliness a regular daily routine and be healthy.

After whole day's playing barefoot in the open grounds in the vicinity of our houses, our legs and feet were soiled with mud etc. She would demand of us," Wash them clean with soap and water before you sit down for meals and before going to bed in the night." Until we washed clean our feet and legs, she won't allow us to sit down for food and later get into bed. She believed; this preventive step was essential to protect the children from numerous infectious ailments. I picked up this habit then and still follow it as a routine, the only exception being that my feet and legs are not much soiled now, unlike in the childhood. It is hands and mouth that need to be taken care before sitting down for food.

The moral; enforcing discipline during childhood has long lasting rewards in life later also.

"Be disciplined and live on principles."

Often, she would repeat; if you wish to make a mark in life, follow high principles and let discipline be the guiding tool and focus in all your daily routines. Remember these two prime attributes always. Don't ever take liberties with discipline and never compromise on principles. "Jeet sada tumhare kadam choomengi" which means, 'the success will always be yours. It will follow you wherever you go; so to say the luck will become your hand-maiden.'

Summing up her vision

Being always hard-pressed for time, she couldn't afford to sit down in formal prayer sessions. While doing house-hold chores she would keep singing in low tones (hardly audible to others) some hymn or shlokas. She explained this enabled her to concentrate on the job in hand besides being a sincere attempt at remembering HIM. I am aware I can't read the scriptures but chanting His Teachings is what I love to do.

She had great reverence for seers and saints like Guru Nanak, Surdas and Kabir. She loved to talk of devotees like Meera, Bhilni and would repeat their tales of love and devotion for Krishna and Rama respectively. She was emphatic and sure that for persons like her who were incapable of reading the scriptures, the way out was applied faith. Remember HIM, pray to HIM to convey your sense of gratitude to HIM for all the bounties, HE has provided to the mankind.

I believe; the canvas of her approach to life was very vast and was laced with unflinching faith and a deep sense of gratitude. She would say, "Let the learned do what they are best placed to do and I will continue to do what I am capable of doing best; recall His Kindness to all the human beings and recite some hymns in His Praise."

When faced with our persistent demands, she would attempt to pacify us in her own unique style, "Have patience and pray to Him, the Almighty. He, surely, will respond and grant your wish in His own style. Do not grumble or complain. He doesn't like it. He will get annoyed if you persist and that could mean still harsher times for all of us."

Our elders; generally simple folk

I believe; our elders were simple by nature, by and large. Faith and devotion to God made life simpler for them. Assimilating the messages contained in holy books and making practical sense of them was their real strength. They truly believed that sermons/messages contained in holy texts were delivered by Gods themselves and, therefore, beyond any scrutiny. No questions entered their minds. They were neither too much analytical nor believed in questioning the authenticity of the holy books. Unfettered deep faith (Shradha in Hindi) and complete devotion for the Lord Almighty was the cornerstone of behavior and thought process for them in matters religious. Faith was their creed. It bred devotion and helped in looking forward to contentment (Trupti in Hindi) so vital for life's journey; peaceful, full of bliss and wholesome (Sampoorn in Hindi). Our mother would often say, "Faith in teachings/sermons as revealed in scriptures is our mainstay, a real support and strength; a genuine hope for our sustenance. The faith endures hope, helps us to look forward to future with confidence. Believe in Him and His Generosity and be happy. His kindness manifests itself in umpteen ways throughout our life. Be worthy of His Kindness by attempting to follow the teachings in scriptures"

My woe of regrets for her

When I look back and recall her great self-less service to us all not only till partition in 1947 but thereafter also, rather till she had seen us make a beginning in work life, a painful feeling haunts me that I could not match the thoughts of reverence and deep love for her with real action; remained busy in meeting the challenges of work-life and responsibility towards my children. Notwithstanding all this, it pains me that I couldn't provide adequate attention, emotional and physical support to her which was my duty as a grown-up son. It is to her credit that she never conveyed her anguish or unhappiness over this neglect.

Getting busy in attending to one's own family's needs is fine but neglecting moral responsibility towards parents and especially to a mother of her stature is unforgivable. It is unfortunate that this happened. I will always feel guilty and carry this burden for all my life or may be beyond it. I know; no amount of repentance is sufficient enough to help me to be free from this pain.

It is of little consolation that for about 3 years when I was in Railways and posted at Delhi Cantonment station as Goods clerk from early 1957 to end 1959, I had the privilege of bringing her to Delhi to live with me, and it seemed, she was happy about it; maybe she thought she was able to provide support to her single son who needed homely food and homely comforts. It was a The short spell of three years in her blessed company enriched my vision thanks to the regular flow of tips of practical wisdom flowing from her mouth regularly many of which of which I have narrated hereinbefore. It was an extremely satisfying and happy phase of my life. She would happily do the house-hold chores herself not allowing me to help her. My responsibility was to arrange grocery etc. and that is all. I was truly a happy free bird, so to say.

Respectful gratitude for my parents

I am proud to have been born to such loving and illustrious parents. Honestly, my attempt hereinbefore highlights, to an extent, their roles as responsible parents but fails to present a complete picture of their persona. In fact my home was a 'pathshala' where we as kids, adolescents and as grown up individuals picked up healthy values. These values got deeply ingrained in our mind/psych and formed the basis for shaping approach to life. I would thank my parents, my stars and say I was lucky. Thanks to the lessons of healthy approach to life provided in the four walls of my home I stayed focused and avoided getting lured by temptations.

Though I didn't have the good luck to grow as a proud sibling in the high profile company of my father, yet his principled sojourn of four decades in this universe greatly impacted my mind. He was an upright person wedded to high principles of integrity, honesty and compassion. I miss him deeply as I do for my mother.

Recently, in a seminar on character-building, I heard a local industrialist saying, "Those who have parents at home need not go to any temple or place of worship. Touch their feet early in the morning after you get up and be blessed."

Chapter 2
My Brief Identity

I was born in October most likely on 19th in the year 1936 in Isa Khel, a small sub-divisional town in Mian Wali district (now a part of Pakistan). As per my mother, it was the second day of Kartik month (Monday) in Hindu calendar (Vikram Samwat) that you came into this world. It was early morning; the time for going to school. She didn't know the year. She would also recall that I was almost three years old when our father breathed his last.

I was number 6 in a family of 7 kids (4 brothers and 3 sisters). Our father was ill for about 10 years and a sizeable portion of family's income was spent on his treatment etc. and, therefore, it can be said that almost since my birth the family faced an extremely difficult situation. Our family, I was told, had a flourishing business of drugs and herbs and owned a lot of landed property but that was a poor consolation now. The family faced a bleak future and our survival was at stake.

My Family's love for Education

Isa Khel and Mian Wali district were backward and an under-developed area. (It is probably so even now in Pakistan). The spread of education was low. The social milieu was poor. With this background, our family's education level and its respect and love for education were praise-worthy. My grand-father was a qualified medical practitioner of Ayurveda, the indigenous system of medicine. My father graduated from High

School in the year 1921-22 which was no mean achievement in those days considering the backwardness of the region and lack of educational facilities. In those days, there was one High School in the entire district at Mian Wali and the students had to take their final examination in Lahore, the capital of the state. It was not surprising, therefore, that a vast majority of population thought formal education to be the waste of time and resources.

Education, family's inheritance and a valuable legacy

I am happy to say with pride that our father had left behind a very valuable legacy in the family; love and respect for education. May be it runs in our blood, as they say? Our eldest sister completed her Primary standard in the year 1935/36 before being married in 1937. Our eldest brother completed his Middle Standard in 1939 but had to give it up thereafter due to unfortunate happening; our father's demise. The second elder sister did her primary standard in 1937/38 and the third sister did her Middle standard (8th) in 1945 by when the girls' school in Isa Khel had been upgraded. That each female member of the family went to school and completed the highest level of education available then, did speak volumes about the love and respect for education in the family.

The lucky beneficiaries of Family's legacy of education; we, the 3 brothers

In hindsight, I thank the legacy of love and respect for education in the family. But for this valuable legacy, I and my two brothers would not have been put in schools in Refugee Camp in Sept., 1947 after the family landed there, completely shaken and destitute refugees. Praise be to our mother and elder brother-in-law who took this benign decision! I am aware that a sizeable population of our contemporaries did not join schools after migration to India. To be honest, we cannot redeem this debt of our elders. We were lucky; the family firmly stood by its resolve and managed, somehow, to allow us to be in schools till our High School. The rationale was that after our High School, we would be eligible for a job in Govt., be self-reliant and be on the path of further growth. Depending upon our personal commitment and determination we could aspire to look ahead to our future with confidence; pursue further studies and/or acquire technical skills. How this long-term vision of our elders proved to be a blessing for me is what my journey of life revealed and what follows in subsequent chapters.

God helps those who help themselves

Believe me, it was obvious that despite all the morals and rationale, such a decision i.e. the three of us (myself and my two brothers) should join regular schools was unthinkable to implement, given the deprivation and non-availability of a regular source of income for the family, except the meagre salary of our eldest brother. However, the family did manage it and overcame the difficulties with every member picking up odd jobs and earning those valuable extra rupees and also taking the help of members of our extended family who were little better off. Praise be to our deceased mother who was the prime mover of the idea and who undertook the burden of collecting extra rupees through hard manual jobs in the neighborhood and also economizing on expenditure in the family by various intelligent moves like (i) buying a goat (sorry, we couldn't afford to buy a cow) for meeting family's requirement of milk even though she knew that goat's milk's taste wasn't good and (ii) breeding of hen to get eggs for her kids. The far-sightedness and vision of hers along with the co-operation of other members helped in achieving what was extremely difficult, if not impossible.

The moral; "God helps those who help themselves."

Chapter 3
The galaxy and its influence

One day, a casual thought made me access internet to satisfy my curiosity to know what is given in my zodiac sign. I am a Libran and as per commentary by known and famous astrologists, a Libran generally is objective, just and wants to do what is best for everyone, hates uncouth behavior, is most pleasant, possesses natural charm in abundance, is easy going mannered, cultured, suave, refined and lover of beautiful things, most of all beautiful people, artistic, stylish and enjoys creating a beautiful world, never manipulative and too nice, amongst many other important attributes and qualities of behavior in him/her.

It was flattering to know that the Librans are endowed with such a vast range of super praise-worthy attributes. To be honest, I got excited top to bottom but soon realized that individual Libran's endowment of these attributes may not be same. But it does indicate that there is a possibility for Librans to possess some of these adorable qualities.

I wonder why knowing about my zodiac sign and its influence didn't occur to me earlier. Probably the dominant influence of 'Karma' theory kept my attention away from the theory of fate. I have seen people talking keenly and wanting to know from astrologers what was in store for them but I never got attracted to any such idea. One thing is clear though; my mother who was my greatest influencer never talked of fate.

The realization that Librans, generally, are a gifted lot boosted my morale and redoubled my determination to push ahead vigorously with the project in hand; writing my memoirs.

My own assessment of myself

I confess; it is really comforting that many of the attributes listed as relevant for my zodiac sign have had impacted me in my life. However, one attribute amongst many others, 'careless and easy-going' is a source of some disturbance to me. Many a times, people around me feel I am easy-going and careless. Yes, this probably could be something to do with my zodiac sign. However, in reality I am neither careless nor easy-going; while people think I am rushing to the conclusion in haste, the correct position is that I firm up my response rather quickly after due study of the situation. I abhor pretensions and feel comfortable in simple and easily acceptable conclusions. When not sure about a given situation I prefer to hold back. And that's it.

Yes, it is true that I was care-free as a child and even now am care-free (but not careless). I carry no inhibitions in my approach to life but cautious I am. I do not take things lightly, study the implications quickly and frame my response without loss of time. I believe; my approach keeps me free of the burden of imaginary consequences or an adverse fall-out. I do not let the burden of anxieties overshadow my rational thinking or being unduly apprehensive. My rationale; I shall face the adversity if and when it comes. Why be apprehensive about outcome when the decision is taken after due deliberation and a rational approach?

Rational and free mind strengthens self-confidence, helps us to seek options considered appropriate for the given situation. This approach also develops analytical skills so necessary for proper evaluation of each option before zeroing in on the most rational and appropriate one.

Long-time back, one of my acquaintance who had a reasonable insight into palmistry informed that I did have a supporting life-line in addition to normal life line which helped me. How far it is true, I don't know for I never consulted a professional palmist about this phenomenon. May be; in a way, it explains my style of being "care-free" in my approach.

Chapter 4
Self-Awareness; an essential pre-requisite for making life meaningful

Aristotle said, "Knowing yourself is the beginning of wisdom."

"He who looks inwardly at the self, revels in the self/ He who revels in the self looks inwardly at the self."

Acarangasutra 2.173

To know one-self fully and precisely true is a challenge, which many of us fail to meet. Why, because generally speaking, we tend to believe in an image of ourselves that is based on superficial assumptions and it rarely reflects what we stand for. We often fail to realize that there is a significant bias in our approach. We tend to believe, "I am fine, reasonable and fair. Why bother about what others say?" Let's remember; true self-awareness generates self-realization which helps in evaluating objectively our values and approach to life. It helps in determining the path ahead rationally and makes the journey of life smooth and hurdle-free. Failing which we tend to assume; our aspirations are justified, our assumptions about others and ourselves are valid. And when our expectations are not met we feel let down easily. The result is disillusionment and dis-satisfaction which multiplies over time. Would all this mean that a fully self-aware person being realistic is not ambitious about his/her growth and would not take risks to achieve his/her goals? No, on the other hand, such a person avoids jumping to conclusions in hurry and thus avoids the pitfalls associated with undue haste and lack of realistic assessment of the project at hands.

Being down to earth practical and realistic are the values that nobody else can give unto us except us ourselves. Being realistic is a virtue par excellence for fulfilling our aims and for a steady growth in life.

Core Beliefs and Values; My Approach

My basic core belief has been, "Be satisfied with the existing situation, avoid unnecessary complaining, perform the tasks diligently with sincerity of purpose. Be fair, just and equitable to all including self. Shun malfeasance in conduct and avoid unscrupulous temptations."

Be regular in prayers and thank Him first thing in the morning and just before going to bed in the evening. It leads to equanimity in conduct during the day and a sound sleep during night. I believe; our busy and hectic daily schedules shouldn't cause us to forget this simple daily routine. All this need not be a long process. Just few minutes are enough provided the feeling genuinely is honest and pure. The universal truth is, "He is the provider and benefactor for all mankind. We owe it to ourselves to be always grateful to Him for His bounty of life to us." He and His aura are omnipresent but we must endeavor to visit His House (a temple, gurdwara or church or other prayer houses as per one's belief/faith) and manifest the pure feelings of respect and love for Him. Be vocal and loud when possible and there is an inner urge for this. How will he know our feelings unless we communicate properly?

Liberal traditions in our religion (Hinduism) allow setting up a temple at home in a separate enclosure or a room. In fact, many people call it "pooja" room and meditations center both. It is believed that given faith and devotion, such an enclosure or the exclusive space manifests itself as His Abode over a period of time. Apart from being a convenient place of choice for meditation and pooja for the seniors in the family, in due course, it also serves as a source of inspiration for the youngsters. Closely observing the elders in meditation etc. is itself enough to create an urge in their minds to follow suit ultimately. It doesn't matter that being in hurry most of the time, they may not find it convenient to spare some moments to sit down there. The real benefit would accrue in the form of a seedling getting a space in their inner-self. I am happy that something similar happened with me.

Many of the followers of some other religions notably Sikhism and Jains are also seen to be following the tradition of setting up a mini gurdwara or meditation center in their houses much like what many Hindus do. The rationale seems to be identical; a well-maintained holy place conveniently located within the house. It is also said that the presence of a holy place sanctifies the entire premises. In my opinion; it is a healthy tradition with far-reaching sub-lime off-shoots, the biggest being continuous awareness in sub-conscious about His Presence so near-by.

A word of caution here is necessary. The place of worship thus created must be kept always clean, well-lighted, decorated with flowers etc. and kept tidy giving a feeling of abundant love of the house-holders for His Abode; a place for purification of mind and making attempts for union with Him; the ultimate end of the journey on this earth. It is also a means of maintaining purity of one's soul and heart too. Not surprising, therefore, that the prayers offered in such a serene atmosphere become an individual's earnest urge for establishing a communication link with the Almighty.

I heard many preachers telling the audience that the Asana on which one sits for prayers/meditation gets blessed with the sacred aura/ environment of the place. True, we do witness scrambles for touching the Asanas of renowned spiritual Gurus in Muths all over the country. Devotees seeking blessings of the Gurus by kneeling before their Asanas is a common sight. I have known a friend who has an Asana in his place and helps people to know their real problems/difficulties by sitting on the Asana while listening to woes of visitors. I am not aware of the mystery but my experience confirms that the Asana does have something mystical about it.

It is said that He is Omnipresent. In fact, we often are told by the Holy men that He resides somewhere in our inner-self. Therefore, a question arises why struggle to create a Place devoted exclusively to Him in our dwelling unit. The answer to this dilemma is, "For undertaking an inward journey in search of Him, one would need to concentrate and what a better place than an exclusive place for sitting down peacefully in a comfortable posture i.e. an appropriate Asana."

The crux of all endeavors for achieving our goal of union with Him is self-less faith in Him and His Propensity to grant us peace of mind and a happy sojourn in His Universe. The learned Pundit ji in Dehra Dun used to repeat almost every day that in 'Kal-yug', chanting of vedic shlokas may be difficult but singing of devotional songs etc. are an easiest way out for common folks or family persons (Grihasthis) for establishing a channel of communications with Him.

In my opinion, an exclusive place for prayers/meditation is a sure means of establishing an easy rapport with our inner-self for further in-depth journey. Being regular in this routine helps retain faith, devotion and a sense of humility. It strengthens our faith in ourselves. Sit down peacefully for a pre-determined duration as a routine every day keeping aside or better forgetting the impending hustle bustle of daily struggles. Do it before embarking on the day's routine and see it takes the anxieties/ apprehensions off your mind.

And let's remember, the real beneficiary, by proxy, of this exercise is the lady of the house who feels blessed as it brings a bigger meaning to her role as the keeper of a pious place of worship. In my opinion, this responsibility should not be delegated to a maid or other helping hand. This would become yet another enjoyable routine provided one is earnestly in love with it for God's duty cannot be assigned or sub-delegated.

Many of us believe and argue that all such activity like prayers/meditation should better be left for old age. The present day competitive environment demands that one devotes his/her 100 % to work-life and also personal/ social life. This is highly debatable. I can speak of my personal experience. I did try to follow what I learnt in my formative years in the company of my elders and also during visits to temples and gurdwaras and I am 100 % happy and satisfied that I did it. Shall I say; my faith paid me rich dividends?

Are rituals necessary for fulfilment in life?

It is a highly debatable issue. I find myself to be incapable of offering any comments. There are very strong views for and against the dividing line. I am aware that the pressures to keep afloat in the society were too big for us, a middle-class family, struggling to find its moorings. Therefore, there was hardly any time left for performing the rituals. And watching some others doing the same under the supervision of a Pundit ji did not evoke any positive response or enthusiasm in our minds. To my innocent mind, it was just a show off and nothing more. We felt that offering prayers as honestly as possible was surely a better and easy option for us and we didn't lag behind. Even as a child I was more fascinated by the serene environment whether in a temple or a gurdwara. Therefore, a feeling grew; pray from the core of heart and do not hanker after formal articulations in the form of rituals.

Beyond Rituals

"God within cannot be apprehended by the eyes, by words, by any of the senses, by mortification of the flesh or by rituals. When the understanding becomes clear and the essential character becomes purified, then in meditation one realizes the one and only God."
Mundakopanishad

The innate impulses that influenced and guided me

Before I start with narrating the travelogue of my life I re-affirm my absolute faith in the teachings in ancient holy texts to which I had a chance to be exposed to while attending the discourses by eminent scholars in the neighborhood temple in Dehra Dun in the impressionable age of 14-16 years. They inspired and motivated me throughout my sojourn: They are:-

(i) "Karmanye vadhikaruste ma phaleshu kada chan (Geeta-chapter 2.47)

Literally, this verse would mean, perform your best and leave the outcome to Me. But as a doctrine, it means the doer need not be bothered by the outcome of his/her act if it falls within the norms of morals and righteousness. To my innocent mind, it meant; "Perform your duty diligently and honestly without any ill thoughts and malice to none. Do not run away from the given responsibility for it may mean weakness of thought process.

This Edict of "Karma and Righteousness" in above-mentioned verse is Lord Krishna's most illuminating and sacrosanct gift to mankind. It is a radical concept indeed which has several deep implications for the humanity. Elaborating on it, an eminent scholar of Geeta says "To work is the sacred right of all, but none can claim its fruits as reward". Yet another thoughtful meaning would be, "While doing his/her act is within the domain and responsibility of an individual, the outcome is the prerogative of God Almighty."

While it is beyond me to attempt to explore further the deeper philosophy of this supreme edict because of limitations of sufficient study of Geeta, I would suggest that the universal interpretation of this Shloka, as widely known and easily understood amongst common folks like us in Hindu fraternity is very simple "Act decisively and perform your duty sincerely and righteously with full commitment without bothering to look for the outcome/reward. Having done your act conscientiously, leave the act of outcome to Supreme Power". And,

(ii)Lord Rama's Persona as "Maryada Purshottam"

Literally, Maryada means time-tested norms of performance with fairness, equity, equality and justice for all. Literally,'Purshottam' means "Purushon mein uttam" which means the tallest and fairest of all and worthy of emulation amongst the human beings. Well this would mean a human being who is beyond compare and is resolutely stead-fast in upholding the principles/attributes of Maryada/Dharma in his conduct. I am conscious that this is no compact and true literary exposition of the depth and significance of the phrase. For me it means it is an ideal which is supreme, is beyond scrutiny and must be adopted by the mortals like us in our endeavor to lead a meaningful life in this universe in the footprints of Rama, the 'Maryada Purshottam, the upholder and follower of all norms of 'Dharma'.

Herein below, I am attempting to present my understanding, though seriously limited, of "Maryada Purshottam's Charitra (Persona) as a Benevolent King of Ayodhya, distinct from Lord Rama as God incarnate, as aptly revealed in Goswami Tulsi Dass's immortal epic 'Ram Charit Manas'.

First and foremost, the well-known and easily understandable couplet "Rghukul Reet Sada Chali Ayi, Pran Jaye par Vachan Na Jayee" coined by Goswami Tulsi Dass and incorporated by him in Ramayana teaches us to be steadfast in honoring the promise, commitment or assurance given to others in day to day conduct.

We must accord due respect and reward our friends and loyalists in appreciation of their support and help as Lord Rama did for many of His loyal warriors, chieftains/princes who provided invaluable support to Him during His troublesome days in exile of fourteen years and during His battle with Ravana, the devil king,

And above all, we must attempt to be worthy of the Lord's munificence, love and appreciation as He showered it whole-heartedly on His devotees/disciples like 'Hanumana'. The heart touching hymn in Ramayana 'Kapi se urin hum nahin, Bharat Bhai' conveys it all. In fact, to be honest, this hymn touches my heart very deep whenever I play/listen it. On return to Ayodhya after exile and victory over the demon king, the Lord tells His brother, Bharat that the self-less services rendered by Hanumana have indebted Him forever to Hanumana.

Be respectful to your elders like Lord Rama was to His parents, Gurus and senior members of His Council of Advisors,

Be truthful, upright and honest while performing our duties like Rama did as a Ruler for his 'praja' and also adopted and implemented the sacred laws of governance, like what we call 'rule of law' in present day jurisprudence,

We must endeavor to live unto one's own and others' expectations of fairness while dealing with matters of State and delivering justice as Rama did as a Ruler of Ayodhya,

Be generous and helpful without discrimination as to caste, religion or faith while handling affairs of the State as an administrator as Rama did for entire people of His Kingdom with openness,

Be sensitive and open to criticism/evaluation of your conduct by your own people as Rama did while handling the issue raised by one washer man (dhobi) amongst His 'praja' even though his comments, objections were not true.

Lord Rama while being a human being on earth symbolizes all that is ideal. His reign is respectfully/proudly referred to as "Ram Rajya" symbolizing that it was a period of absolute security, happiness, bliss and prosperity for all His 'praja'. Even now the phrase "Ram Rajya' is frequently invoked in common parlance to convey as to what an ideal ruler/state ought to be for ushering in an era of peace, equity and all-round prosperity of the ruled. During Lord Rama's rule, the residents of Ayodhya and His entire kingdom enjoyed the fruits of His benign rule.

The present day political class proudly emphasize during the run up to elections and declare that if voted to power, they would spare no efforts to establish 'Ram Rajya' in the country. Such is the deep understanding amongst masses of the phrase 'Ram Rajya'. The contesting political groups, parties and individuals swear by 'Ram Rajya' and assure that they would attempt to usher in peace, prosperity, brotherhood and equity in the society by implementing the basic concepts of public good as enshrined in the phrase 'Ram Rajya'.

The above two edicts, the 'Karma Theory' of Bhagvad Geeta and Charitra of Maryada Purshottam Ram have all along been my guiding principles. The 'Karma Theory' made me feel light and happy. To me, it meant,' Do your job sincerely and feel free of the burden of outcome since it is not in your hands.' What better way than to leave to HIM to own up responsibility for fair-play? And Lord Rama's Charitra as Maryada Purshottam is an ideal I love to cherish. It conveys super-natural messages for our existence. I crave indulgently to seek Lords' Blessings to entitle me to follow the path of Righteousness, Equity and Fairness in my conduct.

(iii) Lord Rama & Krishna's arrival; a spiritual boon for society.

In our mythology, both Lord Rama & Lord Krishna are thought to be Supreme Commander Lord Vishnu's incarnation on earth. Their generous teachings were open to all. They came down from celestial abode to relieve this Universe of the burden of ills this universe and humanity were suffering at the hands of cruel rulers of the times.

I am lucky that I was exposed to the teachings in these holy texts through religious discourses and thus was able to draw inspiration from these discourses. I was not conscious that I was doing it. I believe; what one comes across in childhood and in formative years stays embedded as a benevolent belief provided one is not tempted or overwhelmed by other negative influences. What I have always believed is, "Discretion and steadfastness in values and ethics play a decisive role in our life."

It is often advised, one should not hesitate to consult some close confident(s) to look for alternatives when in two minds. Fine, for it may lead to some better option. But make it a point to find out what is your own inner call and given the circumstances, what is the most appropriate and reasonable option of your own choice.

Do not ever try to take shelter behind an excuse or an alibi. It is your life; face the difficulties with same vigor as you would enjoy the happy moments.

(iv) Synergy between internal values and teachings of holy texts; a cardinal virtue.

Ancient thinkers and philosophers say, "Know thy self to be at peace with self. Relax and struggle not, to be able to make an inward journey. Call it introspection, if you may. Travel as deep as you can unexcited and unbridled. Communicate with inner-self freely and listen attentively to rumblings within. This will reveal and open up a wide vista of knowledge, inherent and inseparable from self. Churn, persist and persevere till you are able to discover the basics and fundamental ethos of your internal values. It is believed; knowing these attributes is as important as being able to pick up and internalize the teachings revealed in holy texts. Synergy between the internal values thus discovered and teachings of holy texts throws up a value chain of life-long import. But it is also a fact that various external influences that one is exposed to day in day out are bound to seek attention and influence the numerous waves of thoughts. How to resolve the conflict between internal values and external influences and find out the streak most preferred for oneself is a moot question. I believe; resolving such contradictions is possible only through meditation and a solemn inward journey. Sit down calmly, discern and communicate patiently with the core within, listen attentively to various urges, let the churning of ideas happen freely, discuss internally various options and then only one can hope to find out the lasting value chain of thoughts that are sure to be a treasure of ever-lasting and significant relevance. Do it as often as possible. It is said, "Practice makes a man perfect." Do not deflect if it takes time. Struggle hard until satisfied with the end result.

Chanakya said, "Who realizes all the happiness he desires? Everything is in the hands of God. Therefore, one should learn to be contented."

Sri Sri Ravi Shankar, the famous Guru and founder of Art of Living, says, "Want or desire arises when you are not happy. Have you seen this? When you are very happy there is contentment. "Contentment" means "no want."

Discovering and firming up value chain closer to oneself is most solemn and worth any amount of struggle. To me, it is like firming up of a mundane policy by a Govt. in an un-chartered territory for the good of its citizenry. Once a policy is firmed up by the govt. after due deliberations and is implemented universally, it brings up quiet satisfaction and its benefits accrue to all the residents. Similarly, once an individual is equipped with a value system of immense significance, the journey of life becomes smooth and satisfying. The approach in both the situations is same; the only difference is in inputs. The correctness and purity of inputs will determine the outcome; a valid and long lasting policy decision by the rulers for common good or a happy satisfying life journey for the individual.

Gurudev Tagore once said, "All men and women have poetry in their hearts". It is a great learning, a revelation of immense value. It implies; God has gifted us with a treasure of good creative values. It is for us to delve in, articulate and attempt to give expression to what lies within us. May be it is dormant until the urge to excel stimulates it and brings it out. Similarly, the basic values, both inherited and acquired, can turn out to be a rhythm/music of life when handled/channelized with care. Do it, repeat it till you learn to write poetry full of bliss and contentment in your journey of life.

Gautam Budha said, "Believe nothing no matter where you read it or who has said it, not even if I have said it, unless it agrees with your own reason and your own common sense." This gem of wisdom teaches us to be our own masters and be guided by reason and our own common sense i.e. the inner call.

(v) A confession.

I am not suggesting that I was aware of this approach to life and its merits in my early years also. But it did have something to do with my visits to temples in childhood along with my mother and sisters in Isa Khel and as a grown up adolescent in Dehra Dun (1949-52).

Now that, with ripened age, I am in a position to have a dispassionate look, I tend to think it could be something celestial that helped me observe keenly and pick up values as I moved along in life. Another possible reason could be the endowment of non-controversial temperament. In a family of seven, I was perhaps the only boy who was not rash or belligerent by nature. On many occasions, I would keep my cool while facing harsh comments or even rebukes. My mother would sympathize with me after the fury was over to help assuage my hurt feelings. She knew; I was right and would hug me and kiss me profusely. I believe; a constant combination of such exposures evolved into a psych of tolerance in me though many a times the rebellious in me would frown and blame my weak attitude for the ignominy I suffered for no fault of mine. One person whom I always respected deeply was my Headmaster of our Primary School. He was a noble person and looked like a saint. I suppose, he too influenced me greatly. Such was his impact on me that I still distinctly remember his figure, his attire and his gait.

A child though not capable of taking decisions on his/her own does take note of happenings around him/her and imbibes values which make sense to him/her little mind or ignores the ones that do not attract his/her attention. This is how a child's thinking process evolves over a period of time. I have not been a student of human psychology but, in my opinion, the values thus gathered during childhood and formative years become a primary factor in laying the foundation for thought process and value system in future.

Chapter 5
Partition of the country; the shattering upheaval for millions

The narration that follows is the eye-witness account of ghastly events that happened in my town, Isa Khel, Dist. Mianwali (Pakistan) in the wake of announcement of partition of our country. The impact of the tragic events was so deep that it is still fresh in my mind even after more than six decades. I have a fairly accurate and clear memory of the events that took place in our town. They were extremely frightening and left a scary vision in my mind. The fear psychosis made us nervous. The highly surcharged atmosphere led to gloom and emotional break-down for us. The imminent threat of large scale violence and threat to our life loomed large on the horizon and it added to anxieties in our mind about safety and security of life and property. The level and intensity of fear was heightening with every passing day after Pakistan was declared as an independent country on 14th August, 1947.

Undercurrent of apprehensions; a reality since long

Till the announcement of acceptance of the demand for partition, the social fabric and relations between the two communities were not healthy, though, on surface, they appeared to be normal. There existed an undercurrent of apprehensions in the minds of Hindus. Being in minority, being traders and land-owners, our elders seemed to have reconciled themselves over long time to accept the hegemony of the majority community. Our elders' message to children like us used to be very clear; do not come into conflict or precipitate the matters even when you are right. Whether in school or otherwise, yield ground and avoid angry exchanges with them especially the 'Khans' who were known to be hot-headed, highly arrogant and had the propensity to take recourse to abusive language and/or physical assault. The rebellious in me was hateful of all this. I would complain to mother about it but her answer was always the same, "Beware, we cannot antagonize them or pick up quarrels. It may mean serious repercussions for the family." We were prohibited even to go to the exclusive locality in the town where 'Khans' had dominant presence. We were told to take a detour even if that meant longer distance.

One can say; Hindus had yielded prime slot to majority community as a quid-pro-quo for survival. It was a practical approach after decades of experience of realities. The native Muslims were dominant in attitude and never let go any opportunity to demonstrate their numerical superiority though they as a whole were far behind Hindus/Sikhs and other minority communities like Christians in matters of education and overall development. The tacit support of administration was instrumental in adding to their (Muslims) belligerence/arrogance. That is why perhaps the approach of minority communities was peaceful and reconciliatory on the surface and cautious and vigilant underneath.

The same attitude was visible amongst our peers of majority community in the school. We were in majority (larger in numbers and disproportionate to our population) in school and far ahead in performance. This led to acrimony many times in the campus but school authorities were able to manage it suitably. Not that merit was very sacrosanct for authorities always but the satisfaction was that it was given to appear as such; a good cover-up, so to say, was thrown up making it look reasonable.

The Muslim League rally in early 1947 in our town

I still remember the Muslim League rally held sometimes in March/April 1947 in our town. It was the harbinger of the calamity and aggression that were to follow. A huge gathering of so-called faithful carrying banners, placards, swords, arms and flags etc. descended in the Maidan not only from all corners of the town but also from nearby villages and habitations. A huge gathering it was. Speaker after speaker exhorted the faithful to rise and fight unitedly till their demand was met i.e. partition of India and creation of Pakistan, the land of Pure. The slogans 'Allah-O-Akbar' "Pakistan Zindabad' reverberated repeatedly regularly in the rally. The environment in the rally was horrifying. The imprint of deep scare and horror on my mind was so strong that I am getting a feel of horror even now while recalling the brute and violent slogans and speeches of leaders, one after the other, exhorting the gathering to fight with all their might till end. The loudspeakers continued to spread venom of communal intolerance till the end. It was a call for rebellion by masses. The leaders' tone was fiery, aggressive and an open challenge to the administration. I along with one of my friends had gone to the rally and stayed there for some time though we were prohibited by elders to do so. I remember the inflammatory speeches, one after the other, were spreading the message very clearly. Partition and creation of Pakistan was the only option. After sometime we were totally horrified and ran home-wards for safety. After this, we never stirred out of our homes and were not allowed to go to school even after the vacations were over. We remained home-bound till we migrated to India sometimes in Sept. 1947.

Pakistan comes into being

The D Day came, Pakistan was created on 14th Aug. 1947, but the atmosphere did not improve for us though we joined in festivities on that day and also thereafter. Hindus; children and elders alike, joined enthusiastically in decorating the streets/bazars and other govt. buildings of the town. Victory rallies and processions to commemorate the historic event saw Hindus participating in large numbers. Festivities for Hindus were organized separately by Hindus in the main Hindu temple of the town, the Gopi Nath Temple. The community elders were very cautious. They did not want to convey unhappiness and discomfort over the difficult situation that was sure to emerge sooner than later. The fear of 'what next' lurked in every Hindu household in spite of the protestations of amity and brotherhood, as before, being conveyed by the Muslim community leaders. Not able to visualize a healthy scenario, our elders were dumbstuck. There was confusion all around and nothing seemed to emerge out of long sessions of confabulations. We were prohibited to talk about this matter either between us or with elders.

Our plight in pre-partition days

Even before the heat and dust of demand for creation of Pakistan had not picked up strength and overall the scenario was normal and peaceful, the lot of Hindus in general was not at par with Muslims. The atmosphere reflected helplessness of the community. The rules of the game were highly against Hindus. An unwritten diktat conveyed; you are number two. 'Do not complain. You may be intelligent, better educated and capable of doing much better in business, trade or fields like games or sports but mind it; you cannot challenge the majority community's hegemony. Understand your limitations well and behave well within the norms spread in atmosphere. As per law, all may be equal but the display of unwritten traditions of superiority by the majority community was supreme.' Follow it OR---?

Generally speaking, the social fabric i.e. relations between the two communities were stable though open criticism of Hindus' religious practices like idol-worship etc. was an on-going affair. It may be irrational and unreasonable to hurt religious sentiments but this is what it was. Hindus were living with it for decades because protests by them were not likely to alter the scene. There may be a genuine grievance but was any redressal mechanism available to Hindus in matters of faith? Obviously, there was none. Acceptance by Hindus of the hegemony of majority community was the fundamental contour of tolerance and a basis for peace between the two communities.

But there were some redeeming features prevalent in the system like joining in each other's celebrations of festivals like Dussehra, Diwali and Eid which were heartening on surface but there was no depth. There did exist the atmosphere of free interaction between the seniors of both the communities on social issues, medical facilities and quality of service provided in Govt. hospital, dispensary, civic issues like water supply, cleanliness and hygiene in the town, and issues relating to day to day governance by sub-divisional authorities. Joint efforts to resolve these issues were a healthy routine.

The ground realities in our town

After the creation of Pakistan, the message of fanatics and they seemed to be in control, was loud and clear, "Infidels have no place here. Embrace Islam or face extinction."

With the grant of freedom and creation of Pakistan based on two-nation theory, it was puerile to expect the fanatics to think and act rationally and not perpetrate atrocities on minorities. The atmosphere of hatred was in the air even months before the final announcement of partition. For the majority community, migration/exodus of minorities seemed to be an opportunity to plunder their wealth, property, business and resultant dominance of trade and other pecuniary resources held till then by minority communities. The society had got polarized along religious divide long back. The demons seemed to have taken charge. Humanity seemed to have given space to intolerance obliterating and squeezing the centuries old laudable tradition of co-existence of different religions in harmony.

The extremely grim situation in our town after creation of Pakistan

The superficial bonhomie on the surface soon evaporated and it was conveyed through public announcements that since Islam now was the only religion of the State, it was essential in the interest of long-term harmony and peace in society that people adopt Islam in large numbers and enjoy the freedom of living with honor. An innocuous announcement conveyed it all, "Join the main stream of society for peaceful living. Otherwise, there could be serious challenges in future."

I am not aware if the civil administration of the town took any steps to stop this veiled diktat or diffuse the tension. Soon there were announcements about the procedure to be followed by masses for conversion to Islam. Elaborate area-wise schedules for the purpose were laid down and announced. There was no choice. Soon the process of mass conversions started. There were long queues in front of all mosques of the town and all people including children and elderly people had to wait for their turn. When our family was in one of such queues, I was asked to be by the side of eldest member of the family, our brother-in-law's mother, who was 92 years then and could not stand for long. I would hold her stick lest it falls from her hand and she gets injured. While with her, I was regularly murmuring and cursing the authorities. She would console me saying 'you are not singled out.' I still remember what she had said then, of-course in local dialect, "ae musibat sab biradri te aye hey, tu kalha nahin". Broadly, it meant, "This curse has not befallen on you alone. The entire community is suffering. Be bold and face it with courage. After all, mere chanting of some verse is superficial, at best. It does not mean anything. In our hearts, we shall always be what we are now."

The ghastly tragedy takes place; violence erupts in town

The overall situation did not improve for our community even after all this tragic episode. Probably, people on both sides of the divide understood the fallacy of this. An unknown undercurrent of fear was obvious. People were not forthcoming much but an uneasy calm prevailed in the community. Anxiety about future was deep and tension prevailed all around. And suddenly, it all happened one night. The main market of the town was ransacked, looted and burnt for it had shops mostly of Hindus only. Next morning, we could see from our houses' roof tops the flames and thick black smoke belching out of the area. It was total devastation. What followed was still more awesome. The orgy of violence erupted all over the town. Vast groups of hooligans and armed gangs were roaming in the streets carrying drums/tins of kerosene oil and petrol etc., shouting slogans and trying to set ablaze the Hindu households. No doubt, our community was overtaken unawares by the magnitude of the violence but was ready to face it. The elders had anticipated something like this knowing the surcharged atmosphere not only in our area but all around the country. Our elders did the re-grouping. Lonely and vulnerable houses were vacated and the inmates were shifted to a cluster of houses which were inter-connected and which had pickets on the roof tops where the seniors took positions and exchange of fire with armed gangs in the street started. There were attempts at burning the cluster, where many families had gathered but the hooligans did not succeed due to effective return of fire by our elders from pickets on the roof-tops. The confrontation lasted for 2/3 days; sporadic firing from both sides continued and thus the lives of inmates of the cluster were saved. Our house was part of this cluster. Inter-connecting doors were opened and food articles were pooled. Community kitchen started functioning and we, the kids, had had nice time playing whole day in the court-yards and enjoying variety of delectable foods being dished out. The atmosphere was fun and frolic for us, though it must have been gloomy and full of anxiety for elders because the mobs were on the rampage in the streets, and intermittent firing was continuing. We used to move up and down the stairs playing and sometimes carrying food etc. On one such occasion, we escaped gun shots fired from a nearby hostile house and that was the end of our jaunts up and down the stairs.

Fateful decision by community leaders of the town; let's migrate to India

After few days, army/armed police took position on roof-tops and strategic places in the town. This helped, to some extent, to restore confidence amongst us. However, the deep undercurrents of tension and anxiety about our future persisted. Local authorities did make attempts to demonstrate, 'all is well' in different ways. The first thing they did was to permit us to stir out of our houses, of-course, under police protection, to fetch potable water from municipal taps in the market place. (There was no piped water supply in homes.) For the next few days, our movements were allowed rather freely; picking up some grocery items, vegetables etc., going to Indus River in batches for fetching extra water for household needs and visiting the main temple in the town all under close supervision. Despite all this, we were face to face with the uncomfortable reality; we would always be second rate citizens and be at the mercy of local Muslim satraps. It was realized that in the long run, the position may worsen further making life more difficult for us.

This led to serious consultations in the community and a most harsh decision was taken collectively; migrate to India knowing its deep implications very well. This collective decision betrayed serious implications for the community and individual house-holds. Get uprooted, be emotionally reconciled to migrate to a land you have neither known nor seen, be ready to face an uncertain future, leave behind all what is yours; your property, your business, your valuables and above all severe the deep emotional attachment that you have with your own 'Matti', the mother earth where you were born, you grew up, created your own unique living world (Ghar Sansar) with love and thoughtful considerations of stable happy living for all your dear and near ones. Despite the collective wisdom of the community to migrate, each individual household had to take its own decision. And some Hindu families, in their own wisdom, did decide to stay on as newly converted Muslims. What could have been their plight or experience is not difficult to guess. Did they get place of honor in society as new converts? A quick response would be 'no'.

Migration starts

The inevitable happened. The en masse exodus started in our town one day. The diktat was that each member of the family was permitted to take with him/her only one piece of luggage and no more and that the bunch of keys of the house should be handed over to the designated person sitting in the street corner. Every family followed the diktat before moving out. Imagine the tragic convulsions the elders would be undergoing then. We, the children, were unable to fully appreciate the implications of all this but the elders who had spent all their life creating a world of their own through decades of sincere efforts and hard work were unable to bear this and many of them started crying bitterly while bidding adieu to their entire life's wages of sacrifices.

I was given the responsibility to carry a canister containing about 8/10 kg of wheat flour. On a given day, we started moving out in the afternoon along with other families of the neighborhood, with permitted luggage on our heads. With anxiety/tension/helplessness writ large on each face about future, the crowd was moving ahead silently; blank-eyed and stone-faced as if in mourning. The migrant families were asked to move to city's pen ('Kanji-House'); the place for keeping stray cattle for the night.

Next morning, elders of some families having spent the night restlessly went back to have a last look at what they had earned and accumulated through hard work and left behind in the house. To their horror, they noticed that not only the locks of all their almeries/cup-boards had been broken open and contents lying there-in the night before had been looted but also the floors and some walls had been pounded to search for hidden treasure, if any. It was no use complaining about all this to anyone. It was obvious that the ring-leaders amongst Muslims had done their job. They had reaped the fruits of partition in one night.

After some time, the orders for 'march' came. "Move and board the trucks with your luggage for being transported to the transit camp in district town, Mian-wali." How much distance it was, I do not know but I do remember that we had to cross mighty river Indus on foot since it was told that movement of vehicles was not permitted on the newly constructed barrage which was very long and walking with load on head was surely very painful for me. I along with my school pal and close friend, Yash Pal Gandhi, were left behind the group. Yash was afflicted with polio and could not walk fast. By the time we two crossed the barrage, the trucks were full and ready to move. This was serious situation. It was clear that I was unlikely to board the truck where my mother and other members of the family were standing and crying for me. She was not being permitted to get down and pick me up. I started crying too and ran to catch hold of mother's hand leaving behind the canister of wheat flour. Providence

50

had it that one army man took pity on us and helped me and my friend, Yash, to board the truck.

Inhuman conditions and un-certain future in camp at Mianwali

We stayed in the refugee camp at Mian Wali for about 10/12 days waiting for our turn to board a train to take us to India. The life in the camp was miserable with no arrangement either for food or lodging. Probably, it was some school or other govt. building converted into a camp. The whole place was chaotic. You were lucky if you were able to pick up some food packets being dropped by planes. I believe; we survived against all odds only because of HIS Benevolence and strong will-power.

What was happening in the camp was tragic and pity-some indeed. But the news of killings, arson, and kidnapping of children and women in other parts of the district were adding to our concern for safety. Our worst fears were; anything could happen even in the camp itself. The atmosphere all around was of mayhem and anarchy. It was total failure of governance. Fully armed blood thirsty gangs were roaming everywhere. Humanity seemed to have conceded place to demons suddenly everywhere. The victims like us were at His Mercy and prayed to Him for safe passage to India, which, we believed was our destination and hopefully we would be safe there.

My happy brush with luck

The memory of my brush with two incidents, one benevolent and the other dastardly, while in Isa Khel is too deep to be forgotten. It was a very important Hindu festival (most likely Janamashtmi) when the holocaust started in our town. Unaware of what was happening in the market place, our mother told us (we two brothers) to fetch some fruits for her fast. As we were heading towards the market, we saw a crowd at distance shouting slogans. We ignored it and kept on walking. Seeing us going in the same direction where the crowd was gathered, and realizing the threat to our life, the massage man by the name Thothar sitting in the nearby tea-café, came out of the café and told us to go back to our home. He had recognized us. Seeing us adamant to go forward, he started pelting stones at us and made us run back. But for his rebuke and stone-pelting we would have faced a fatal risk. The market was closed and violent mobs were on the rampage. Riots had started in the town and we were open to serious harm to our life. As soon as, we entered our lane and were near our house's gate, two gun shots were fired at us from the house in front of our house, where a Muslim family lived. Luckily for us, the shots missed us and our mother dragged us in. And we survived.

Frustrating and agonizing messages being relayed from Delhi on All India Radio

I distinctly remember even today the anger/disenchantment amongst elders in the community regarding the messages being relayed on All India Radio from Delhi and also published in Newspapers/magazines, urging the Hindus in Pakistan not to plan to migrate to India. It was being conveyed that exchange of population was not envisaged in the concept of partition as if the scheme of partition meant drawing of new boundaries only. The leaders seemed to be either unaware or pretended to be unaware of the ground realities especially in Pakistan. Our elders were highly critical of the obnoxious wisdom of the political leaders in Delhi who seemed to convey through these announcements that soon the situation would calm down. They wondered how to let the authorities know about the explosive situation being faced by us. The Govt. machinery of the day could hardly be expected to help and convey our elders' views to authorities in India. The elders realized soon that all this really amounted to, 'take your own decision based on the actual ground position.' And they decided in their wisdom to look for opportunities for safe passage to India.

Karmath Jeevan

Stark failure of political class

Considering the explosive situation in many parts of the country, it appears in hind-sight that the political leadership of undivided India failed miserably to understand the implications of partition per se. Given the surcharged atmosphere for years before the partition, it was fallacious to think that there would be peaceful transition from British rule to self-rule and there would be no movement of population from across the borders for safety and protection. Knowing fully well that the policy of divide and rule festered by British for centuries was responsible for chasm between the two large communities and was their mainstay for prolonging their rule; one cannot accept that the native political class didn't foresee the horrible consequences of partition. The political class failed to do what was critical; an open discussion between the local leaders on ground of both the communities at national as well as in affected provinces on the modalities of peaceful exchange of population. It was rather fool-hardy to assume that the transition would not lead to riots even when sporadic violence had been raising its ugly head in all corners from Bengal to Punjab much before a formal announcement of partition was made. The failure of political class to learn from history was a callous act. They let down the innocent masses and be a party to the genocide by not anticipating the upheaval and failing to provide security and safety to poor masses. After all what was the fault of hapless masses? The pertinent cries were "Save us. Give us protection" The victims of this severely tragic and devastating decision, like us, have not understood even till date the wisdom and compulsions, if any, behind succumbing to the pressure of divisive forces to put this great country on the chopping block.

Political analysts and historians have produced huge volumes of write-ups on this great tragedy and some have probably described it as inevitable. Most of these post-mortems reflect the opinions of those ensconced in safe environs far removed from realities and actual happenings.

Krishan Aneja

The idea of partition; a cover up for fulfilment of personal ambitions of political class?

As I mentioned elsewhere, in spite of occasional stray outbursts of strife, sometimes very serious also, in some pockets in the country, the underlying feeling at zero level i.e. between common people of different communities betrayed that all was not difficult to manage. The ambitions and vested interests of political leaders at different levels of spectrum were the prime reason for the tragic decision of dividing the country on ethnic lines. I am sure, if an impartial referendum was conducted in affected areas i.e. which were witnessing the demand for partition, the majority of mature citizenry would have voted against it. Rather than being party to nefarious designs of British, the main political leadership should have attempted to find a midway approach like granting political autonomy at different levels. I know the idea was discussed and abandoned, but why? Was there no space for persuasion and negotiations to succeed or the process was given up too soon? Many such questions remain un-answered even till today. I know; the blind pursuit of nefarious idea of partition by religious and sectarian leaders on both sides in the name of superiority of one religion over the other did exist then, as it has always been or is a serious impediment even today. But it begs a question. Is it such a strong force that it cannot be handled rationally through overtures/persuasions/negotiations nor is it being practiced even now? Is the social scene very homogenous now even after over six decades of independence and conflicts are not being resolved through negotiations etc.?

Yes, I was too young at that time to be able to present an inside story or offer a scholarly viewpoint but I can say with confidence that except some fanatics in lunatic fringe, vast majority of citizens were comfortable to live together as before. Leaving hearth and homes and getting dislocated is always the last option for human beings. The idea of partition gained some ground and started being listened to in political rallies which exhorted the masses to stand up and demand nothing less than partition. Based on inter-action between elders of two communities in our town and ideas flowing in from other distant areas, I am positive in saying that the social fabric in pre-partition days was, more or less, lively and homogenous at ground level in spite of occasional differences. It was well-known that the consequences of partition were enormous and were sure to lead to catastrophe thanks to regular incitement by vested interests; the British rulers, the so-called religious leaders, the lunatic fringe and failure of decision makers on both sides of the divide. After all, it is a well-known reality that differences do erupt when some common pool of assets needs to be shared. Does history, local or elsewhere, tell us that partition did lead to a solution of the problem? The answer is an emphatic 'no'.

One cannot escape the conclusion that the personal greed of leading political figures of the day was the prime-mover behind this decision which had inherent immense catastrophic implications. Even if those leaders are resurrected now somehow, say with the providence of Lord Almighty, and see for themselves the misery this so-called wise decision of their making, has brought about on millions of innocent people, they would go back to their habitations (whether hell or elsewhere) crying in bewilderment.

Chapter 6
Our journey of escape

Sometime in second week of Sept. 1947, we boarded the train from Mianwali camp for India. Anxiety for safety was writ large on every face. The unconfirmed news of slaughter of whole population of some trains on way to India had started pouring in. It seemed the religious fanatics and criminals had joined hands in this heinous act for reasons of their own; one group believing in eliminating the so-called infidels in the name of jihad and the other looking to loot the valuables etc. and kidnapping of children, girls and young women. The atmosphere was thick with all sorts of horrifying rumors. Everybody was alarmed at the prospect of meeting the same fate. The only hope was the safe passage and safe, unharmed arrival in India somehow. Nothing else mattered then. We were hungry, thirsty, completely helpless and destitute. How did we survive in these circumstances, I do not know. The will power to survive probably saved us. Our group boarded the train when our turn came and this was the moment of some hope, though nobody was sure about what may happen the next moment. People on board reminded each other, "God is Great. He is Merciful. He has helped us so far. Let's pray and leave it to Him".

It is proverbial for human beings to look to God for help, when in trouble. It gives emotional stability and mental strength. The chanting of hymns, religious discourses were a common sight in the train. And sometimes when the train slowed down or stopped at some station or somewhere else enroute, this became louder and shriller, to ward away the thought of some tragic happening. Nobody complained of hunger etc. Whatever food was available was being shared. Pale faces, blank eyes betrayed the deep anxiety within. The thrills and joy of a ride in train were missing for us, the children. Everybody wished the journey to end soon and train enters India safe.

Lucky, we land safe in India

It was God's merciful boon that we survived and entered India, our own country. It was the hour of deliverance for us; a virtual second birth. It was nothing but providence that protected us. Prayers and Faith had triumphed. The thought that we were in our own country was enchanting and soothing for nerves. Ours was a lucky train for the reason that it travelled unharmed for 3/4 days through the surcharged atmosphere of un-bridled violence. Sitting in the train we could see mobs moving around with all the tools of destruction, butchery and arson. They looked determined to wreak havoc on innocent hapless population, whether in trains or on roads or just on bullock carts or just walking bare feet in an attempt to cross over to India, their dream-land of safety and protection. The prime reason for our safe arrival was the deployment of a small contingent of Hindu/Sikh army personnel in our train. Otherwise, there was total failure of the Govt. apparatus. The civil administration and police force had ceased to function. Rather the local administration and police were in collusion with the gangs of anarchists and providing support to them. The only hope was armed forces deployed by govt. from India.

As soon as, our train entered the railway station Attari, the entire population of the train knelt down to earth, kissed it to make sure it was the dream come true, after all. There were jubilations and spontaneous recitation of prayers of Thanks to Lord Almighty. The motley crowd in the train had seen with its own eyes the ghastly and nerve-shattering scenes of some trains full of corpses and some survivors severely injured lying therein crying for help. As if, a sort of heinous competition of taking revenge by groups on each side of the dividing line had taken charge. For each train of dead would result in mass killings in the next train coming from the other side. I still remember people talking of complete elimination of occupants of train which originated from Bannu on 10th of the month. It had the elite of the town, the rich and wealthy, and most prosperous people on board. The riches and wealth was, probably the prime target. It was said that the occupants of this particular train had had most cruel end; women were abducted, raped, all the valuables were looted and then the occupants including children were killed mercilessly. Even now, while recalling this tragedy, the elderly people like us, who had known this tragedy first hand, start crying ceaselessly. It was a tragedy, most cruel, barbaric and worse than a beastly act.

The charm of being safe and in our own country

That we were not dead seemed unbelievable for a while. All sorts of opinions were being expressed but everybody was busy embracing and congratulating each other; probably to be doubly sure that we had really survived. The reality of being alive in these circumstances was a true bliss. A miracle had happened in our life, with God's Grace and Benevolence. Soon we heard the slogans, 'Bole So Nihal, Sat Sri Akal' 'Hindustan Zindabad' 'Sanatan Dharm ki Jai' and we realized we were in our motherland and safe. For a while, the deep anxieties about our future vanished. We were amongst the people we could call our own. Strangely, the loss of hearth and home in the land of our birth and where our ancestors had lived for ages did not occur in our mind then. The critical first phase of our 'Journey of Escape' had completed. We could dare to breathe normally, have hope and believe there was a future for us. Probably for security reasons, the train did not stop for long at Attari. At the next stop(I do not remember the name, but probably it was Amritsar) there was huge crowd at the platform ready with buckets of drinking water, plenty of cooked food and other necessities of daily use etc. with smiles of welcome on each face. Suddenly we realized we were hungry and thirsty. Not only, we were fed well on the spot but also given packets of cooked food, some utensils and other goodies before the train moved ahead. My mother's and some other elders' eyes became moist. Probably, the idea of being a refugee and recipient of doles and aid was discomforting for them.

Chapter 7
Our First Abode in India;
the Refugee Camp at Kurukshetra

After a brief stop at Amritsar the train started moving out. And soon, the anxieties about future re-surfaced for we did not know where we were headed to. A few hours journey and we were at Kurukshetra, where a huge camp was set up by the Govt. for arrivals from across the border. A new title awaited us there. We were 'Refugees' and had to register ourselves there and furnish details of our identity and domicile in Pakistan. A Refugee Card was issued to each family giving details of each member. This entitled us to tent accommodation in the camp for a specified period and also other perks and facilities like free ration, medical aid, and education facility for children. Free rations, grocery and other necessities were being provided by the Govt. outlets, while other social/religious organizations were generous in distributing other necessities like utensils, clothes, blankets, foot-wear and linen etc. Virtually every article necessary for living was being made available either at govt. ration shops or by philanthropic organizations. On surface, life started rolling on though the bigger questions were begging answers. Our family consisting of our mother and three of us brothers and our eldest brother-in-law's family consisting of our sister and their daughter (Pushpa) got living accommodation in two separate tents. All this arrangement meant that the primary needs of food and shelter had been taken care now. And it provided the families with peace of mind so badly needed after the debilitating turmoil. It was let known by the camp authorities that stay in the camp was surely available for a reasonable period to enable the families to make arrangements for settlement. It was a great relief.

Elders' benign gift for us, the children

No sooner had the dust settled down and the family got into some routine, our elders decided to send us to school in the camp to continue our studies unlike large numbers who were seen in the lanes hawking some odd items. It was an epoch making decision which put us on the road to a meaningful life. I joined there in class 6 having passed class 5 in Pakistan. It was good for us to begin our studies without interruption. The school was good and it functioned like any other school. It had class rooms in different tents. Classes were held regularly and teachers were helpful. The Hindi teacher used to take great pains since all his students were new to this subject. I finished my class 6 in the camp school and was happy with the level of satisfactory standards of education there.

I am always deeply grateful to my elders for the benign gift of education.

Family starts looking at possible options for settlement

Our eldest brother-in-law, who along with his own family was with us throughout this turmoil, was a qualified medical Dispenser and got a job in camp's hospital. In a way, it meant the future got on track for them and the camp was their regular abode now. As always, the family depended upon him for a mature and correct decision for future plans of settlement. The harsh reality was that there was no adult member amongst us who could pick a job and support the family. Our eldest brother Manohar Lal was already in India working as a salesman in one of our uncle's army canteens but on a very meager salary, which by no imagination was enough to support the family. The struggle for survival being faced now appeared insurmountable than the threat to life faced earlier. Having survived the holocaust was Bliss. How to continue to live now was an enormous challenge. For how long, could the family live on doles. In any case, the doles of the refugee camp were available for a limited period only. The family had to decide and move out fast. Besides the limitations of access to stay in the camp, my hunch is that it was hurting the self-pride of the family though nobody brought it up in discussions.

Our mother had a painful feeling that doles and depressing environment in the camp was an antithesis to growth and an honorable life. The sooner we moved out the better it is. In spite of the harshness of lack of resources at Isa Khel after the death of our father, our mother did not give up to temptations and continued to lead and inspire us all with her determination to face the odds courageously. She always believed in herself and her mentor, God.

After few months, the camp authorities let it be known that we could no longer continue to be there. The suggestion was that we move to Rewari town (now in Haryana), which as per Government's decision was allocated as a place for settlement of persons from Isa Khel. It was given to understand that the state govt. would help us with support to settle down there on regular basis. However, on arrival there, a temporary stop gap accommodation was provided to us in govt. school for a limited period and we were required to fend for ourselves. This was in stark contrast to the assurance given by camp authorities at Kurukshetra but to no avail. It was disgusting and soon it became apparent that it was the end of govt. support.

Bareilly emerges as family's destination

After due deliberations, our elders decided not to prolong our stay in the Refugee camp. Considering all aspects, the elders decided to move to Bareilly where the eldest male member of the family, our brother Shri Manohar Lal was already working in Jat Regimental Centre's canteen as a salesman. The final view was that there was no other option except to face the difficult situation together and endeavor to make a new beginning in free India jointly. Accordingly, the family moved to Bareilly sometimes in 1948.

Thanks to the Refugee Card issued by camp authorities in Kurukshetra, we were provided with accommodation in a temporary refugee camp set up in empty army barracks in Bareilly Cantonment. I cannot recall how the family managed its affairs but gradually a feeling started creping in our minds that a beginning had been made. Everybody was struggling in whatever manner possible and making contribution in his/her own way but the real responsibility was on our eldest brother's shoulders. I must confess he lived up to family's tradition of facing the challenge head on and with confidence.

To us, the children, life in Bareilly refugee camp appeared to be stable and normal. It was totally different from the overall environ of painful cries and shrills witnessed in Kurukshetra camp. Gradually, we made friends and got busy in our routine; going to school regularly, playing with new friends in the open like what was in Isa Khel. Our elders had decided to send us to school here again. The target was the High School Examination which would entitle us to seek a job of a clerk.

A Refugee's plight and urge for integration in society

Being a refugee is not only a curse but a social stigma too. While in Bareilly, fingers were pointed at us, wherever we went. There was language barrier; we did not know Hindi. Our dress and social customs were different. Sometimes, it appeared we were looked down upon for we were thought to be aliens and a burden and were sure to usurp the native social structure. Probably, our community demonstrated its independence too openly and sought no alms or charity, which, normally would appear to be necessary for refugees in the land of adoption. Social integration with natives appeared difficult and time consuming, in any case. Patience and waiting for opportune time was the sine-qua-non of the difficult situation facing our community. We, the children were frequently admonished for picking up quarrels or controversies if any, in school or in the neighborhood.

The seniors; our mother, eldest brother and sister-in-law were careful and focused on not creating any controversies with natives. Gradually, this approach brought about the results. The hostility gave way to resistance and then to 'couldn't care less' attitude towards us. Ignore them (refugees) seemed to be general feeling now. The realization that the refugees were here to stay started sinking in. The vast majority of the local population was sympathetic and willing to accept the inevitable; gradual integration of the refugees. A large number of social welfare and religious organizations and officials of the 'Relief and Rehabilitation' department of the G.O.I. were helping to mitigate our hardships and also contributing to the process of gradual integration in the society. I remember; there was no general environment of hostility or non-acceptance amongst children and teachers in the school.

To sum up, over a period of time, there was general acceptance and there were no bars. The integration of refugees with the local society started happening fairly early. Credit for this goes to local populace, political and community leaders for helping the process of integration.

Our brother's presence in Bareilly; a boon

Thanks to family's determination to face the adversities jointly with courage and firm conviction in the adage "united we stand, divided we fall", the journey hereafter proved to be ok in spite of harsh realities of deprivation and continuous struggles for survival.

It is said, the agony and misery diminishes, when faced together. You have the pleasure and satisfaction of sharing whatever little is available, so to say. And bits of success achieved in adverse and difficult circumstances, stimulate us to do more, achieve more; more so when the success/accomplishment is the result of joint endeavor. To boost our morale and to reinforce our confidence in the concept of unity, our mother would narrate the old famous story of a wise old man, demonstrating to his sons the strength of unity in a bundle of logs which nobody could break when tied together but when untied, each log could be broken without much effort.

Virtues of Joint Family living

The family comprising of our mother, eldest brother and Bhabi ji (they were married in April/May, 1947), and three of us, lived in the camp accommodation provided by the Govt. for about 2/3 years. All the 3 elder sisters were living in different places with their husbands who were lucky to have secured govt. jobs. The impact of hardship and deprivation was rendered less harsh with fixed salary income of eldest brother, stable shelter for living and willing efforts of seniors to supplement family's income by taking up odd jobs. Gradually, the tragic events and travails of partition started loosening their grip on family's psyche. Or it appeared so to me. Life seemed to be moving ahead as it could be in those difficult times. Lack of basic facilities and resources were accepted as inevitable and sine-qua-non in the circumstances prevailing then. The family learnt the art of sharing and being satisfied broadly with what was available. There used to be differences and divergent views but they used to be reconciled by discussions. To me, it appears, the basic factor of limitations was the prime mover behind this reconciliatory attitude. Work hard honestly and live on the hopes of better days ahead was the rallying point.

Expectations of better days ahead start materializing

It was hoped that when the two of us brothers finish our schooling and get a job, things will improve and change for the better. And it did start happening after 1950 when the elder brother passed his High School exam. He got a job of a clerk in the office of Custodian of Evacuee Property in Bareilly sometimes in 1952, after he turned 18. His pay package was Rs 85/p.m. which was a handsome amount considering the level of inflation at that time. You could buy day's requirement of vegetables and some fruits for the whole family for just one rupee. Unbelievable; but it is true. In any case for us it was a big relief. The family did start thinking of going in for some aromatic and nutritious food articles especially some fruits and milk products. Occasional treat of eggs also started happening. It was a welcome change and helped the ladies to bring about some variety in the food.

There was hope now. The family could now think of buying some gadgets/utensils for the kitchen and some new clothes on occasions like birthdays or festivals. Few months later, all members insisted that the elder brother buys a bicycle for going to office instead of going on foot or in the bus. Such small goodies were a source of great satisfaction and happiness for all of us.

Now the family could think of future instead of just bothering for daily needs only. The very thought of planning for future was an elixir; invigorating to full brim and motivating us all to put in more efforts for making a success of our endeavors.

A shelter of our own

By virtue of devotion to job and good performance in office, the elder brother was allotted a small house by his office on a nominal rent out of the lot of houses lying vacant and in the legal custody of the Govt. With this facility, the life for us became more organized. We started looking forward to still better days ahead. The noble judgment of the elders had brought about a marked improvement.

The house lying vacant for years after its owners migrated to Pakistan was in real bad shape. It (the house) being about 70 years old needed extensive repairs and strengthening. The family got busy in making it habitable and suitable for its needs. By then I was earning attractive amount as my wages of labor as rent-collector on commission basis. It took us few months to complete the repair and renovation work in the house. It was a significant milestone of genuine satisfaction and happiness for the family. In fact, it made the elders feel relieved of the pain of leaving behind our house in Pakistan.

Charms of being part of a
free democratic society; our India

Soon we realized that a refugee's life in free India was a boon compared to the scenario that obtained for us in Pakistan and which was sure to deteriorate further with every passing day. Here in India, you breathed freedom, lived as a free person, felt secure, enjoyed the freedom of holding on to your faith, got closer to your dreams for future, could look forward to pursuing personal aims and goals, and support from Govt. authorities and social and religious organizations. There was Hope. There was satisfaction with the life as it was unfolding. There was contentment.

We could believe in ourselves and visualize a bright future for ourselves. It was our own country, a free society, no discrimination of any type; opportunities were open to us like they were to native inhabitants.

Other fascinating attractions of happy life in Bareilly

The other good attractions here were a good weather, good facilities for education (good schools and colleges) and availability of basic urban facilities like electricity, piped water supply, street lights and good roads. People wearing Gandhi caps, white and starched, was a welcome change compared to long and big turbans that were compulsory in our high school.

Talking of weather, I must tell that we came from a place where there were only two dominant seasons; severe bitter cold and harsh, scorching sultry summer. There was no rainy season like what we witnessed here. The words 'Sawan' and 'Chaumasa' heard by us here were refreshing and soothing. They not only were the harbinger of heavy rains after the scorching summer, which itself was a great relief but also represented the rich folklore associated with the arrival of monsoon. People would welcome the auspicious month 'Sawan' and heavy down-pour associated with it by enjoying the folk songs like 'sawan ke jhoole', happily riding in swings, dancing with joy in traditional costumes, making merriment with friends and family members during the festival of 'Teej', savor sweets and other dishes closely identified with 'chaumasa', like puri/kachori, kheer (rice pudding of rice and milk) and vast variety of Ghevar which is prepared only in the month of 'Sawan'. These rich social and cultural events were mesmerizing. I am sorry; I must refrain from attempting to describe the magic of the word "Sawan". This can be done best by persons with creative talent like poets.

That people go crazy in 'Sawan" is a well-known reality both in Pakistan and India. After all, we have a common heritage and culture going back to centuries. I am not suggesting that people in Punjab (Pakistan) from where we migrated were not familiar with the pleasures of 'Sawan' or no traditional folklore was known to be associated with this golden month. However, our area in Pakistan though part of Punjab was in the extreme North West where nature's bounty of 'Monsoon' and plentiful rains associated with it were not so common. Of course, I remember the big community feasts that were organized during this period on the banks of river Indus in our town. They were called 'Dhawani' in local dialect which meant a community outing of men, women and children by the side of river bank. It included bathing for long hours in the river, community cooking of variety of food and games for all. It used to be a day-long affair. Men and women would jointly do the cooking; the 'puris', 'kheer' and 'chhole, aloo ki sabzi' along with 'salads'and pickles. Enjoy the dip in the river and eat in between the dips. Children like us would not only enjoy but also indulged in pranks while playing and keeping the Moms anxious, as usual, about kids safety; the prominent fear being getting drowned.

The greenery all around in Bareilly in rainy season was a feast for eyes; soothing, charming and bringing in the hopes for vast variety of vegetables and fruits. We had not experienced such a wonderful bounty. We used to have a variety of fruits in Isa-khel but they were all coming from far off places in Punjab, NWFP, Afghanistan and Bulochistan. The harsh local climate and paucity of rains in our town was not helpful in the production of vegetables in abundance. The most well-known fruit grown in our area was dates. We did have musk-melon and water-melons grown in abundance on the banks of Indus River. There were no canals for irrigation then to help produce vegetables in large quantities.

In Isa-Khel, there was hardly any rain in summer and if on some day, it did rain, we would go berserk with happiness, rush out to call friends, remove our shirts, rush out to enjoy it and get wet as long as it lasted. Kids; boys and girls alike enjoyed it together. Everybody would claim that he or she was the first to have received the first drop on his/her back and this was thought to be a lucky omen. We would chant the colloquial lines "pehli kani main jhallai, jeevay mera peo te bhai" which means 'I received the first drop of rain on my back, God Bless my father and brother.

Some other happy signs of prosperity which fascinated us in Bareilly were cinema halls, big bazars with well-stocked shops, good eateries,

'Chaat' kiosks and motor transport for local travel. Betel shops were surprise attraction which we had neither heard of nor known in Isa Khel. Obviously, these were some of the signs of development which had escaped us till then.

Soothing salutations in vogue amongst people of Bareilly

Life in Bareilly unfolded a few welcome surprises. The congenial environment for redemption of our faith was the first and foremost bliss here. The phrases 'Jai Ram ji ki' and 'Jai Shri Ram' which were commonly used here as salutations by people were soothing not only to ears but also to the inner-self which embodies faith and deep respects (Shradha) for Hindus' most revered religious icon. Being refreshingly new for us, the phrases meant a new world to us. We developed a great fancy for them. For us, it was happy satisfaction galore; we were now free to believe in our religion, practice it and feel proud of being closer to our religious traditions. We were totally unaware of them so far. Use of any such salutation was unthinkable while in Pakistan. We were happy to hear them repeatedly during the day. People will salute each other like this every time they met. We loved to utter them, occasion or no occasion. I believe; it was a natural instinct considering the harassment in the name of religion which we were subjected to, not long ago.

Chapter 8
Brave New India and Valiant migrant Punjabis

It is said, 'Adversities make a man perfect and bring out the best in him/her.' People like us, the refugees, who did not have enough financial and human resources, were around in large numbers but the spirit of moving ahead by hard work was visible almost in every household. The brave Punjabis, victim of circumstances, were in no mood to give up and suffer. They were determined to leave the past behind and make it big in free India, their own country. Realistically speaking, they had no other option; work hard or perish.

The business acumen of Punjabis came to their rescue during those harsh days. It was a big challenge to compete with the already established business houses and vendors of goods and services and that too without sufficient capital or infrastructure. Innovation and new trading skills were the only options that could give Punjabis a foothold in trade and they demonstrated that they could do it. Therefore, they adopted the time-tested formulae to meet the challenge; low margins which would generate high volumes. The other intelligent move was; buy in bulk on credit, spread your ware on road-side, keep smiling and be attentive while talking to the customer. Yet another distinctly different and meaningful step was; hand over the goods duly packed in paper bags rather than asking the customer to bring his/her own bags as was the practice with the established shop-keepers. This innovative practice gave the Punjabis an edge and boosted their turn-over. Carrying own bags was hassles for large majority of customers who preferred the sellers on the foot-path.

The result was obvious; handsome profit thanks to handsome increase in sales.

The times were acutely difficult. Antagonizing the local population was the last thing refugees could do. They needed support from all quarters; govt. agencies, political groups, socially important and active groups of people, and people at large. Punjabis had no option but to adjust to the local environment and they did it willingly keeping in mind a long-term vision.

It is true that Punjabis, by nature, are hard-working and can rise high to meet the challenges. History is witness that they faced the repeated onslaughts of aggressions from the North which made them hard-willed. Whether it was Alexander the Great or other invaders from the North like Mohd. Gauri of Ghazni, Changez Khan or Babar of Central Asia who came to India to plunder its wealth or conquer a part of its territory, Punjabis were the first to suffer at their hands but they never gave up. This indomitable spirit gave them positive energy at the time of holocaust in 1947 and thereafter in the interim period of struggles to settle down. The self-pride and confidence in their ability to face the adversities coolly helped Punjabis to carve out a niche for themselves in the society very soon.

Punjabis give themselves a new identity; "Pursharthi"

Punjabis resented being addressed as "Sharnarthi" (Refugee) which suggested they were asylum seekers. "We have come to our own country; we do not want doles, rather we want support with dignity and integration with honor." The word "Sharnarthi" hurt their self-pride and was a double-whammy. A new adage, "Pursharthi" (believer in self and hard work) was coined by them for themselves which meant a person who has faith in himself and is keen to succeed by dint of his ability to work hard.

Karmath Jeevan

Similarity of challenges before newly independent India and hapless, struggling migrants

An interesting parallel existed between the struggles being waged by newly independent India and migrants from across the border. While our leaders were busy making efforts for bringing about stability in the newly independent country and were working hard to lay a sound base for its progress, the refugees like us were struggling to find their moorings in the vast land. Again, while the political leaders were busy in framing a constitution appropriate for an equitable, just and democratic rule in the country and to lay the foundation for an egalitarian society for its vast population, the refugees were busy in adjusting themselves and creating their identity for integration in the new environment.

The challenges confronting the political leaders and refugees were same. It was an uphill task for both. While the spectrum for the political leaders was vast and they were face to face with an herculean task of peaceful integration of princely states with the rest of the country, building of infrastructure, and establishing rule of law in the newly independent country of about 350 million with a focus and vision for a stable democratic institutions for meeting the aspirations of the people, the refugees had before them similar questions of ensuring a stable future with honor for themselves and their kith and kin.

Apart from above, the country needed huge resources for development and growth and this was a serious question before the refugees as well. Having overcome all odds, the country getting independence after long drawn struggle and refugees escaping the murderous mobs, the immediate task before both was the same; work hard and lay foundation for all round growth to overcome the environment of despondence. Plan for innovative development to satisfy the urge for making a new beginning based on equity and equality and look forward to an era of prosperity and growth.

The first important milestone of framing a democratic constitution was completed rather expeditiously and India became a Republic on 26th January, 1950. Here again, a parallel was achieved by migrants by virtue

71

of making a beginning, though very small, for themselves. By about this time, majority of refugee camps were wound up, the implication being that by then the majority of migrants had stopped receiving doles and had made a beginning on their own. The parallel continued beyond this period. The Govt. successfully conducted country-wide first general election in 1952 and the migrants not only exercised their franchise in large numbers but also actively joined the political process by joining the cadres of political parties and taking active part in campaigns.

A good beginning had been made by both the govt. of the day and the migrants. An era of hope subsisted for both; the political class and the refugees.

Chapter 9
Mighty Indus to Holy Ganga;
my journey of fortitude

My life's journey of fortitude and perseverance spread over 78 years transcends vast stretch of territories forming part of Pakistan and India. Like many others' (victims of partition), my journey embodies cyclical movement of ups and downs, joys and sorrows, and scaling of heights as it chugged along the cycle of life. It is a tale of struggles of an orphan. Not deterred by serious impediments, I faced the challenges with determination, picked up petty jobs when in school to contribute to family's resources for survival like other members of the family. My whole-time work-life began just after finishing the High School exam when I started working at the young age of 17, as a rent collector on commission basis for a contractor of the govt. Soon after I turned major, I qualified in competition and secured the regular job of a clerk in Railways. I persisted with my efforts to acquire higher qualification along with job as a result of which I continued to push ahead and secured higher jobs in different offices/organizations. And in the end, achieved what would have been a dream; the position of General Manager in a prestigious national oil co. of the country.

It is said, "In adversities lies an opportunity."

The real satisfaction is that after a tumultuous work-life of nearly four decades, we have settled down at Dehra Dun, a beautiful town in lush green Dun valley in the foot-hills of Himalayas near holy river Ganga.

From a place near Waziristan (Isa Khel), now a notorious epicenter of terrorism, to the shores of peaceful territory of holy river Ganga and Himalayas, my journey witnessed a multitude of varying social milieu. It is gratifying that though my place of birth, Isa Khel, was away from Mohan Judaro and Harapa in Sind, the famous archeological finds/sites of ancient Indus-Valley Civilization, Indus River is known to be home to civilized societies living all along its route starting from Ladakh in Himalayas. My reasonable assumption is that our territory also must have witnessed the imprint of this ancient glorious civilization.

Majestic Himalayas in the North; a glorious canopy

The majestic Himalayas stretching from Kashmir to Sikkim in the north of India constitute a glorious cap-like canopy for the country. They are famous not only for their glorious peaks, mighty glaciers and rivers and scenic beauty but are also known to be home to hermits, saints and rishis for centuries. These holy and outwardly rustic persons are known to be doing 'ghor tapasya' (deep meditation) for centuries for realizing inner peace, self-realization and Nirvana/'Moksha'. Himalayas' serene environment provides ideal support to these noble souls who seek re-union with Him..

In fact, it is widely believed that India's rich and world-famous treasure of deep spiritual heritage (Gyana) contained in the Holy Scriptures was revealed to 'rishis' while meditating in Himalayas and over a period of time these revelations acquired the form of texts. The universal view is that these holy texts are cumulative contribution of unknown scholars/ rishis and were not authored by any single individual.

Garhwal Himalayas; a spiritual sanctuary

Garhwal Himalayas aptly known as "Dev Bhoomi" (Gods' Abode) are home to sacred ancient temples like 'Badrinath', and 'Kedarnath' amongst others where hundreds of thousands of devotees pay their obeisance every year during summers to seek the blessings of ruling deities, Lord Vishnu and Lord Shiva. These temples are at heights of 12000/13000 feet and remain closed for 6 months of winter. Legend has it that these two shrines were established by 'Adi Shankracharya' in the 8th century AD when the vast majority of followers of Hindu dharma had fallen into a slumber. The Adi Shankracharya, a learned saint, travelled from the southern edge of the country in Kerala to all the four corners of the country and re-established the four sacred Dhams as citadels of Divinity to reinvigorate the dharma and spread the message of peace with dignity. His was a noble mission necessary to save the Hindu religion from getting into oblivion. The Garhwal Himalayas are also home to 'Gangotri' and 'Yamnotri Dham' from where the holy rivers Ganga and Yamuna respectively originate. The ancient Gurdwara of 'Hemkunt Sahib' where Guru Gobind Singh meditated for years in his previous birth to attain the supreme knowledge is situated here. This Gurudwara being located in high altitudes is thrown open for few months in summer when thousands of devotees from all parts of the country throng it to pay their obeisance.

Dehra Dun; my final moorings of choice

I am indeed privileged and lucky that after a tumultuous and hectic spell of 35 years of my journey after independence, Lord blessed me to find my moorings in 1982 in ONGC, Dehra Dun; a location I had aspired since long for settling down after my retirement. Dehra Dun's dominant attractions are its peaceful and relatively crime-free environs and a healthy climate. It is true that population explosion and un-planned urban growth has severely impacted Dehra Dun and deprived the town greatly of its unique peaceful hue but the question is which other habitation, whether urban or country side, has remained untouched by the hurricane of so-called development which is mostly ill-planned rather non-planned and ad-hoc in nature, in the country as a whole. Un-wittingly, we became an accomplice to the rat-race of un-planned growth when I bought a parcel of land in an under-developed location. And who can be said to be responsible for this sordid state? Obviously, the State Govt. and local administration who failed to act to meet the growing demand for housing needs of the people. The result was obvious; people like us would grab what was on offer, was reasonably priced and had the potential to grow and develop into a reasonably good and safe location in due course. This exactly happened with us. Starting with four houses in the midst of orchards of litchi, mango and other tropical fruits built simultaneously by four of us in 1983-84, the colony today is a well-developed habitation, secure, gated and well-taken care by a society headed by a President supported by a Secretary and treasurer. No wonder, today our Green Park is the most sought after residential address in this part of the town. And the icing on the cake, as they say, is the spirit of mutual regards, support and co-operation amongst its residents. Give a call in the midst of night, if in distress, and see your neighbors coming out in support. Green Park people are like that only and hopefully it will always be like that only.

Chapter 10
Childhood; the innocent phase of life

Childhood reminds me of a popular Hindi movie song's first line, "Sapne suhane ladakpan ke mere nainon mein dolein bahar ban ke" which means broadly, 'Dreamy days of childhood dangle like spring before my eyes'. The significant meaning of this catch-line would be, 'childhood is like spring when every-thing around is charming and colorful.' An eminent scholar defined childhood as dreamy-eyed, romantic notion of childhood as a time of un-alloyed joy and golden sun-sets. Along with the above crisp and short description of childhood, I would like to add that a care-free mind, innocence and openness are the hallmarks of childhood. It is natural to say, therefore, that longer the childhood the better it is for a healthy future growth. Given this, who would want to disconnect with childhood and childlike attitude even during adulthood or ripe years of 70s and beyond. This is one treasure that makes life truly cherishing.

Childhood in our times

I believe; we were lucky to be children in those good old times. Let me explain 'we were lucky' and 'good old times'. We were lucky because we had the privilege of being closer to our elders. They had lot of time for us, listened attentively to our small anxieties and concerns, helped us to resolve them and feel happy, demonstrated through their conduct the virtues of being patient and careful while dealing with others, made us aware of our glorious heritage, exposed us to the religion of our forefathers, narrated stories of valor, sacrifice and self-less service to humanity, society and country by our Gurus, saints, rishis and Vedic scholars and above all, knew how to get closer to us and communicate freely with us. The social scientists call it 'spending quality time' and rightly it is so. However, the phrase 'quality time' just doesn't imply being together, sharing happy golden moments and enjoying each other's company. To be meaningful to a child and being effective in helping the child to pick up vital valuable inputs, the time spent together has to be all inclusive. It calls for depth of knowledge with conviction and ability to disseminate it unobtrusively whatever is intended to be communicated by parents and the elders.

It is imperative for seniors to be gifted with rich personal experiences and possess ability to capture the imagination of the child. Paying close attention to what the child conveys during inter-action, giving due weight to it, making visible attempts to allay anxieties and doubts in child's mind is important. It demands listening skills to be able to build confidence and help the child to open up freely. It has to be an environment of mutual understanding.

Now, what are good old times? The times were good because the social and domestic environment, by and large, was free and open. By and large, it was free of unnecessary conflicts, was rustic suggesting people felt confident to share each other's experiences and views. People were not too secretive and self-centered and generally felt happy to share their happiness and sorrows. The flavor of bliss prevailed generally.

The limitations childhood faces in present times

What follows are my franks views. I am not suggesting that now childhood is no more vibrant, no more precious or it has lost its virtuous charm of innocence and a free mind, as it were. It is still a time of unalloyed joys and golden sun-sets. These wonderful attributes are still the preserve of this golden phase in a human being's life. However, what has happened over years, for whatever reasons, has brought about certain limitations and changed the complexion. In my opinion:-

The joint families which were the bed-rock of equipping the children with important/critical learning are getting fewer. The result is that in most cases now the children grow up in isolation and get deprived of the valuable examples of meaningful personal conduct of elders. Good real-time examples of conduct of elders blazed a trail of far-reaching depth and value before the children. In addition, now the children in nuclear families do not get opportunities to listen to tales of heroics and exemplary conduct from ancient history and glorious past. They have to contend with reading the relevant books, if interested, but listening orally from elders with value-addition by them has unique charms and significance of its own. The delicate responsibility of exposing children to our heritage laced with the wisdom in scriptures and supported by anecdotes and lessons of history was best performed by elders in a unique amiable style. Thus the children had the soothing privilege and pride of being aware of the past cultural heritage of the family and their country.

It won't be an exaggeration if I suggest that children were the top most priority for elders and attention to self was secondary for them. It was fine if in the process one's own routine was disturbed. A child getting full attention and that too in plenty was the norm.

The advent of nuclear families and present day compulsions for working couples to be not able to spend sufficient time with children has impacted children's growth. When alone, they either tend to indulge in superficial activities or just while away their time. The concept of utilizing their time for their own benefit in a productive activity gets ignored in absence of proper guidance.

The perceptible change in life styles, parents being more busy in pursuing personal ambitions more vigorously to meet the challenges of competition whether in work place or in personal life means lesser attention to matters influencing the children's mind. Some other issues like engaging maids who are not professionally competent to take proper care for healthy grooming of children and creeping belief in the veracity of gadgets being a

79

good companion for a child are serious issues needing attention. They do have long-term implications for development of 'healthy mind in healthy body.'

Social and peer pressures queer the pitch and squeeze more time of couples now to get involved more in societal issues/problems thus reducing the window of time for children. Another aspect which often affects the children is the explosion of information and availability of multiple means/gadgets of communication which a child is face to face with every day. This is a game changer; making children mature in childhood itself and robbing them early of the innocent charms of childhood.

Further to what is stated hereinabove, it is also a fact that a child is exposed to influences of conduct of peers and teachers in school, pals in the neighborhood and extended family, if any. The child picks up some of these attributes also besides the ones the child is exposed to in his/her own family.

Innocence thy name is childhood

The universal fact is that the child quietly accepts and internalizes only those traits in sub-conscious mind which attract his/her innocent mind without any extra efforts. The attributes so imbibed and internalized by the child continue to develop and grow, as the child advances in age. And these qualities get settled at the bottom of the pyramid of child's value-chain. Therefore to be satisfied and happy with the child's grooming, the parents/elders have to lead by example like a successful leader, an armed forces commander or a businessman.

Chapter 11
My Glorious Childhood

I am lucky; a happy carefree attitude has been my legacy in childhood. Like I mentioned before, I was truly a free bird unmindful of anxieties or fear complex for future. Would enjoy playing with pals in the neighborhood, whether boys or girls, for long hours till getting tired or feeling hungry or thirsty. After we finished playing in the afternoons, we were encouraged and provided with healthy nutritious snacks easily manageable in the neighborhood. One such item was rustic village type roasted grains especially chick peas and jaggery in the afternoons when we were hungry after long hours of play. We would go home, pick up some quantity of raw chick peas, corns or wheat whatever available and go to the fellow in the neighborhood who had big sand blasting iron pan (wok) and get the grains roasted. All the children would share each other's item and enjoy it happily together. It was indeed a sort of feast which we looked forward to everyday. No other snacks were permitted and of course, no packaged snacks like potato chips, patties and juices or other so-called healthy drinks were known to be available.

Before being allowed to go out for playing with my friends, the seniors in the family were careful that I completed my homework or any special assignment in time. And I would finish it very fast to be able to enjoy the games and the company of my friends to the maximum. The games we played were mostly country side rustic type; like 'Gili Danda', 'kabaddi', 'hide and seek','Kho Kho' and similar other games where no formal play ground or costly items were required. Our play field was neighborhood for our parents would not want us to be far away.

A favorite pastime during summer months used to be a trip to the river bank for a dip there. The mighty Indus River was about a mile and a half away from our home and it was a big relief from scorching sultry summer to have a dip in it for as long as possible. Of course, we were there under the supervision of a senior person who would monitor our movements and ensure safe conduct. He had full authority and control on us while we were enjoying the trip. Yes, this permission was not given so freely. We had to earn it.

The mighty Indus was huge, full of gushing streams of water. The sound of running water sometimes sounded like the thunder of a lion. The river looked like an ocean and was very vast. The other end of the river was not visible to us. People feared boarding a boat for going to the other bank. In any case, we were not permitted for it. I remember having travelled once in a boat along with my mother and some other relatives in mighty Indus River. Water could be seen to be gushing at terrific speed creating whirls and it was the boating skills that helped the boatman to navigate safely through the river. We were in the boat for few hours before we reached the destination on the other end of the river. It was a pilgrimage trip to some widely revered saint's Samadhi. Our elders like other pilgrims believed that this visit shall grant them their wish. For us, the children, it was a journey of fun, merriment and freedom.

Factors that helped shape the values in my childhood and adolescence

(i) Freedom to believe in self and influence of holy texts

The freedom I enjoyed during those formative years in Isa Khel and later in Dehra Dun helped me build up an attitude of plain, simple and rational thinking. I developed an antipathy to things I considered abhorring. May be, in the process, I also developed a strong sense of intolerance to things wrong. My mind wouldn't accept that there could be some valid reason or a justification for a wrong that was happening around. To me, a wrong was a wrong and accepting it was also wrong. The influence of stories from holy books I heard from time to time from my mother and other elders was ingrained deeply in my thought process. I believed in their authenticity or maybe I just liked the characters and their conduct.

(ii) Firm belief in truth and being honest in dealings.

Anyway, notwithstanding some other shortcomings in me like fear complex, lack of leadership traits, shying away to face difficult situations and not exhibiting strong will when required, I continued to develop and live with a firm belief in truth, simple and straightforward attitude and being fair and honestly good in my dealings with others. I didn't feel ever the necessity to be malicious in my conduct. I never felt compelled or thought of indulging in 'tit for tat' when face to face with an obnoxious situation.

Thanks to my elders especially my mother during my childhood days and brother-in-law in Dehra Dun later, I firmly started believing that ultimately the truth prevails. Follow it and be happy. I was told, "Truth builds nerves, invigorates self-confidence and in spite of odds and resistance by others, the journey is rendered smooth. It is always a "win win" situation notwithstanding some setbacks now and then."

(iii) Wise counsel of elder sisters.

The environment in my early childhood days was complex; sometimes very congenial but at times I felt confused to understand what was right and what was not. In such difficult situations, both my elder sisters and mother were great support. They would spend time with me, listen and try to make out what the problem was, give bits of advice relevant to the occasion and narrate some incident or a tale to clear the confusion/ misgiving. The underlying approach/advice would normally be; have patience, all will be well. They knew; my problems were more imaginary than real as is normally so with children of our age.

I believed in not hurting others with my conduct or loose and harsh comments and was careful to avoid controversies. I was told, "It would be counter-productive for a person like you. Hence avoid it." I never understood why people stoop down to misbehavior when not in agreement with a point of view. While getting annoyed and conveying unhappiness vocally and rigidly may be alright in a given desperate situation, there is no room for misbehavior or misconduct. Therefore, be careful in communication and dealings with others. Be persuasive and not being seen as unreasonable, argumentative or unwilling to listen to others' point. Speaking loud and harsh results in confrontation and brings about a negative response. When confronted with an unreasonable situation, leave the matter to rest there. Give time to passions to calm down. The phrase "let's agree to disagree" would be helpful most of the times. It may bring about a positive and reasonable response sooner than later.

(iv) Balancing gift of Almighty.

Although the weaknesses/shortcomings enumerated above were basic and could have hampered my balanced growth, I didn't encounter any obstacle on the path to a healthy growth. I genuinely believe that my firm faith in straightforward dealings with an open mind did help in smoothening the journey going forward. I never felt compelled to take recourse to unfair or corrupt practices. Even, for argument sake, if I wanted to indulge in all this, I am sure, I would have done a miserable job and landed myself in trouble. I must confess; it was/is simply beyond me. In hindsight, I realize it helped me all along and saved me of the ordeal of living a miserable corrupt life. There were no regrets when I faced an adverse or difficult situation because of my conduct for I knew I had done no wrong and ultimately the true position will emerge. I was conscious that it may not happen always soon thus resulting in some anxious moments. Doesn't it all appear to be too good to be acceptable? The answer lies in appreciating and accepting this tenet as a matter of faith and internalizing and following it sincerely and truthfully. The taste of pudding lies in eating it, as they say. I concede I was too young and couldn't have fully comprehended the merits of this approach. But it happened with me and is still ingrained in my psych. I have followed it all my life sincerely and honestly. In the process, though there have been occasions/instances of disbelief by others. I have been simply ignoring them and thus making light others' comments of disbelief.

Sum total of my value system

Once, when I was about 24 years and working in AG's office in Shimla, I had a discussion with one of my colleagues about my basic instinct in dealing with others. I remember having said then, "I start with the assumption that the person I am dealing with is nice, honest and sincere until it is revealed otherwise by his/her conduct, to which my friend replied that the person has to be under careful watch till he/she demonstrates that he/she is reliable and honest". I am happy that I lived all my life with this basic valuable instinct. I feel I am lucky to have been like that only.

The innocent pleasures I enjoyed in my childhood

Apart from school and games, I enjoyed going for a walk in the morning with friends on Sundays and holidays. We would go to the city park, stealthily pluck flowers, and cover them up in our pockets lest the gardener sees them and have fun in running after chirping and flying birds. We loved listening to cuckoo's melody and would imitate her voice loudly and she would respond repeatedly with her sweet and mesmerizing tone. We would enjoy it gleefully and share our happiness by laughing loudly repeatedly after each act of imitation and cuckoo's response thereto. It is gratifying to recall that our town had a big park well-laid and well-maintained with walk ways, lawns and vast variety of flowers and tall shady trees. There was a separate wing of fruit bearing trees. Like any child, we too would want to pluck or pick some of the fruits going back, if possible. Alas, the window of this pleasure was short because of harsh weather; either sultry summer or biting cold during 8/9 months in a year.

The environment of shared happiness between elders and us

The memory of listening to riveting stories, tales of valor and travelogue from an uncle in the neighborhood is still fresh in my mind. He had an unending treasure of ancient tales of Arabian nights, emperors, kings and queens of our land, valorous Afghans, travelogues of ancient Arabs, European visitors and stories of ancient 'jadugars and mystics.

'Sindbad the Sailor','Ali Baba and forty thieves", 'Laila Majnu', 'Queen Elizabeth' 'The stories of Emperors Chandragupt Maurya and Ashoka and the famous Guru Chanakya' were some of his favorite ones. His narratives, style of delivery along with his explanatory notes were lucid and juicy. On request, he would also tell the stories of sufi saints and preachers like Guru Nanak, Kabir, Tulsi, Sur Das, and Meera. The story telling sessions would begin in the night after dinner and would continue till late night subject to fulfillment of certain conditions by the gathering of listeners who were children of the neighborhood like me. He didn't encourage grown-ups to be part of the gathering. In fact, the story telling would start only after he was satisfied that we would abide by the terms of the game. And all these sessions were held at the second floor roof top of his house mostly during summer vacations.

His name was 'Sidhu chacha'. He was an elderly person and was a mason by profession. His terms were simple and business-like. Being a manual hard worker, he would be dead tired and would lie on his bed upside down. The requirement was that some of the children would do the errands of messaging his head and entire body continuously to relieve him of the day's fatigue, while some others would run the hand-held fans made of straw etc. to keep him cool. The narrative would continue till the service continued. Any breach or slowing down of the service would instantly result in stoppage of the narration. It was very interesting phenomena. Both the deliverer and receivers of the service were aware of their respective obligations. The quid pro quo of the game was well known to both the parties and that is the reason the deal was working well.

My harmless pranks in childhood

As I mentioned earlier, the summers in our area were very harsh and virtually intolerable. It was unthinkable to keep any mattress of cotton on the cot while sleeping in the night. Therefore, we used to spread mats made of straw and would sprinkle water on them before lying on the cot. There was no electricity; hence we used to have our cots on the roof tops. God alone knows how the nights passed. The temperatures improved somewhat in late nights. I remember; I had picked up a nauseating habit then. At about 4 in the morning every day, I would start crying demanding a bowl of curd. I would yell, "lalli, lalli". Poor mother or elder sister who were up and busy in house-hold routine would rush with the bowl of curd, I would gulp it fast and go to sleep again. Doesn't it sound funny now? Is it possible now to even imagine that a Mom or a sister would tolerate it and not call it a silly nuisance? I am not suggesting that it was a normal happily acceptable situation. But look at the kind and generously benevolent heart of a mother or a sister who accepted it as something normal and complied with the silly demand.

Fussy about food

I was quite fussy about food since my childhood. I was very demanding and kept my mother guessing and anxious about my tricks in the matter. Probably, I enjoyed keeping her on tenterhooks in matters of food especially the food on week-ends and lunch time on weekdays after I came back from school. Soon after reaching home from school, I will reject whatever she had cooked and will start cribbing and making complaints, "you never cook what I want. It is always the same routine stuff that you offer every day. I am not going to eat it and better remain hungry and that is probably what you like." Virtually terrified at display of an adamant attitude by me, she would start offering different dishes and as soon as she uttered an item's name that I had set my mind on, I would yell in harshest pitch, "Will you bring it or just keep standing?" Was it just her love for me that I exploited or I was really a spoilt brat in matters culinary, I don't know? She had lot of patience in putting up with such an idiotic behavior though the real reason for her inability to provide us with big variety of food was the financial constraint. To the extent possible within her limited resources, the poor lady always tried to keep us satisfied and when seeing us in calmer mood, would try to rationalize her problems and difficulties with us.

Mother, thy name is sacrifice, compassion and love

The relationship between a mother and a child is always enameled with deep emotions; mesmerizing and so sweet that it is beyond the realms of any analysis. The inter-action between a mother and a child has its own unique attributes that makes them both oblivious of happenings around. It is pure simple bliss unending for life though the child when grown up and busy in his own affairs may tend to miss this truth. Just try to imagine what happens when a child goes hungry, for whatever reason, before the eyes of a mother? She will be restless, silently crying until the child eats.

Our mother used to tell the story of a grown up boy who was carrying the heart of his mother, after killing her, to his beloved who had put this as a condition for marrying him. In hurry, the boy hit a boulder and got hurt when mother's heart cried, "Careful my boy, lest you get hurt". That is mother (Maa), an apostle of love, compassion and self-less care for her kids. Nobody else in this universe is closer to this definition. Nobody can take mother's place for her child. Happily and without any expectations, she would genuinely sacrifice her own comforts to provide for and look after the welfare of her child. No sacrifice is too big for her when necessary for her kids.

An ode to wonderful years- childhood

Before I bid-adieu to childhood here in this write-up, let me confess, it was really wonderful to be a child; innocent, care-free and open-minded. The first opening lines of a popular Bollywood movie's song sum up my sentiments for childhood in general:-

"Bachpan ke din bhi kya din theiy, udte phirte titli bun ke- bachpan!"

Chapter 12
My schooling in Pakistan

I must confess, initially I was reluctant to go to school and my elders had difficult time in making me understand its necessity in life. Most likely, the free time spent in playing in the company of my neighborhood friends was too tempting. Under pressure from all corners, I relented and became regular in going to school. Like many children of my age, I let it be known in the first few weeks after admission that I was not happy to be in school primarily because, to my mind, there was hardly any interesting activity there other than studies. And the temptation back home of being a free bird and enjoying the company of my pals by loitering around with them was more luring then the discipline etc. in the school. My mother's goading as also display of un-happiness by her, fear of punishment by elder brother and finally skillful handling with care by the headmaster of the school did the trick and I stopped protesting and got busy in studies willingly.

The Headmaster of Primary School

The headmaster was a very gentle and nice person. His talk of few minutes in the morning assembly was easily understandable and touched some interesting topic. Most of us would listen to him attentively. I believe; he left a strong impression in my mind. I remember his name and figure still. He was Mr. Ganga Ram, (one of my father's cousins) a very sober person, soft spoken, always dressed like a saintly elder. He was widely respected in the school. Students would obey him willingly and happily. I am still fascinated by the simple style of his turban; tied low on his head and without starch. And his looks in a simple set of spectacles added grace to his person. There was great charm associated with him.

The Math teacher

I also remember the name of another teacher. Our Math's Teacher, Mr. Noor Mohd. He was tall and of a strong built. He adored his moustaches and supported very long hairs which were always colored red with henna. Probably, there were no hair-dyes then. He used to teach us Mathematics. Though his style of teaching was not inspiring yet no body dare utter a word for fear of backlash. The stick he carried was awe-inspiring. He used to take his lunch in our class. A few selected boys laid his table, fetch water and made him comfortable, while two boys would pull with full vigor the strings of celling fan of cloth hanging in the room so that it dispelled maximum air while he was eating. Yet another group of students would take up the teaching of lesson of the day either orally or explaining it on the black-board in a hesitant and cautious manner lest there was some mistake and it invoked his anger. And to cap it all, after finishing his meals and washing hands etc. he would stretch his legs for rest. All this looks funny now though even now in govt. schools the situation is more or less same; nay I would say it has deteriorated for there is hardly any supervision or accountability. Teacher absenteeism in govt. schools is an acknowledged fact. During our times, the fear of sudden visit by the headmaster was scaring for teachers. Our Math's teacher would tell some of us to keep an eye on the corridor and entry door of the class room while he was taking his food.

Our primary school campus

Our school campus was spacious; it had properly equipped classrooms, playground, a well-kept open ground and a stage where apart from morning assembly, other functions/events were also organized. There was no electricity then but the rooms were well ventilated. Toilets were reasonably clean and there was arrangement for water supply in the school premises. There was neither a canteen nor a separate eating place. A hawker with candies and other small goodies used to be there. On the whole, the environment and atmosphere in the school was congenial. Students were encouraged to participate in games and sports. I was fond of Kabaddi and Kho-Kho which we used to play back home also.

The time (4 years) I was in this school passed off without any hassles. My performance was thought to be good. The punishment regime in the school was not harsh or brute. The student concerned would be asked to go out of class room for a specified duration, depending upon the mistakes committed or some act of indiscipline, and stand in the corridor facing the pillar in the veranda and his back to the walk-way. Frankly speaking, this punishment, though appearing to be mild on the face of it, had harsher and lasting impact than the physical handling. The passers-by would watch with a glee and the student would get exposed to large numbers rather than only pals of the class. No lashes or other similar harsh punishment was permitted, thanks to our great headmaster. It was a sort of noble decision.

The High School

The successful students of class 4 like me from all the middle schools of the town were enrolled in class 5 in High School after completing the required formalities. There was only one Govt. High School in our town and it was over-crowded. What a contrast it was from the Primary school; everything in High School was awe-some. The campus and school building were huge. The school gate was massive, built of steel. The boundary wall was very high; the idea seemed to be that nobody should be able to scale it and jump out. I was there in class 5 for one year (1946-47 Session) where after we migrated to India after partition.

High School's code of conduct for students

The code of conduct for students was strict. All of us were required to be in neat and clean school-dress; which comprised of a loosely stitched long white shirt and a white salwar, black shoes/sandals and a white turban of about 5 yards so that it was sufficient to cover the head fully. Strands of hair were not to be seen. It had to be worn throughout the day in the school. Anybody spotted without turban in the school was liable to be punished. And surely, wearing a huge turban whole day in scorching summer was a big punishment by itself. Heavy sweating in harsh summer was no excuse for taking it off anytime. The teachers also were required to have a head-gear, while in school. As a corollary to this harsh diktat, a very interesting scene could be seen just outside the school gate every morning. Students carrying their folded turbans on their shoulders were seen hastily tying them up before entering the school. It was a pathetic but a hilarious situation; fresher like us cribbing and seeking simultaneously the cooperation of seniors in tying it up fast and tidily. Seniors heartily enjoyed all this but did help us. Just the opposite happened outside the school gate in the evening; students removing their turbans with vengeance just after leaving. The poor turban would be no more than a sack now. Nobody was bothered that poor mothers will have tough time cleaning the badly soiled turbans and getting them ready for use the next morning. And all these acts whether in the morning or in the evening had to be done discreetly lest the school headmaster passes by. And if you are spotted doing all this, you sure would be gifted with special treatment in his office. For this reason and other actions, the poor creature had earned a sobriquet, "Jallad", the person who handles the gallows in the prison.

Our High School Headmaster; a strict disciplinarian

When I try to recall the overall environment in the School, the profile of our Headmaster there comes out as very striking. He was short not only in length but also in temperament. His gait, overall mannerism and conduct in the school campus displayed clearly his penchant for discipline.

His name was Mr. Imam Din Bhatti. He was about 5' feet high, had a black dark color, always stiff-faced, never smiling and would be seen taking rounds in the school during the day. He was disliked by almost everybody including teachers and school staff. In hindsight, I think, the discipline in our primary school was no less. However, it didn't occur to us any time that we were under leash. There was no sense of fear. Probably, its enforcement was done in a pliable manner. It didn't look high-handed or unduly harsh.

However, there was a positive fall-out of discipline in the High School. Thanks to headmaster's vigilance and strictness, the level of hygiene and cleanliness in class rooms, toilets, drinking water kiosks and school premises as a whole was very high. May be, the Headmaster was correct in enforcing it strictly because the students in primary school were like kids and not prone to defying the instructions whereas the grown up students in high school were likely to create problems if not kept under strict check. There can be two opinions in this matter but the environment and the times probably justified what our Headmaster did.

The funny punishment regime practiced by the Headmaster

Our Headmaster's style of awarding punishment to errant students was funny, to say the least, and was a source of immense pleasure to lucky onlookers. His short stature was an impediment for him since the students in senior classes were very tall. They were in their late teens or early twenties and most of them married. Compared to them, the headmaster was about 5' high and looked like a pygmy and may be this was one of the reasons for his stiff temperament on the campus. Who knows, he may have been behaving differently in his social circle and back home. Whatever it may be, it was fun watching him standing on a bench while wanting to punish tall students in senior classes. Many a times, he would ask the student facing the punishment to pull a bench and keep it in his own front to enable the headmaster board it and deliver the punishment. It was high voltage fun witnessing this drama. Juniors like us yearned breathlessly to watch any such episode. However, one ran a big risk attached to it. If somebody happened to pass nearby and seen to be watching it from outside, he would be summoned in immediately and given his share of the punishment on the spot. Though, we the juniors were mortally afraid of getting caught, yet each one of us was crazy about it for it would give us an opportunity to narrate it cheeringly to other students in the class. I still vividly remember having seen twice such a wonderful feast for eyes and the grace was I was not caught. The fellow students were jealous of those like me who were lucky.

The corporal punishment of this and more severe type was quite common in schools in those times. The adage was, "Spare the rod and spoil the child". Such type of punishments was quite common with parents also. The school's gate was closed immediately after the bell, which was very big and heavy. Being made of some alloy, bell's sound reverberated heavily and could be heard till very far off. We would start running if, as per our estimate, we were likely to get late. Of course, the time needed for tying up the turban would also be factored in. We would pity and curse our luck if on some day we really got late. The late comers would have rough time facing the headmaster. There used to be pin-drop silence during the assembly. The daily routine included drill and march-past, hoisting of flag, prayer and day's announcements by the headmaster. The P.T. teacher would conduct the program aided by class monitors. After the function, the students would march in queues in pin-drop silence. No noise in the school premises whether in class rooms or outside was the strict rule.

High standard of teaching in High School

I was in High School for one year in class 5. Thereafter, we migrated to India.

Our teachers in high school were very sincere, committed and paid full attention to each student. Of course, the brilliant ones would get closer attention and be encouraged to take the lead; a sort of grooming. Our Math's teacher, Mir Haji Shah, was one such outstanding example of commitment to his students. Math was considered to be a tough and boring subject, which even today is considered so. His style of teaching was lucid. His attempt used to be to make it simpler and easily comprehensible. He would repeat and explain again when so requested by students. If any student was seen to be non-attentive, he would have it. Be sincere and careful in the class was the unambiguous message. He was a very hard task master. Students loved him and feared him simultaneously. He was fair to all in matters of teaching and awarding punishment; the students from rich and wealthy families were not spared. And that is why; there were no protests when he took action. His style of punishment was not only unique but too scary. He would pinch very hard on defaulting students' under-arm with his thumb and index-finger and keep twisting it harsh. The recipient would keep stretching his legs in slow motion not being able to withstand the severe pain. And this punishment would last till the student made a fervent appeal and promised not to neglect his lessons.

Our English teacher (sorry, I am not able to recall his name) was equally good at teaching. He was soft-spoken, well-mannered and easily approachable. I believe, during this one year, he was successful in shedding-off from the minds of rustic students like us the fear complex associated with English language which was thought to be a hollowed difficult foreign language. It was a good beginning for us indeed. He would divide the class into two groups, organize question/answer sessions between the two; aim being to build up an environment of healthy competition. I was always in the fore-front in his class and enjoyed participating in these sessions. This gentleman commanded lot of respect in the school. We heard he had a long experience of teaching English language in schools in developed towns like Rawalpindi, Lahore.

Sweet lingering memories of High School

When I look back, I realize, the one year spent in high school was a trend-setter for me. The discipline, overall vibrant environment, teachers' well-meaning approach and healthy style of teaching helped develop amongst students the importance of being serious and committed to studies. The reward and punishment system was well known. Meritorious students were properly identified and encouraged. The rewards for them were like monitor's position, a chance to deliver a small talk on an important topic, an opportunity to be amongst the teachers on the Dias in the morning assembly and grant of merit certificates. Display of innovation by the students was encouraged and appreciated. During half-yearly and annual exams, the students were required to bring their own answer sheets. Students would decorate the answer sheets artistically and creatively with multi-color crayons/color pencils/pens. While evaluating the answers, the teacher would reward the better artistic talent with extra marks for it. If I am recalling correctly, I had put in lot of efforts in artistically decorating the top sheet of all my answer books. Arithmetic was my favorite subject. In the annual exam of standard five I had secured first position in the class and at the time of announcement of results I was called to the dais and open appreciation was conveyed by the class teacher in the open assembly of students and teachers. I still remember; I had got very excited then and quickly ran out of school to convey this happy news to my mother and also to escape the harsh pranks of my class-mates and others.

Partition disrupts education and outdoor activities

Our session of class five ended sometimes in April, 1947 but we couldn't continue with further studies after the school re-opened in July after summer vacations. By then the communal environment had degenerated significantly and our elders were not comfortable with our going out or to school either. There was fear complex and a sense of insecurity all around. Going to River Indus was now out of question. "Be indoors. Do not stir out. It may mean harm to your person," were the general comments of all the seniors. We used to while away time aimlessly. Most times, we the close bunch of friends would gather in the vacant rooms on the first floor of one of our friend's house and indulge in useless pranks and play some innovative unstructured indoor games. It was frustrating to be indoors whole day long without any meaningful activity. No books, no school, no studies, no playing in the open neighborhood and nothing to look forward to. The normal daily routine had vanished. Our innocent minds didn't know how to respond to this vacuum and perspiring void.

Chapter 13
Anxious adolescence; a challenge & an opportunity both

Before I start narrating the struggles I faced in my life during this critical phase, I wish to delve into my assessment of adolescence in general.

Adolescence is a very critical phase in a human being's life. It is a great opportunity for learning because in this phase one gets the instinct to discern and discriminate between what is good and what is bad, what is worth adopting and what is not. The critical faculties of observing, learning/retaining, absorbing what appears to be interesting and rejecting what is not appealing are at work subtly. The individual's capacity to analyze, evaluate and to accept or ignore the happenings around him/her keeps developing as one grows in age. One starts learning the skills to understand the implications of one's own actions and those of others, whether one's own family members, school mates or other friends and pals in the neighborhood and other contacts. In this phase of life, the discreet skills of observing and drawing one's own conclusions based on internal assessment is at work. Nuanced guidance and help by parents and other seniors in the family plays a very critical role in helping the adolescents learn to be uninfluenced by inhibitions and prejudices or other similar negative nuances. This process also helps in developing discretion and ability of firming up of views. Here a question comes up why the ability or inclination to use this useful support mechanism is not universal in all human beings. While some are really keen observers, others are not. And this difference is seen not only in people with identical social background, same age-group and close friends but also amongst brothers/sisters in the same family. The answer to this variation may lie somewhere in gene or surrounding circumstances or undue influence of some individual of strong will with whom one may be in regular contact and/or combination of some other peripheral influences. Yet, another reason could be individual's self-indulgent and/or careless attitude. Whatever it may be, it is an interesting phenomenon.

Elders' role in helping/guiding adolescents

Adolescence is a gateway to maturity and parents have to be enablers to be effective and seen to be supporting. It is a phase of life when the child has an urge, potential and free choice to discuss and talk about any misgivings and confusions with elders. Encourage this tendency in the child and see; it helps smoothen the relationship with the child and proves to be rewarding to both, the child and the eldersan on-going routine and thus are in a position to enjoy the fruits of this behavioral wisdom. The observation skills when used objectively help us to take decisions devoid of bias and prejudice. However, those who do not focus on this critical learning ability miss the boat and suffer from an imaginary alibi of manipulation and discrimination by others towards them. I believe; the adolescent age is a fountain of energy and enthusiasm in abundance. One has to galvanize it and channelize it in positive direction for own benefit. During this phase we get an opportunity to firm up our fundamental and basic approach in life and build up a stable foundation for our personal and distinct value system (Sanskars as we call them in Hindi). A value system picked up after due internal churning during adolescence is the sine-qua-non of a happy, satisfying and meaningful future.

Difficult circumstances for migrant adolescents like us

For those of us in this age group who came to India after partition, this phase of life turned out to be totally different from what we were used to earlier in normal conditions. Traumatized by the painful harrowing experiences in Pakistan and after escaping the possible butchering and killing in train itself, we had landed in the refugee camp at Kurukshetra. It was an environment of insecurity and unknown fears. I am clear that for a sizeable population of migrants, the trauma of pains related to partition was hard to forget so quickly. Though secure now and free from the worries of shelter and food, the bitter and shattering memories of the recent past would often lead to sporadic wailings and cries in one corner or the other of the camp. And each time a new batch of refugees arrived, the wailing shrills would get louder and emotionally unsettle all those who were there already. Such outbursts would overshadow every move, adversely impact us the adolescents and cloud our decision making ability. Being totally in dark about our future and being not mature enough, we would often get nonplussed and confused. It is not difficult to imagine how our adolescent mind got divided between hope and despair.

They say; time (Samay in Hindi) is a great healer and it helps people come out of the shadows of the past. I would say; it did happen to some quickly though on totality basis, this number was a small fraction. One could listen to complaints against the very concept of partition and its fall-out; the barbaric atrocities on the hapless innocent minorities on both sides of the divide. For many, the sufferings heaped on them were unforgettable. Millions of innocent and hapless men, women, children, and toddlers were butchered in their homes, in trains or whatever place they were in mad frenzy of violence on both sides. Thousands of women were abducted and forced to convert to the other religion and forcibly married in captivity against their will. The gruesome memory of such atrocities was an ever-lasting ache in the hearts of family members who escaped and were now in the camp. It was impossible to console such victims and many a times the sympathizers would let them cry hoping this would relieve them.

My adolescent mind was often at a loss to think rationally. I would rue our fate and curse the powers that be who were thought to be responsible for our miserable plight. Virtually, the faculties of observation and rational thinking had ceased to function. I cannot explain how long this lasted and how we overcame all this. But, as they say 'time and tide wait for no man', life moved on as it came because there was no easy solution for our problems. They were huge, manifold and too complex.

Family faces a difficult situation after landing in Bareilly

Upon all landing in Bareilly, all the three of us brothers were admitted into a school by the name "Rookes High School" in the cantonment area. I joined in class seven in July, 1948 and passed out in 1949. I do not remember the details but I have a lingering impression that the standard of education here was just average. My performance in this school was just satisfactory. One reason for this could be my inability to adjust in the given environment there. The teaching staffs on the whole, was not as caring as were those in the school in Kurukshetra Camp.

To start with, we came across lot of problems after coming to Bareilly. There were no free rations as was the case in Kurukshetra Camp. Getting two meals a day was a problem many a times. Survival was a serious issue for the family. The family was face to face with serious financial constraints. It was under these circumstances that a decision was taken to send me to Dehra Dun to live with my elder sister (Raj Rani) and brother-in-law, D.C.Kalra to reduce the burden of finances on our family.

Chapter 14
Family's landmark decision to re-locate me to Dehra Dun

Finding it difficult to manage the finances of the family and keeping in mind my sincere devotion to studies, my elders decided to send me to Dehra Dun. This decision heralded a new beginning for me; a beginning of bright prospects of growth, promise of proper education and availability of reasonable facilities for a reasonably good standard of living. Upon arrival there, my sister (Raj Rani) and brother-in-law (D.C.Kalra) took great care to make me feel at home soon.

My brother-in-law was working as a Booking Clerk in Railways at Dehra Dun. He was known to be a very honest, simple, and hard-working person. In personal conduct he was rather a strict person (no non-sense type). He was a gentle, plain-speaking (whenever he spoke) and an introvert. He was highly religious too. Getting up early in the morning, he would visit the nearby temple for prayers and listening to religious discourse and kirtan etc. On special religious occasions/days or even months like Sawan or Kartik of Hindu calendar, he would perform pooja as ordained for the day and observe fast with proper rituals. My sister also joined him in many of such activities but not to the extent he would do.

Being a member of the family and also being under their tutelage, I too was expected to follow suit. My routine in the temple may not be as rigid and strict as his but getting up in time, getting ready after bath etc. and accompanying them to temple was a necessary routine. This routine reinforced my faith in matters religious and helped in getting some insight into what the Hindu religion stood for, and also being aware about the important role the faith plays in our life. Nothing was forced on me. I was free to listen to discourses, join in the kirtan and prayers and be free to ask questions when and where they came up in my mind. All through this churning, I am sure, I was comfortable to learn, absorb and retain subtly what I saw, listened and got familiar with. I realized later that all this helped build up a strong inclination in me about being aware of my forefathers' religion, learn to be true to it, and respect what transpires in religious discourses. I didn't see any merit in doing rituals blindly and thanks to the discretion developed then, I am not keen about rituals even now.

Raj Rani, my sister at Dehra Dun

She turned out to be my second mother; caressing, loving and an angel for me. The genuinely deep love and affection showered by her during these three years was God's sweetest Gift for me. To her, I was like her own son. She would take great care to see that I was comfortable, all my needs were given due attention and were met with an open mind. I never felt I was away from my mother. She was a deeply religious lady, was very kind-hearted, generous and helpful and an innocently honest person. She believed in the virtue of straight-forward behavior and practiced it in her own life through and through. Any Sadhu, alms seeker or a beggar would not go back disappointed. She would listen to them attentively, try to assess their expectations/needs and do try to help within her means. On such occasions, her theme would be, "Sai itna deejiye ja mein grihast samaye, maen bhi bhookhi na rahoon, sadhoo bhi na bhookha jaye". Literally, it means, "God provide me with resources enough to meet my family's needs and also no alms seekers may go back disappointed from my door"

I tried to live up to her expectations of being seriously committed to my studies, secure high grades to help me secure admission in an engineering institute after finishing my high school. She was keen I do at least a diploma course in engineering and start my career as a Junior Engineer and not start as a clerk. The idea of being a clerk was not o.k. with her. She would say, "Junior Engineer means a respectable position and that helping me to pursue it was not beyond her means." That it didn't happen is a different story. On my part, I can say I deeply admired her from the core of my heart and made sincere attempts to keep her happy and give no occasion to her for regrets about my conduct towards her, my brother-in-law and their family. I was always helpful to her in as much as I would happily do all the errands for her necessary to run the household. I would not say no to her any time even if I was busy in my homework.

Her sweet lingering memory is always fresh in my mind. I owe a lot to her. It was her initiative that got me to Dehra Dun. Her vision was that I would pursue my studies unhindered and without hiccups and would also provide support to her for she had no child of her own. It was tragic that I couldn't continue to be with her after my high school. My elders in Bareilly, in their wisdom, had thought it fit to recall me to Bareilly in 1952 after I finished my high school.

My alma-mater in Dehra Dun, Sadhu Ram H.S. School

The new beginning in life which I made at Dehra Dun in 1949 brought to an end the phase of uncertainty about my education. Justifiably, this turned out to be a game-changing event of my life for it helped me re-discover my passion for education. Therefore, I was quite happy on being admitted in class eight in the nearby school, S.R.Higher Secondary School, which was considered to be one of the good institutions of the town then. The teachers in this school were good, classes were held regularly, discipline and punctuality were enforced strictly under the able supervision and guidance of the founder Principal of the school, Mr. Sadhu Ram Mahendru. Teaching schedules for different classes were drawn in such a way that there were no free periods. The students were kept busy either in classes or in some other co-curricular activities or games/sports.

The morning assembly was an impressive affair and was solemnized with proper care and attention of the sports teacher. The presence of all the senior teachers including Principal himself on the Dias was a big morale booster. The school management availed of the opportunity to make announcements of important matters/events in the assembly itself. The atmospherics generated in the assembly percolated down to classes leading to enthusiasm amongst students for studies. No loitering of students in the campus was permitted except during break. This school was in competition with other schools of the town to earn a high rank for itself. I was happy to be a student of this school.

The teachers in Hindi section were charged with the responsibility of preparing students for debates, intra-school, inter-school, district level and at state level. One of the teachers, Mr. Kaushik, had great literary background and was highly experienced in writing scripts. He was ably supported in this effort by the headmaster, Mr. Shekhar. With the efforts and guidance of this competent duo, S.R.H.S.School was winning awards in debates year after year. It was a matter of prestige for the school. I remember; our school was always in positive news in this regard.

One of our Hindi teachers, Mr. Goel, was extra considerate to migrants like us who required extra support in this subject. The Math teacher, Mr. DR Bhasin, the English teachers, Mr. Shekhar the headmaster, Mr. BM Sharma and Mr. OP Gupta, were highly committed to providing good learning opportunities to their students. These two subjects were thought to be difficult and critical for future growth and were under continuous focus. The weak students were paid extra attention in the 'after-school' classes. Overall, the standard of education in the school was very good and the school enjoyed high reputation in academics.

A shining example of coordinated team work in school

A Dance and Drama festival lasting about two weeks was organized by teachers/students in full cooperation with each other every year in the school campus. The entire preparatory work for the festival was handled by students and teachers as a team; the arts teacher and his team of selected students would do the paintings of screens/curtains depicting the theme of the festival, the Hindi and English teachers would do script/

dialogue writing, the Scouts brigade of the school do the construction and erection of stage and allied activities and the crafts teacher and his team would take up the illumination and decoration of the stage and the campus. It was a wonderful co-operative effort; highly successful and praiseworthy. The actors in the drama would be school students only. The make-up of actors and costume designing would be handled by some designated group of teachers and senior students who had past experience. The drama was open to public viewing and there used to be an entry ticket for the same. The proceeds of sale of tickets were meant for school building fund.

The three years in Dehra Dun; bed-rock of my future growth

The three years' stint in Dehra Dun came about as a turning point in my life. The unhindered spell of regular education at critical stage (class eight to ten) and hassle-free environment of a stable life meant I was free to pursue my studies with confidence and be not bothered by any constraints. In a way, it meant we were refugees no more. We had started believing in ourselves, once again. And this did reflect in my will to work hard and aim to excel. I was always amongst the top few students in my class and earned laurels now and then. Though good at studies, I was not confident enough to demonstrate my skills freely. Some unknown anxiety always persisted. May be, it had something to do with the over-arching spell of discipline and strictness of my brother-in-law. However, to be honest and fair to him, I must say, he never meant any wrong to me. He was always quite anxious and keen about his role as my mentor. He would often say, "What face shall I show to your family if you do not do well in studies? I must fulfil my obligation as a responsible senior." He did his best to help me in studies, especially in English and Mathematics. I passed my High School in 1952 in First Division securing 317 marks out of 500 i.e. 63.4% which, as per present trend, appears insignificant. However, during those days, the evaluation standards were rigid, as a policy. Only 4 students in my class of 115 students achieved that distinction. That fulfilled my dream but more than me, my brother-in-law was happy and not happy at the same time; happy at my getting First Division but unhappy that I had missed distinction in Math (75%) about which he was too sure. On the whole, he felt relieved that he was successful in his role of a mentor.

A hilarious scene was witnessed on the day my result was declared. During those days, the result was published in one designated news-paper only. And on the anticipated day, all the students of different schools were on the roads since morning awaiting the arrival of pack of the designated news-paper. After day long wait, the paper was received in the evening and after great struggle, I could grab a copy. Seeing that I had passed in First Division, I rushed home happily with the paper. I wanted my brother-in-law to be the first to see the result. Not seeing him there (he had not returned from his office by then), I rushed to the roof top of our house and started pacing the roof floor waiting for him. As soon as he came, he shouted at me to come down. For the first time in three years, I saw him smiling, after he saw the print in the news-paper. That was a great moment for us; him, myself and my sister.

My saviors; the saintly couple at Dehra Dun

My words fail me to express my deep gratitude to the noble souls, my brother-in-law and my sister for laying at critical stage in my life, a sound foundation of education, growth and making an honorable living possible for me. But for them, probably, I couldn't have achieved the target most cherished then i.e. finishing my high school program. The consequences were obvious was it not done. God forbid, I might have suffered the indignity of living a miserable life. That is how I am indebted to them as long as I live. I cherish humble respects for them in my heart, always. Apart from this virtuous dispensation of theirs to me, I do acknowledge they led me by example. They believed in truth and lived by it all their lives. Dishonesty, malice and ill thoughts for others were unknown to them. The honest, simple and plain disposition that they possessed was a great influence during this critical phase of my life; adolescence. My brother-in-law's nick-name in his work place was 'Bhagat ji'. You go to Dehra Dun railway station and ask for him by his real name (Mr. Duni Chand), nobody will help you but if you ask, where is 'Bhagat ji', there will be instant response and you will be told where he was at the moment. 'Bhagat ji in common parlance means a noble soul committed to God's Bhakti/ service. I was lucky that such a virtuous person was my mentor, guide and benign helper during those formative years in my life. Grateful and indebted, indeed, I am to him and my sister for all what I am!

Dehra Dun a charming Green City of yore

The Dun valley is surrounded by Reserve Forests of variety of trees mostly the 'Sal' which is a timber of great strength and is used extensively in making wooden frames for doors/windows. The pristine Mussoorie Hills in the north (height approximately 6000 sq. feet) give a majestic look especially during night when the entire stretch of the town is lit with lights. Mussoorie is popularly known as the queen of hills. Being close to major north Indian towns and conveniently accessible by road, it is thronged by tourists in large numbers from all over the country all the year round. It is at a distance of about 35 Kms from Dehra Dun.

In the not too distant past, Dehra Dun (at a height of 2200 feet above MSL) was a beautiful place to live in. The climate was moderate, pollution-free and had a distinct charm of its own. There was limited number of vehicles (four-wheelers and two-wheelers both) on roads. The only public transport available was 'tanga', a horse-driven carriage. People used to walk long distances on feet. Even bicycles were not a common sight. It received heavy rains and there was no need for fans etc. during summers. It was a peaceful small town with all the amenities of decent urban living conveniently available. There was no big population pressure in the town. Rates of land for building houses were affordable. It was thought to be an ideal place for senior citizens to settle down after long hectic work life. Dehra Dun had a lot of unique and distinct attractions of its own. It was a small town spread in a radius of about three kilometers from the central place, Clock Tower. Beyond this and within the town also, there were orchards of 'Litchi' and other tropical fruits. The luscious litchi of D Dun was very famous for its taste. You mention Dehra Dun and the first thing that came to mind was 'litchi' and the Basmati rice. Its distinct aroma and unique sweet taste separate it from other varieties of Basmati rice.

Nature's bounty for Dehra Dun is a lot of picnic spots in and around the town. Streams of fresh cold water flowing from hills, incessant drips of water from hillocks and a pool of hot sulphur water, all at one place in Sahstradhara was a unique location for outings. The lush green forests, magnificent view of Mussoorie hills and perennial streams of clear, sweet natural water from Mussoorie hills were the envy of many a visitors. In short, Dehra Dun was nature lovers' paradise; serene and peaceful in a universe of its own away from the hustle and bustle of Metros and other big towns. The world class schools like Doon School and Welham's added to its glory as a hub of high standards of education. These schools even now are education loving parents' preferred choice for their children.

Dehra Dun had a very rich social life. The unique distinction of housing thirteen cinema theatres way back in forties and fifties when its population was just a fraction of its present mad rush speaks volumes about its residents' preference for entertainment and love for movies. It had cafes, restaurants and other eateries of high standard. Odeon cinema and its café was the favorite haunt of cadets of Indian Military Academy, India's premier Academy for training of officers for Army. It was a privilege and indeed good luck to be a resident of this beautiful town.

The present day Dehra Dun

The present day Dehra Dun is just the opposite of its past; chaotic, heavily populated, polluted, bursting at seams with large number of vehicles of all sorts and traffic jams. However, considering the population explosion and unplanned urban growth in the country as a whole, it is still a better place to live in. It is relatively calm and peaceful. Much of the credit for this goes to the local populace, well-educated (most of it) and cosmopolitan in character. Maintaining its earlier glorious tradition of being an educational hub, it has drawn attention of enthusiast entrepreneurs and educationists to open a large number of Institutes of Technical Education, Medical Colleges and Universities which draw students from all parts of the country. It has a big presence of Army units in Cantonment area. It is also house to many Govt. Institutes of strategic and national importance. The vast majority of residents of the town are Govt. employees. After the formation of Uttrakhand as a separate state in Nov. 2000, Dehra Dun is its temporary capital. This has added to its woes and hiccups of all kinds. The abnormal growth of population has stretched beyond limits the civic services. All said and done, Dehra Dun is facing severe problems of un-regulated urbanization and the problems associated with this malady. Considering, however, the unbridled and un-regulated chaotic scene in urban habitations in the country as a whole, Dehra Dun still scores well on the barometer of satisfaction. On the scale of ten, it should still score 7.

Back to Bareilly from Dehra Dun

Not knowing what was in store for me and full of anxieties for further education I landed in Bareilly in mid-1952. During the interim period when a debate was on between Dehra Dun and Bareilly about shifting me back to Bareilly, my anxiety about my future especially the prospects of continuing with further education was at its peak. I was surely unhappy at Bareilly's insistence on my leaving Dehra Dun when, it appeared, I was at the threshold of a bright future if permitted to stay on with my sister. She was keen to send me to Engineering Institute for a three year diploma course so that I could make a respectable beginning in life and I too was keen to continue there to be a support to her. I knew; my presence in Dehra Dun was really a big help to her. She was under the regular care of some gynaecologist and was not keeping good health. Due to this reason also I was not comfortable with the idea of letting her be on her own. It was genuinely painful for me to go away when she was in dire need of support. Above all, the relationship of love and respect that existed between her and me was a very strong bond of attachment. I respected her from the core of my heart and she showered her genuine love on me as she would do to her own child. But that was not to be. And that was the beginning of yet another phase in my life. Continuity and stability had given way to uncertainty and its concomitant off-shoots of anxiety and fear complex.

While in Dehra Dun, I got used to a stable routine with no overpowering signs of financial constraints. Living conditions were normal as they are expected to be for a middle class family. Regular salary income of brother-in-law, though limited, enabled the family to fend for itself with a careful and cautious approach of thrift. However, in Bareilly, financial outlook was still not stable, though it had improved quite a bit. Eldest brother had quit his job in uncle's army canteen and had started his own business of general merchant at a very modest scale in a small outlet taken on rent. However, the expectations of growth, in due course, were the hope of better days ahead. The other elder brother had secured a job of clerk in a govt. office and that was a welcome relief for the family.

I pick up a temporary job; education disrupted

After coming from Dehra Dun, I joined Bareilly College in Class XI in 1952 and passed the First Year exam a year later. However, I couldn't continue my college education soon. My elder brother who had secured a job of a clerk in the Office of Assistant Custodian of Evacuee Property, Bareilly, was able to find an ad-hoc job for me. I was to work a member of the team of rent collectors for the Manager (rent collection) on commission basis. I was just 17 when started working whole time as a rent collector to be able to collect more and earn more. The job was very tiring as it entailed going from door to door. I devoted whole-heartedly to this work and soon started earning a handsome amount as my remuneration. It was a welcome addition to family's finances. We could now plan to buy some new clothes, shoes and other items of personal use apart from some additional items for the kitchen like crockery and utensils and many other small additions in the house. It was an on-going monthly effort but not a regular solution of my career needs. The job was uncertain, the remuneration was uncertain being linked to the total collection of rent in a month and the percentage of the commission was not commensurate with efforts and time required to be put in everyday; rain or shine, scorching heat or biting winter. And going from house to house and knocking at the doors was absurd and uncomfortable. With male members of the households away to work, the women's responses were niggardly hopeless and most of the time highly irrational and irritating. And this was more so for me because the area under my charge was vastly spread in down-town and it called for extensive cycling whole day, seven days of the week. The area was mostly the habitation of poor daily wage earning Muslims. Repeated visits to each household for collection of rent were a norm. It was a dream to expect to get the amount in one or two visits. Though deeply frustrated with the job, I continued with it because I was able to earn, in spite of all the hiccups, an amount that was substantial and it did enable the family to gain confidence to organize the house-hold more rationally. The monetary income was more satisfying to all of us even though it meant a lot of emotional and physical stress to me. Life dragged on like this and in due course, I got used to it. Leaving it without an alternative job was out of question. I continued with it for about 3 years. I am not able to recall the exact period now.

Chapter 15
My early joint-family life at Bareilly

Financial security induces an urge for normal life

After about six years of our arrival in Bareilly, family's financial position started stabilizing. Having overcome the basic problems, having secured minimum educational qualification and having been successful in finding a job by both of us, i.e. on acquiring financial stability and seeing better prospects for future, the urge to aspire more grew stronger. Organizing ourselves properly to pick up a normal routine for the family came up strongly. The family started getting a feeling of looking forward to future with hopes for better days ahead. We all realized that living in the past meant nothing but status quo. As we all know, this only inhibits and dampens desire for any major initiative.

My thought process started inducing me to think of something that was normal at that stage for a person of my age-group; build up friendships, have a bunch of pals for company in hours of leisure to indulge in frivolities, indulge in and enjoy gossiping, go to an outlet occasionally for small snacks etc. in friends' company, go for leisure walk in the evenings, go to theatres and enjoy movies. That is how, we a bunch of ex-college mates who enjoyed each other's company started sharing our evenings together. We used to indulge in free-lancing harmless pranks in each other's company. Frankly, we were not into any serious violations of ethics or morals. We were a close group of bosom friends and together believed in not indulging in deviations of any sorts. Each one of us had known each other pretty well and was conscious of upholding group's un-impeachable identity. Fresh entrants were not welcome. We were careful that our elders were not offended by any action of ours; a sort of disciplined lot. Sometimes, the group did play cards with stakes but not very high. I personally was not fond of it but didn't muster enough courage to say no to it openly. I would mostly avoid this activity advancing some reason or the other. In fact, playing cards with stake never clicked with me though playing simple games of cards were welcome. On the whole, I enjoyed being a part of this group though my elders were critical of my propensity to devote time to my friends and indulge in all this. To them, it was a waste of time and money both.

Mixed feelings about me surface in the family

The memories of acute financial sufferings that the family had undergone were too harsh to be forgotten so early. Everybody had made great sacrifices in holding back the urge to splurge and it appeared to them that the tendency to spend even little money or a few coins by me on my small pleasures was a waste of precious money. It is true that financially, we were not very comfortable even now. Every rupee mattered. On the other hand, my young mind considered spending some amount on small goodies in the company of my friends as not a waste. It gave me some happiness and a sense of fulfilment of my minimum aspirations. I always tried to reason it out with logic with my mother. She would accept my pleadings for what I wanted to do or was doing but would advise me to lie low occasionally to avoid irritation in the family. Do it discreetly and avoid controversies, she would caution. Probably she didn't want to hurt me harsh and often advised against any confrontation. She had faith in me and my ability to be firm in my conviction and not get astray.

Hard work; eldest brother's only passion

Divergent views in the family about my association with friends and spending some money in their company notwithstanding, I felt sorry for my eldest brother who quit his school after the untimely demise of

113

our father and had started working as a help in uncle's canteen at partly sum at the delicate age of 14. Therefore having known from close angles the worth of every paisa; he was justified and realistic to entertain his views of restraint and being conservative in spending money. To him my behavior was hardly justified. He knew the worth of money more than all of us. My eldest brother's unhappiness made me sad for I never intended to dis-obey him. I had highest regards in my mind for his self-less huge sacrifices. Above all, the harshest routine that he was following even now was really a disturbing and painful matter for us. Often, I reached out to him with help in his business affairs with a view to reduce his drudgery. All his life, he had not known the taste of rest and recreation. Work was the only passion he had known. Many a times the mother attempted to induce him to think of at least half a day's rest on week-end if not the whole day. He would agree to it sometime and this was the occasion for our sister-in-law to prepare some sweet and special dish for him or take him for a walk in the evening. I don't think he ever went to a movie. I am sorry; he did not care about himself. The idea of just relaxing and not doing any work was alien to him. The harsh crude realities and deprivation he had faced all along had conditioned his mind.

He used to tell, 'Continue to persist and persevere till last. Sitting idle is a sin. Time is money. Time lost is opportunity lost. Keep busy and be happy.'

Elder brother's marriage brings cheers and signals a welcome change in family's mood

My elder brother, VP Aneja had joined railways as Booking Clerk at Bikaner sometime in April, 1954. In line with popular social thinking prevailing then, he was fit to be tied in a wed-lock. As soon as the family let this inclination be known, the offers/proposals started pouring in for him and ultimately in early 1955, he was engaged and got married in July, 1955. This was a welcome change of mood in the family. Our Bhabi hailed from Kaithal a small urban settlement in Haryana. I suppose, she was about 16/17 years at the time of marriage. This marriage was the first major event of enjoyment for the family. It reflected the collective thinking of normalcy in family's psyche. We had lot of merry-making at Bareilly before the marriage party travelled to Kaithal. The fun, hospitality and gracious warm welcome by bride's family were much beyond expectations. Bhabi's extended family of uncles, cousins were in large numbers and all of them proved to be great hosts. The younger lot was vibrant and flamboyant. I enjoyed their company and made friends with some of them. This first major function in the family was the harbinger of the happy days ahead.

It is God's Grace that this loving couple has had the blissful conjugal happiness of over 58 years before the Bhabi breathed her last in 2013.

"The customary poetic compilation (**Sehra**) of good wishes presented by me for a happy married life to my elder brother VP Aneja on his Wedding Day (8th July 1955).

115

PART - II

৯০ ০৪

Chapter 1
A welcome beginning; first regular govt. job

Most likely, it was sometime in December, 1955, that I got an offer of appointment from Divisional Office, Bikaner, advising me to join in training school at Saharanpur. I left Bareilly to join in there, successfully completed the training and joined at Hanumangarh as a Relieving Goods Clerk. I was happy; I had achieved what was the dream of many in my age-group. The idea of a regular job in Indian Railways was highly encouraging. Now I had a stable future before me.

However, on joining at Hanumangarh, I realized that the job profile was monotonous. There was no regular work for me there. Go to office early morning every day, mark your presence and find out if any message had been received from HQ at Bikaner for any duty at some outstation in my beat. Let me explain; RGC meant being available to relieve a goods clerk when he proceeds on leave/vacation. This rarely happened as going on leave by these people was rare and therefore I was free all the time. This was indeed boring and an anti-climax to aspirations of a budding employee who was keen to get involved in his job and to learn his office routine/work.

The work environment that rattles my conscience

The boring routine mentioned above continued for some months when one day a message was received from HQ advising me to go to Mandi Dabwali railway station to relieve a goods clerk there who was to proceed on leave for 10 days due to sudden death of his father. I joined there as directed and took charge of the assignment. It was then that I learnt why people didn't go on leave except in emergencies. Proceeding on leave meant losing extra earnings of slush money which was substantial. My share of this slush money during my stay of 10 days there was about Rs. 100 which was almost equal to my one month's regular salary. The amount was tempting but not for me. In fact, it would have been much more if I was to work on some other seat. Frankly, this temptation did not catch my fancy for two reasons; the illegal nature of the earning was unethical and the job entailed a lot of slugging from morning to late evening. And top of it, the surroundings and conditions in the work place were deplorable. I was not happy to be in such an environment. It didn't enthuse me, to say the least. I offered not to accept my share but the official in charge refused and simultaneously tried to convince me that it was my due share of earnings in the system. He warned me that my refusal may isolate me and later it may lead to some difficulty.

The game changing move that shaped my future

Disillusioned thoroughly with what I saw at Mandi Dabwali, I rushed to Bikaner, the Divisional HQ, to discuss the matter with my elder brother who was working there and also to look for possibility of some escape route. I was shocked when my brother did not see anything wrong in the practice I witnessed at Dabwali. According to him, it was a regular feature in all Goods offices. Rather he was happy that I was in a position to make some extra bucks which the family badly needed. My idea of wanting to get rid of the situation was repulsive to him. I was, however, firm in my views and requested him to help me find out a place of posting where nothing of this type was necessary, where I could get more time for my studies and which helped me in pursuing my under-graduate program to improve prospects for my future. He was sure; prudence demanded that the family had more cash to take care of various pressing needs. I had a bigger picture before me for my future. I had different views about my job profile and career. The work culture and environment in Goods Offices was suffocating and highly repulsive to me. There was no openness in mutual dealings. People were suspicious of each other and appeared least concerned about fairness.

Ultimately, I succeeded in persuading my brother to take me to the clerk in HQ office, who was into postings and transfers of employees like us. I explained my requirement to the clerk who, too, was aghast after listening to me. Probably, this was the first instance and most likely the last one of such madness before him. I remember; he rebuked me and suggested to post me to a plum seat, of course for a consideration. I repeated my request. Finding me adamant, he informed that there was a vacant seat in Delhi Cant. C.O.D Siding, which was thought to be a sort of punishment posting but it had all the important attributes which I was looking for. I immediately put in an application requesting for posting there. I was double-happy because it was Delhi, where the facility for taking up the UG program of Punjab University was available in its extension campus. A few days later, the posting order came and I rushed to Delhi Cant. to grab it in hurry forgetting that there was nobody in competition with me for this posting.

Ultimately, this proved to be the real game changer in my career.

Posting in Delhi; being a graduate a sure possibility now.

After getting a posting in Delhi Cant I could visualize and foresee some pleasant times ahead. After all, taking up UG program of Punjab University as a private candidate was an opportunity of consequence. As subsequent events revealed I was right. I knew I would be in different trajectory after I successfully completed my UG program. Being a graduate in those days opened up vast avenues for higher jobs in Govt of India and State Govts.

I joined in Delhi Cant. C.O.D Siding office sometimes in January, 1957. The job here did not entail any strenuous efforts and would finish mostly by mid-day. Therefore, like my other colleagues who devoted their free time reading news-papers, magazines and books etc. or talking politics as a pastime, I would take out my course books of UG program or just take permission to go out to the public library which was in Delhi. During this period of struggle and preparations for the program, I also availed of the company of one of my distant relative in Delhi who too was a candidate like me for UG program of Punjab University. We would study together discussing the difficult chapters extensively and trying to finalize the final view. His elder brother was a PG and was pursuing his Law in DU. He was quite a help. On the whole, the preparation was satisfactory. Many a times, I would stay for the night with them. Luckily, my efforts were blessed with success by the Lord Almighty and I passed out in April, 1959 session. I was now a Graduate and could aspire to seek a job higher than my present job in Railways which was equivalent to a Lower Division clerk in Govt.

A blissful spell of togetherness with mother

During my stay in Delhi Cant. my gross emoluments were Rs. 125 inclusive of all allowances. Considering the price level of those days, this amount was sufficient enough for a family of 2/3 persons. My love and gratitude for my mother made me think of bringing her to live with me. I knew; she badly needed a break from her difficult past and would be happy to accede to my suggestion. After some time, she and my younger brother, Atam Prakash, joined me at Delhi Cant. The younger brother too needed support to secure some professional qualification and considering his aptitude, he was admitted in a vocational course of two years duration in Delhi Govt.'s Industrial Training Institute. He successfully completed his course and after a few selection interviews, was successful in getting a job of an artisan in BHEL, Bhopal. The three years that we were together was a period full of bliss, happiness and satisfaction for each one of us. I had taken on rent a two bed-room house in Delhi Cant near railway station. Our mother had the satisfaction of managing the affairs of a small house-hold as per her convenience and her choice. My salary income was good enough to meet our requirements of food, clothing etc. and other living expenses. There was no high inflation and in any case, our present financial condition was far happier compared to the acute problems we got used to after arrival in India as migrants. Spending liberally and freely was not our tradition since long, in any case. Managing our affairs within the means available was the norm. The real satisfaction was the happy family living that we were enjoying. I believe; these three years were a good change for my mother. She had the satisfaction of having seen her two sons moving ahead in life and securing independent economic status for themselves.

Mother goes back to Bareilly

Not being sure of arrangements for my stay in Shimla where I was to join my new job and considering the harsh winters there, she decided to go back to Bareilly to live with dear "Veer ji's" family. In any case, Bareilly was family's HQ after migration from Pakistan. It was family's permanent address and was recorded as such in our service records. Bareilly became her permanent abode once again. She used to visit Bikaner where the elder brother was posted or Shimla or Bhopal where the younger brother was working in BHEL for a change was a routine. Over a period of time, her movements outside Bareilly got reduced. Her attention shifted to temple/ gurdwara visits and prayers at home. With age, her health parameters got affected and even visits to temple/gurdwara became less and less but she continued to be agile and self-supporting till her last moments. Dear "Veer ji" and Bhabi ji spared no efforts to look after her well. I can believe, she breathed her last as a contented and satisfied person. She was about 85, when on 9th June, 1989; she left for her heavenly abode. Being posted in Bombay, I was not lucky to be by her bed-side when the end came; regret I carry with me always.

Chapter 2
When I thought I had arrived

Audit & Accounts Dept. emerges as a viable option of growth
During studies for UG program, I and my friend used to explore the avenues available after successfully completing our UG program. The Govt. job that attracted our attention the most was that of an Auditor in Audit and Accounts Dept. This was equivalent to UDC in Govt., a step higher than LDC. The main attraction in this job was the bright prospect of future growth. There was a system of departmental exam. After working as an Auditor for 3 years, one was eligible to take it. The exam was in 2 parts; Inter and Final. We visited few offices of Audit and Accounts to get a feel of the actual position. The visits revealed that qualifying the departmental exam was better said than done. Not only the syllabus was vast and a real challenge but the success ratio in Part I averaged about 3% at the most and a maximum of 5 chances in entire career were permissible. The very low success ratio and limit of a maximum of 5 chances in life were seriously dis-heartening, rather a big deterrent. I felt, it would be a challenge no doubt but was a real opportunity also and with determination and sincere hard labor, one could clear it. After all, nothing can be achieved without putting in efforts. The redeeming feature was that the exam was a qualifying exam and not a competitive one. We gathered during visits that many a tame-hearted persons would not take it up at all thinking the final failure could lead to depression for the entire life. In fact, there were a lot of terrible tales of failures doing rounds in the office corridors. You talk to some such candidate who would advise you

to take it only if you are prepared to devote at least 8 to 10 hours per day. God forbid, if you finally fail in the last chance which could be around 40 to 45 years of age, how would you show your face to others and especially to your own grown up kids. These depressing voices were enough to kill the enthusiasm of many. On the other hand, there were others who had succeeded in the first attempt itself. For aspirants like us it was a mixed bag of despair or hope depending upon which voice seemed closer to you. Despite all the talk of low chances of success in the exam, my mind got enamored of the prospects of growth in this Dept. I set my mind on trying to go in for the job of an Auditor in the Indian Audit and Accounts Dept. and I started looking for opportunities for this.

Apart from this option, the other widely talked-about options for growth for a graduate were the open competitive exams for various levels of civil services conducted by UPSC. The intelligence I gathered about these exams conveyed that the competition was very tough indeed. There were multi-layered tests which called for thorough knowledge of the subjects chosen by a candidate as optional. And the competence expected in English paper, which was compulsory and other optional subjects was equivalent to Honors course. I knew I didn't possess such a high level of competence in any subject since I had qualified in UG program only as a private candidate and had no benefit of exposure to regular classes in any college/university. All this led me to the conclusion that choice of an Auditor's position for my career was more appropriate at that stage. I told myself it was no use running after UPSC competitions when the reality was that I was not equipped for them.

Self-actualization; a significant help

The search for determining a viable growth option in work-life for a simple graduate like me gave me a very healthy lesson. For being happy in life, it is important to be aware of one's strengths/weaknesses realistically and objectively before setting mind on an objective for it is no use following the mirages. It doesn't really work. It doesn't take us anywhere. Rather, it breeds dis-satisfaction. The limitations one is aware of about oneself should not be brushed aside. Some people believe it is being negative to focus on one's weakness. In my opinion, being aware of certain limitations saves energy for other viable options. Aspiring for higher objects is a welcome approach to success but it calls for matching depth/strengths in competence, abilities and an unflinching determination in walking the harshest territory.

The basic salt and critical mass for an individual to be successful is to have a strong will power to perform come what may, have patience to neglect/ignore one's own comforts, be able to work out and pursue a gruelling routine of hard work of long hours every day. I knew that the path of open competitions was highly challenging for one's stamina and demanded putting up with hardships of all sorts. But still I went ahead and appeared in All India Services exam of UPSC; the aim being to test my knowledge base. No soon, had I finished the written papers in this exam, it was clear I stood no chance even though I had put in serious efforts. Yet I can say this effort didn't go waste; it made me aware of my limitations and helped me to gain experience for other exams in future.

Key factor for developing broad vision in life

In the course of my work-life I got the opportunity to travel extensively thus coming into contact with different people of diverse cultures, languages and social backgrounds. Not only that; the work environment in different locations being not the same, it helped me to develop and appreciate the significance of adjustment and give and take in work life for mutual benefit and growth in diverse environment. In hind-sight, I thank my stars for all this otherwise my story would have been similar to that of a 'frog in a well.'

I believe; one's vision becomes vastly open and broadened thanks to the power of adjustment acquired in different locations and circumstances. I am pretty confident; this experience contributed significantly in my story of growth.

Self-analysis; a valuable strength for me

I am sure and conscious that I am capable of doing an honest and objective assessment of where do I stand? I have never spared myself of the scrutiny/evaluation of my actions, when warranted and am aware; it has always been a clean job, un-influenced by any consideration that it is me who is under scrutiny. Whenever, I have been part of a problem, I have not hesitated to put myself on the block and be subjected to an objective scrutiny of my role in it. Being a matter-of-fact oriented person committed to integrity, I did not spare myself of the blame, if it fell in my lap. I think it is my big strength. It helped me to keep myself under check. I have lived through it all my life. It has been an extremely satisfying and rewarding experience. It built up capacity and confidence and helped me in doing deeper analysis and induced me to do course correction when warranted. That I always succeeded in this attempt, I can't say but not shying away from it or not excusing me of the scrutiny, is by itself a step in the right direction. It always induced me to face the realty with courage. The basic tenet for me has been honesty, integrity and truthfulness in my dealings.

First inner call; an intuitive strength

I believe; the first inner-call when face to face with a dilemma is always a best option for those who believe in and practice fairness and shun self-indulgence. What is first inner call? To me, this means an intuition which surfaces when one is at peace with self and is in a care-free serene mood. The vibrations and signals received then can help crystalize the message behind the intuition and help in firming up the future line of action for filling the void or making a move on the path of creative activity. Self-reprimand and control, when necessary, help one to stay focused. It provides strength to one's character; a vital input for success in life. It generates a huge amount of self-confidence toned by realism. There is no place for self-arrogance. Excusing one-self under the garb of some alibi and pointing an accusing finger at others comes easily. Indeed, it is very tempting. It tends to lighten the burden and props up a justification for the act. Once one falls into this trap, it repeats itself regularly and becomes a justifiable norm in conduct and gradually settles down in psych as a valid option. One needs to have a vision to see through the pitfalls in such an approach. Blessed are those who seek His Intervention and Guidance in all decision making phases, when at cross-roads. It is no exercise at preaching; just an outpouring which came out by itself.

Soon after I qualified as a Graduate in April, 1959, I started looking for opportunities for a job in Audit and Accounts Department in which, I knew, good avenues for growth existed. My and my mother's happiness knew no bounds when my efforts paid off and I was successful in securing a job of an Auditor in Accountant General, Punjab's office at Shimla. It was a real pleasure. It was not only a job I had set my mind on after due deliberations, but it also relieved me of the anxieties and drudgery of the job of a Goods Clerk in the Railways. I was not only the first graduate in the family but also had succeeded in securing a job higher than others in the family.

My mother advised me to meet and convey my respects to my uncle (mother' cousin) who was a retired professor and was living in Delhi. I used to visit him otherwise too to seek his advice about my plans. On hearing about my selection as Auditor, he was very happy and congratulated me too. His gems of wisdom were, "It is just a good beginning but not the end in itself. It is not very big achievement. Lot more avenues of growth are open to you. Work hard, aim high and be sure you do not relent so early in life." I explained to him in some details the prospects of further growth in the Dept. by qualifying in the departmental exams. He was quite happy to listen to my explanation since it conveyed that I was conscious of the need for future growth and seemed to have done the exploratory work before deciding to go in for this job.

I always sincerely valued his advice since it was borne out of his concern for me.

Chapter 3
A most happening phase begins

The sweet and lingering smell of satisfaction was palpable on securing a job I liked. With huge expectations and dreams in my eyes, I landed in Shimla in Nov., 1959, to join as an Auditor in AG Punjab's office. It was a stupendous moment; a momentous occasion for realization of my dreams. I had set my mind on this opportunity after a lot of serious thought. It was an opening which made me feel sure about my future.

Now, when I have the pleasure of looking back, I can re-affirm that the beginning that I made at Shimla in 1959 was a true harbinger of a great future that lied before me. It was a welcome step forward not only in my work life but also a welcome foot-print of life that was to follow; the life in its entire spectrum. Though, I had started working in 1953 first as rent-collector on commission basis followed by a job of Goods Clerk in Railways I never accepted either of them as an ultimate job/position of my liking. Therefore, it enthralled me to live the happiness I had earned by getting a job I liked.

Quite naturally, I believed then, "I have arrived. The future is mine. I have a big opportunity before me. I will seize it and do all what is necessary to convert dreams into a reality." Indeed, it was a meaningful step forward for a hapless migrant.

I told myself, "Be happy, it is indeed a good beginning. You have an exciting future before you now. Make sure, you make it worth looking forward to. Be clear, it is an opportunity for unleashing your potential. Dream, have a vision, be sure what you want out of this life. True, you have had lot of struggles till now but your consistent efforts have catapulted you to this position; a position that opens up avenues for growth, for success and of course for happiness. Grab it with all the sincerity and commitment to achieve what is really good for you. Have a road-map, keep pushing and spare no efforts for meeting your objectives."

I still vividly cherish the sense of satisfaction I gained on landing in Shimla encouraged by the overwhelming thought of a bright future. I had known that I would be eligible to take up a departmental Examination called S.A.S (Subordinate Accounts Service) after 3 years and which, after qualifying it, would entitle me to promotion as an Accountant followed by next promotion as an Audit Officer. It was a dream within the realms of sure possibility; not too difficult to achieve and that too in a short spell of 5/6 years. I was also aware that in no other department such an opportunity existed. And that made this job very attractive to a fellow who was innocently ambitious about his future.

Snowfall in Shimla, an enticing attraction for me

The idea of being in Shimla, thanks to this job, was thrilling for me for more than one reason. And it filled me with an unknown sense of fulfilment. I genuinely believed it was great to be in a wonderful place like Shimla. The first thing that immensely attracted me about Shimla was the thought of witnessing 'live' the snow-fall. I had seen it all happening in movies but experiencing it live was heavenly for me. It was a paradigm shift; an absolutely different scenario from rains to which we were used to for long. I can't describe how crazy I was about it. I would ask my colleagues number of times every day, 'when is the snowfall likely to happen this year? In the heart of my heart I wished it happened just then. My excitement would lead to hysteria on seeing the clouds on the horizon. And my query to my colleagues and friends would get shriller. My senior colleagues who had been there for long and had long experience of facing the harshness of severe winters in Shimla, would smilingly say, "Wait my dear; you shall have plenty of it along with the accompanying misery of chilling winters." I would just not care to listen to all this and repeat my query," how it happens, how it feels like when it falls, does it last for days or finishes in few hours, how can one walk on such a magnificently white snow and spoil it (without a feeling of guilt)?" And one line answer would be," Have some patience. You will get to know all this and more after it snows." Of-course, such a response was enough to shut me down for a while but it didn't affect my enthusiasm at all. I continued to look forward to the cherished scene impatiently.

My first encounter with Snowfall

A joyful happening for which I was waiting breathlessly since my arrival happened one day. To be precise, it was 13th of January, 1960 when it started around mid-day and continued for many hours. Witnessing it live choked me with emotions; overwhelming with happiness beyond compare. It was indeed a dream come-true. I became almost hysterical and was restless to run out of office and be in the open; touch it, pick it up in my hands, experience the sheer joy of having touched it, seeing it fall on my clothes and make balls and play like what many enthusiasts like me were doing. And I did manage to get a 'furlough' in the afternoon. I dragged with me one of my friends. Though he was not new to Shimla like me but was quite an enthusiast. We spent few hours out in the falling snow on The Mall and the Ridge, running and chasing each other with balls of snow, having fun in trying to make with snow some miniature statue-like figures and watching scores of people enjoying like us the miracle called 'snow-fall'. The environment all over was a treat; watching people giggle and laugh as if there would be no more falls. Thanks to enthusiastic excitement, playing in the open for hours gave us energy; unlimited and boundless. We neither got tired nor felt hungry and continued to enjoy like this till sun-set. I wasn't wearing proper and heavy winter clothes and gear like hand-gloves, gum-boots and thick woollen scarf etc. weren't with me then. The freezing cold started its effect in the evening when we rushed to the 'Coffee House' on The Mall; a wonderful joint where apart from steaming hot coffee, one could enjoy the South-Indian fare;

like Dosa, Vada Sambar, Idli etc. and could simultaneously relax in the warmth of coal-fired stoves.

The first encounter with snow was a mesmerizing and unforgettable spell of heavenly bliss for me. It reinforced my deep love for the place called Shimla. I thanked my stars for this wonderful gift; the satisfaction, pleasure and happiness of being in Shimla.

The travails of harshest winter

If I am not wrong, it was the winters of 1961-62 which brought havoc for the town. The snow-storms, the blizzards and heavy snow-fall every day for about 10/12 days threw life out of gear. It would snow during night as if in tandem with its daily routine. You get up in the morning and find there is a layer of fresh snow. The result was; frozen water-taps all over, power net-work totally crippled, huge piles of snow everywhere, transport and movement of vehicles at stand-still, huge shortage of food items and vast population suffering from cold-induced ailments. We ran out of rations like bread, butter, milk, eggs, snacks and other groceries very soon. With no prospects of supplies coming from plains, the prices shot up beyond wildest levels. Even the train service from Kalka remained disrupted for few days due to huge piles of snow on the tracks. Offices and markets were virtually closed. People lived like prisoners in their own houses. The mounds of snow got converted into ice soon thus hindering movement. The Municipal Committee deployed laborers to clear a small stretch in the middle of the 'Mall' to help in movement of people but the layer of frozen snow (ice) at the bottom resulted in bone-fractures and serious injuries for many. The Gum boots and sticks with chisels were in-effective but that was the only aid/ help available. Braving the odds, we would go to Coffee House or to Dhaba or 'Lower Bazar' (market) for picking up necessities and grocery etc. notwithstanding the fear of slipping down and getting hurt. The rebellious in us would force us to take the risk and move out. Being at home and in bed for long was more painful than the fear of being caught in a storm and getting hurt.

Karmath Jeevan

A dreadful incident averted

An incident that sent down shivers in our spine at that time is still fresh in my mind. One Sunday A/N, my room-mate, Ved, and I set out of our house in search of food after being trapped inside the house for two consecutive days. On the way, we picked up our friends, Raj and Sudarshan, who were also without any food for 48 hours. On reaching the Mall, we found our dear resort, Coffee House, was closed. We headed to one of our colleague's house in Lower Bazar in the hope of getting something to eat but his kitchen too was almost empty. The gentleman offered some drinks and both Raj and Sudarshan accepted the offer. While Sudarshan had limited intake of alcohol, Raj was liberal with it. After sometime, we were at the 'Scandal Point' on the Mall and by then our friend Raj was in the other world being fully inebriated by now. Seeing him in blown up state, we got terrified and made attempts to take him back home but he wouldn't agree. "We are all hungry. We must have food before we go home. Do you think I am drunk?" he yelled. And he started pushing towards the Ridge Maidan limping because of the intoxication. Our requests/pleadings were falling flat and he was enjoying his acrobats on the snow. Waving his stick at us, he would not let us go near him. We were waiting helplessly when an experienced gentleman who was passing nearby saw him and whispered in my ears, "Take him home and put him in warm bed before the cold impacts him. Do not delay otherwise his whole system would get stiffened due to cold." That whisper set the alarm bells ringing for us. We mustered courage, caught hold of him and started dragging him on our shoulders in spite of his protests. After few minutes, his resistance and shouts weakened. But by now the strong possibility of his catching serious cold was clear and our houses were surely an hour's walk away. A good sense prevailed to his good luck. We took him to the Dhaba where we were taking our food those days, explained the difficult position to the owner and requested him to provide shelter to Raj for few hours to enable him to get the warmth he badly needed. And thus Raj was put in the beds of Dhaba's staff which made us feel comfortable and awkwardly bad simultaneously; comfortable to have found a warm place but bad looking to the condition of the beds and cleanliness/hygiene of the accommodation. It was first time we were face to face with the miserable living conditions of the boys who always smilingly served us food but were there because of their poverty and ignorance. After 3/4 hours, we felt he was breathing normally but certainly he was not in a condition to do the walking. We, therefore, engaged few laborers from the nearby 'chawl', covered him with some blankets and he was carried home. Thank God, he was safe now!!

The aftermath of snow-storms

Even after the snow-storms stopped, life/activity remained paralyzed for weeks. And probably, we the singles were the worst sufferers by all means. We were without a bath for days. Even for making tea or brushing our teeth or washing our face etc. we would pick up a pile of snow from the roof, melt it and use it. The staircase of our house which was in the open was blocked by heaps of snow making our movement up and down a real challenge. It took more than a month for the infrastructure to get back to some shape. The heaps of snow, nay ice, were got somewhat cleared by the Municipality in March. The real relief was provided by the perpetrator of the havoc, the nature; the melting of snow/ice in the sun brought life back to normal. The poor infrastructure notwithstanding, the poor economic position of majority of people was equally responsible for sufferings during such natural calamities.

My initial struggles in fixing up residence

On arrival in Shimla I stayed in a hotel for few days. A few days later, with the help of one of my colleagues, I managed to get a room in barracks of staff quarters of 'Cecil Hotel' and started living there. This hotel used to open for 2, 3 months during summers and that is how some quarters were available for hire on regular basis. The distance to my office was about a km and the locality was known as 'Chaura Maidan'. It was clear that this room was at best a stop-gap arrangement and I remained on the look-out for a proper accommodation. A few months later, my boss, Mr.

J.R.Pasricha, arranged to let me share accommodation in 'Eleslie Cottage' as a sub-tenant of Mr. G.R.Sood, a colleague officer of my boss. It was a beautiful duplex bungalow located in peaceful and serene environment of pine and deodar trees away from the main road. This house was way beyond even wild dreams of a lower middle class employee like me. Thanks to Mr. Pasricha it happened and I continued to live there till 1965.

Chapter 4
A panoramic view of work-life in Shimla

The magnificent office building; 'Gorton Castle

'Gorton Castle' is indeed a castle, majestic and magnificent. Built atop a hillock, it commands a clear view of the entire town. During British Raj this building served as Central Secretariat when the Govt. of the day functioned during summers from Shimla. It is a huge multi-story building in the middle of the town conveniently accessible from the Mall, the railway station and the highway connecting Shimla with the plains. The foundation-stone of the building mentions that it was built in 1904 at a cost of about Rs 4 lakh. It is utterly unbelievable now that such a huge magnificent building made up of chiseled stone and steel structures was built in this paltry amount. Other important buildings like Legislature building, Viceroy's residence, other important offices and Bungalows for Ministers, dignitaries and senior bureaucrats were nearby. Even the race-course was about 3 kms down below connected with a motor-able road.

Work-life begins; I am posted in Pension Audit section

After scrutiny of my credentials/testimonials of educational qualifications, date of birth and identity as an Indian national by Establishment Section staff, I was asked to report for duty in Pension Audit Section, which was located in an adjacent building known as 'Railway Board' building. This building too was a huge mansion. It was a multi-storied structure built of stone and steel sections.

My main assignment in this section was authorizing payment of pension to retired personnel of Punjab and HP Govt. The authorization for pension normally was in 2 parts; 'Anticipatory Pension', which was authorized as an interim measure if scrutiny of pension papers revealed some deficiency. It was pegged at not more than 90 % of the likely final entitlement. On satisfactory compliance of the deficiency by the concerned dept., full and 'Final Pension' was authorized. It was called Final Pension Payment Order entitling the individual to present this PPO before the concerned Treasury Officer and start getting his/her pension.

Made strenuous efforts to clear the back-log in office

On joining my duty in Pension Audit Section, I found to my surprise that there were huge delays in issuing of Pension Payment Orders (PPOs). This scenario was appalling to me. In my view, the delay for whatever reason was reprehensible. How could it be thought that a person can survive if he/she is deprived of his/her pension for such a long period? On scrutiny, it pained me to see that many of the pending cases could have been cleared either for Anticipatory Pension or for final pension. I brought this sorry state to the notice of my Supervisor, the Accountant and he in turn briefed our boss, the Accounts Officer in charge. Luckily for the pensioners and me (I was feeling guilty for the delay as if I had committed it); both the Accountant and the Accounts Officer were sympathetic, were possessed of liberal disposition, took a lenient view and agreed to authorize Anticipatory Pension in most of the pension cases. This human face of my seniors impacted my mind and served as a positive guidance in my work-life later. I put in extra efforts to clear the backlog after office hours and that too in severe cold winter.

This sincere effort was highly appreciated by my seniors and probably this was the reason that prompted Mr. Pasricha to put me into 'Eleslie Cottage' as a sub-tenant of his friend, Mr. GR Sood. This gesture and my sincere efforts in office work built up over a period of time a warm and close personal relationship with Mr. Pasricha. I will attempt to describe it in details later as to how this relationship blossomed into a cementing and everlasting bond of closeness between us in matters both official as well as social/personal. However, I wonder if I shall be able to describe it well and touch the depth that was the 'sine qua non' of this mutual deep respect between us.

I continued with my zeal to perform well in other assignments also with speed and this also earned for me the goodwill of my Accountant who encouraged me to think of taking up All India Services Examinations conducted by UPSC. He himself had been pursuing his efforts in this direction and ultimately, he was successful in clearing the coveted Indian Audit and Accounts Service.

The overall atmosphere in this section was too good and healthy. My senior colleagues helped and also encouraged me, the new-comer, a lot in building up my confidence. To name a few; Mr. BS Nayyar, SL Kumar, Raj Malhotra took personal interest in building up my morale. Each one of them was a class by himself. Thanks to them, I could clear the backlog happily.

I continued to be in this section for about four years and was transferred out to GAD 4 section, as desired by Mr. Pasricha.

GAD 4; a still more challenging assignment

The saga of my transfer to GAD 4 section makes an interesting reading. Mr. Pasricha who was my boss in Pension Audit section was given the charge of GAD 4 section to stem the rot that had set in there for long. This section dealt with authorizing salary and other entitlements to Gazetted Officers of Himachal Pradesh Govt. There were in-ordinate delays which resulted in serious complaints from the officers' community and the Govt. The Chief Secretary and other top bureaucrats were voicing their concern and were keen that the situation was brought under control urgently and authorizations started happening in time. This challenging assignment was handed over to Mr. Pasricha considering his reputation as a hard task master.

The first most urgent and tough task for breaking the logjam in this section was breaking the citadel of employees' union leaders posted there. And Mr. Pasricha handled the situation deftly. In the process, the laggards and union leaders were shifted out and in came the staff of Mr. Pasricha's choice; staff who enjoyed his confidence and about whom he was sure they will face the odds confidently and deliver in a time frame decided by the top management.

I was the first choice of Mr. Pasricha followed by VC Jauhri who was well-known to be a great performer. Jauhri was given the responsibility of handling the cases of top bureaucrats; IAS, IPS & PCS officers which was a serious challenge and he met it gracefully. This process of bringing in new hands in GAD 4 section continued till all the sanctioned posts to Mr. Pasricha's satisfaction were filled up.

I was assigned the charge of handling two important Depts.; Ministers, MLAs and Medical and Public Health Dept. The assignment was a real challenge. There were in-ordinate delays in issue of salary authorizations to many Doctors. There was hue and cry by the Doctors' community and the head of dept., the Director of Health Services. Most of the Doctors were working without any salary and allowances for months. In addition to this, the revised pay-scales which had been introduced for Doctors under the Central Health Service Scheme were not given effect to. The clamor for quick action increased after the word spread that there was complete overhaul in the section and new staff had been posted. No surprise that the expectations rose high and pressure for quick issue of authorizations called 'Pay Slip' built up immensely. Written reminders, personal visits by concerned officers and meetings between the Chief Secretary and Director of Health Services and our officers added to the pressure. We were required to clear the backlog in a time-bound period agreed to between the Govt. representatives and our office. Well, we met the challenge by devoting extra hours. Of-course, there was no extra remuneration for us for doing so. Our reward was profuse appreciation. Unlike now, those were conservative days. Even no tea or snacks were provided to us at office cost during extended duty hours. Rules didn't permit all this and A.G's office administration was expected to set an example.

Implemented the Central Health Service pay scales & allowances etc. for Doctors of HP Govt

Apart from clearing the backlog of issue of Pay Slips for payment of current salaries, the next important assignment for me was to give effect to the revised pay scales announced in Central Health Service Rules for the Doctors. It meant revising salaries of Doctors in accordance with these rules and authorise payment of arrears for the past period. The number of Doctors covered by this scheme was about 150. This was a herculean task for this scheme was effective from a back date and this called for detailed scrutiny of service record of each Doctor to work out his/her entitlements taking into account the changes in status i.e. promotion etc. And all this had to be done by preparing a spread-sheet manually for each Doctor separately to enable working out his/her revised entitlement and facilitating its scrutiny by the Accountant and approval by the Accounts Officer. And there were no electronic calculators even what to talk of computing machines. Using mechanical calculators appeared to be cumbersome and rather time-consuming to me. Therefore, we used to utilize our mathematical skills for determining the final amount. An additional complicating feature was that some of these doctors were being paid the salary etc. as per their entitlement under the rules of the princely state to which they belonged. Their entitlement under the HP Govt. rules after their integration into H.P. Govt. Service were also to be worked out before revising it further as per the CHS rules; a long drawn and complicated process. The number of such Doctors was large. I remember, in nut-shell, it took me about six to eight months to clear the backlog and authorize payment of arrears due as per CHS rules.

Doctors shower their gratitude

No doubt, there was huge appreciation by my office and the Director of Health Services when this task was completed. Warm messages of thanks started pouring in from the community of Doctors soon after the revised Pay Slips authorizing payment of arrears of salary and allowances were sent to them. I was happy to have completed this arduous exercise with speed to enable the concerned doctors to get the arrears which ran into thousands of rupees for each one of them. And at that time thousands meant quite a lot. Almost all the doctors including those posted in far-off places and had no chance of meeting me personally, started knowing me by name. Aneja became a very familiar name in the Medical and Public Health dept. To express their gratitude, many doctors sent invitations to me to pay a visit to their place and meet them personally. I was not sure whether I should accept the invitations and kept on lingering the matter and ultimately the enthusiasm for a visit slowed down but for one Doctor, who continued to press for it.

Warm hospitality that deeply touched us

Dr. GL Tuli who was posted at Theog, a distance of about 25 miles from Shimla continued to persist and kept up his pressure for the visit. And one Saturday, his son dropped in suddenly and insisted we accompany him. We myself, my wife and daughter who was few months old, went to Theog. It was a memorable visit. The welcome accorded to us by the entire family was genuinely warm and full of love. Our stay with them was as if we were part of the family; each member eager to attend to us to make our stay comfortable. On arrival in the house and during the first night that we spent with them in their house, we were given a royal welcome with every member including his family members taking good care and seeing that we were comfortable. The guest room, where we were made comfortable was keenly furnished. It was an out-of-world experience, unbelievably exciting and much beyond our imagination. The dinner table reflected that minute attention had been paid to selection of the fare and great care was paid to preparing of variety of dishes. The whole scene was amazing. Both, the daughter and daughters-in-law, stood in attention while we were busy savoring the variety of delectable preparations. After dinner, the entire family sat with us chatting freely and happily as if we were an old and close acquaintance for long. For the next two days, we were in Dr. Tuli's orchard of apples. It was an enchanting experience. Dr. Tuli, his wife and elder son accompanied us and took us round the orchard. Here also, a great care was taken to make sure our trip was really enjoyable. We did hitch-hiking and were taken for sight-seeing to nearby places. After hiking and extensive walks during the day, we got tired when the maids treated us to a spa like activity; massaging our legs in a bucket of warm water to reduce the fatigue and help us get sound sleep in warm beddings. It was a heart-rending experience and even now when I and my wife recall it, our eyes get moist. To be honest, such a warm hospitality full of love and affection touched us deeply. The departure time made us cry in conveying our sincere thanks and regards to the elderly couple and their loving children.

Another equally touching and poignant experience of warmth for us

I am at a loss to decide where to begin. A lady doctor by name, Dr. S. Abel, used to visit me in office, off and on, with some queries about her entitlements. As usual, I would listen to her small anxieties with care and try to allay her fears. She was due for superannuation from service in about six months and had an apprehension that her pension would be delayed since the dept. had yet not sent her pension papers to our Pension Report Section. Her concern was genuine since the delay in submission of papers could really delay the issue of Pension Payment Order. She asked me if I could help her in this matter. Though, normally, our office had no role at this stage and we could help expedite the process of clearance once the pension papers were received by us but on her pleading I talked to some senior people in Director of Health Services office and District Medical Officer's office to request them to expedite the process of submission of her papers to our office. I guided the concerned dealing staff in DMO's office as to how to complete the documents. I also advised the concerned staff member to come and meet me personally if he had some difficulty in doing so. During all this conversation, Dr. Abel was sitting with me. She was deeply moved by this gesture of genuine initiative of mine. To cut the long story short, there were some problems since her past years' service record was not complete but due to my intervention, her office people put in extra efforts and sorted out the problems. In the process, her pension was not delayed and of course, she was too happy.

One day, the gracious lady came to thank me and asked me if I could take her to my residence because she was keen to meet Mrs. Aneja. And we went to our house together. Mrs. Aneja welcomed her and offered tea etc. which she enjoyed. What followed after this was unbelievable. She asked if we could let her adopt our daughter legally and thus make our daughter her own legal heir because she was unmarried. She conveyed she was afraid that when she goes to her native place, Pune, her relatives would forcibly grab her money, property and valuables. To guard against all this, she wanted to have a legal heir of her own. Though her proposal was a genuine gesture, we politely declined her suggestion and begged her excuse.

High drama for my transfer from GAD 4 section

After clearing the mess in GAD 4 section, Mr. Pasricha was given the charge of Establishment section primarily to initiate and handle the disciplinary proceedings against the union leader, who it was considered, was responsible for vitiating the work atmosphere in the office as a whole apart from instigating and intimidating his colleagues in GAD 4 section. I had earned Mr. Pasricha's full trust while working with him in Pension Audit and GAD 4 sections. Therefore, Mr. Pasricha wanted me to join him as 'Confidential Assistant' in his personal cell to deal with strictly confidential papers. Accordingly orders were issued by Establishment section for my transfer from GAD 4 section. This was not acceptable to my current boss, Mr. Thakar Singh. The issue transformed into a confrontation between both the officers and quite a number of meetings were held at different levels to resolve the matter but to no avail. I do not know how but Mr. Thakar Singh had his way and orders were cancelled. Apparently, the matter appeared to have ended there but Mr. Pasricha had some different plans. He was clear that he must have me with him as 'Confidential Assistant'. It became a prestige issue for him. In-fact, Accounts Officer, Establishment, enjoyed a distinctly high position in

Accounts Officers' hierarchy. He felt offended when his orders had to be cancelled. He worked out a strategy to get me in his office. It was planned that I proceed on long leave of more than thirty days and as per rules in force, a substitute was required to be given to GAD 4 section in my place and on return from leave I would be part of the general pool of auditors available at the disposal of Establishment section who could post me in a new section according to vacant positions then. Accordingly, I proceeded on long leave though I never wanted it. Mr. Thakar Singh was equally smart. He refused to accept any substitute in my place and kept the seat vacant. Obviously, he was determined to outsmart Mr. Pasricha. On my joining back from leave, he insisted that I be sent back to my original place which was not acceptable to Mr. Pasricha. A battle of wits ensued between the two of them and I remained idle and without any assignment for about four weeks. I am not aware precisely how but ultimately Mr. Pasricha succeeded and I was posted as his "C.A'. I know; this episode was subject matter of gossip and heated exchanges between many of our colleagues. It became obvious that I was Mr. Pasricha's trusted lieutenant. Well, I enjoyed being the focus of this high-caliber drama and I became known amongst the senior officers.

The culmination

Now my formal office designation was 'Confidential Assistant' to the Accounts Officer, Establishment. This was a most coveted and sought after posting. It meant I enjoyed full confidence of my boss who, by virtue of critical nature of the assignment, would want a trustworthy person to occupy this seat. My new assignment meant that I sit in the office room of my boss. That was my work-place. I was not free to move around and spend some time with friends in the canteen. Nor could my friends come to our room and meet me. The office room, I worked in, was out of bounds for them or, for that matter for any person who had no appointment with the boss. With boss present in the room, even the attendant hesitated to come in, unless called for. Any/every paper in the room was confidential. I normally waited for lunch-break to stir out

144

and meet my friends. It is not correct to say that the boss was haughty or boorish. The nature of job he was handling being strictly confidential demanded that nobody should have free access to the room and the confidential papers. As far as I was concerned I was free to move out but it involved caution lest he is disturbed. It was virtually a solitary place for me. I was not free to leave office in the evening until the boss had left. Whatever transpired in meetings or was otherwise discussed in the room by the establishment section staff with the boss was confidential. Every matter here was confidential and I had to ensure that the sanctity of confidential matters becoming known to me every day while discharging my responsibility was maintained. In line with the designation, C.A, my job was to assist the boss in all confidential matters.

After about a year and a half, Mr. Pasricha was enrolled into Audit and Accounts Service after being selected as such through a rigorous competition, interviews and selection procedures. I was extremely happy on his well-deserved elevation. He had a very respectable place in my inner-self. I will attempt to profile him later in a chapter that follows

Another feather in my cap

In April, 1965, I proceeded on long leave to get married and on return was posted in TM section; one of the top important sections in the office. This section was concerned with interpretation of Codes called Fundamentals Rules, Supplementary Rules, and amendments thereto and decisions conveyed by the GOI and CAG from time to time for regulating the service conditions of Govt. employees. The interpretation/opinion given by this section in cases referred to it by other sections was considered to be the last word. Where, of course, there was some doubt or possibility of two interpretations, this section alone was authorized to seek clarification from GOI or CAG, as the case may be. The posting in this section was considered to be recognition of one's competence and ability to handle difficult assignment of interpreting Govt. Rules. This section was under the direct charge of Senior Deputy Accountant General himself and therefore postings to this section were done after he was satisfied about the suitability/ competence of the person concerned. In a way, posting in this section put the incumbent in a separate and prized category. I was transferred out of this section after I was due for promotion as S.A.S Accountant.

Glory associated with Audit and Accounts dept. of our times

Accountant General's office of our times was responsible for maintenance of accounts and also for carrying out the audit thereof; of-course these two important functions were handled by separate independent groups in the office. The separation of audit and accounts under two separate offices was done later. The Audit wing of the office had a vast pool of talent. Conducting audit objectively to ensure compliance in true spirit and intention of the rules and regulations and preparing audit reports keeping in mind the sole objective of highlighting irregularities, non-compliance of statutory provisions, pointing out instances of wastage of public funds was kept in focus by the audit teams. In those days, the audit reports were receiving full attention of the Govt. of the day as well as legislatures. These reports were discussed thread-bare in Public Accounts Committees of the respective legislatures. After exhaustive analysis and debates, the concerned departmental heads and Ministers were hauled up in the committee by the Chief Ministers who were assisted in this task by the Accountant General and his team. The follow-up action or action taken report as they call it now was debated threadbare in the PAC and the Legislature and many a times rules of governance were amended based on A.G's Audit Reports. The Constituent Assembly in their wisdom created the institution of PAC as an important feature of checks and balances between Legislature and Executive wings and to keep a healthy check on the tendency of profligacy of various Govt. functionaries.

Chapter 5
My vision of growth materializes

I qualified in the sacred (to me) S.A.S Exam. in November, 1967, but continued to function as an auditor till there was a vacancy in SAS cadre in 1968 when I got promoted as Accountant and was given the charge of Administration III section. This section dealt with all sundry matters for smooth functioning of the office like accommodation, both office and residential, its maintenance and liaison with CPWD, furniture and fixtures and other office equipment (procurement as well as maintenance), stationery, care-taking of the premises, making arrangements for seminars, conferences and other events, logistics, liaison with Govt. hospitals/dispensaries and evacuation of seriously ill/injured employees and last but not the least up-keep of lawns and gardens in the office premises. Virtually every activity necessary for smooth functioning, care-taking and safety and security of the office involving regular inter-action with police and district administration was included in our charter of responsibility. Maintaining leave records of the entire work-force was another function of this section. A very large staff contingent was part of the section. Needless to say, the functions our section took care of were critical but not recognized as such compared to the other two Administration Sections which were handling establishment matters and pay-rolls and other entitlements.

Krishan Aneja

The first major challenge I successfully met as an Accountant

A very critical and urgent assignment awaited us (myself and my team) soon after I took charge. In the wake of trifurcation of the state of Punjab in 1966 into three states of Punjab, Haryana and Himachal Pradesh, a decision was taken by CAG in 1968 to trifurcate the Accountant General Punjab office into three offices; one each for each state. Soon two Accountant Generals one for Haryana and one for H.P. along with one Deputy A.G. each arrived in 1968. The first urgent task before me, therefore, was to provide to these worthies a suitable office accommodation and furnish it properly. This assignment, though small, turned out to be ticklish. The office rooms identified by us for the purpose were not o.k. with them though this was supposed to be a stop-gap arrangement. After great difficulty and persuasion at the highest level, this issue was resolved.

Thereafter, the real tough exercise started; making an inventory of furniture, fixtures and other equipment followed by a plan of distribution of these assets amongst the three entities. A nerve-wrecking exercise followed still. Physical rounds of inspection of all this started. I, my Accounts Officer and the concerned staff members had to be on the move whole day till late evening with each of these worthies together or separately. I would be dead –tired daily when we called it a day. And all this continued for more than three months before the three worthies jointly agreed to the physical allocation plan. Thereafter, the movement of the staff/officers to the allocated building/rooms along with the relevant records, furniture, fixture and other equipment started. There was no escape for me till the whole exercise was completed even though I and many of my team members were physical wrecks at the end.

A valuable opportunity to work with inspiring seniors

I was allocated to the A.G. Haryana office as per my option and was given the old charge in the new office. My new Accountant General, Mr. AC Bose, was a thoroughly gentle, soft-spoken, a scholarly person not given to speaking much, mostly busy in his literary pursuits for the office work

148

didn't take him long to finish. He believed in delegating powers to his worthy Deputy, Mr. Akbar Hamid Jung. Mr. Bose's office table was almost always empty. He possessed an elegant, artistic taste and distinct choices. To furnish his office room and ante-room was simply challenging. His needs were very few but specific. He was very clear about the ambience and over-all look. His choice of each item of furniture, wall-hangings and the artefacts for his office spoke volumes about his high and exquisite choice. Mr. Jung too like Mr. Bose was blessed with distinct tastes and preferences. No compromises were acceptable to either of them. The duo, Mr. Bose and Mr. Jung, were my dear favorites. A hard task master, clear-headed, concise and precise in conveying his view-point, very particular about details, willing to listen to suggestions with an open-mind, thoroughly gentle to deal with and always well-prepared with his plans was how Mr. Jung was. It was known that he did a lot of home-work at night before taking a final view. It was a pleasure working with him. I felt I was lucky and privileged to have got an opportunity to work with him and Mr. Bose though my direct contacts with Mr. Bose were few. In hindsight, I can say, my association with these two worthies for about a year or so was truly rewarding. I picked up quite a lot in matters of inter-personal relationship management during this short period.

The work environment in office changed significantly for the better thanks to the initiatives and positive decisions taken by them. It is note-worthy that Mr. Bose was hardly in the fore-front though the decisions were mostly his but Mr. Jung was seen as the management's inter-face with the staff. It appears, it was a deliberate style and a message to the staff that top boss was the ultimate authority for appeals/redressal, if any. AG Haryana's office became a torch-bearer for other two A.G. offices not only in matters of hygiene, cleanliness and other similar facilities but also in matters of improved work-culture. The staff including union leaders hailed these improvements positively; there weren't any issues on which to agitate or convey unhappiness in the staff meetings.

My stay in Shimla ended in June, 1969, when I proceeded on deputation to BHEL, Hardwar.

Krishan Aneja

Summing up my work-life in Shimla

Exhilaration, a deep sense of satisfaction and achievements worthy of recounting and being happy about, comes to mind while recalling a crucial and most important leg (almost a decade long) of my work life at Shimla.

Let me recount/recall certain anecdotes that make me proud and enable me to substantiate the answer I have given above:-

Upon joining in Pension Audit section, I found that a very large number of pension cases were pending on my seat. It was a painful realization which deeply moved me and I resolved to clear the backlog as quickly as possible. The job was easier said than done. I was new to the job and needed time to grasp the rules and regulations. After about two weeks, I got going. Gradually I gained confidence and picked up speed in clearing the back-log. It was heartening that the huge arrears of pending cases were cleared in record time thus mitigating the hardships of a large number of the retired personnel. This initiative was of my own volition without any prodding of seniors. Of course, their appreciation from time to time was an encouragement that I cherished and which induced me to do more and more always. My efforts didn't end at clearing the back-log only. It also set-up a positive trend for future; authorize Anticipatory Pension in cases, where possible, to mitigate to some extent the immediate financial hardships of the retirees,

Cleared the backlog of issue of Salary Slips to officers of H.P. Govt. which were held up for no valid reasons except lethargy of my predecessors,

Implemented the scheme of revised pay scales and entitlements under the CHS Rules for Doctors of H.P. Govt. The rules of the scheme were fairly complex and called for seeking clarifications from the Govt. of India. The entire process of seeking clarifications from the G.O.I and thereafter implementation was completed quite expeditiously.

150

Worked hard to unravel the Pay and Allowances Codes of some erstwhile princely states for integrating them with the entitlements under H.P. Govt. rules in the first instance and then working out the entitlements under CHS rules for the Doctors who were absorbed in the Medical and Public Health Dept. of H.P. Govt. on merger of the princely states into it. This assignment was pending for long and the concerned Doctors had given up hopes long back. Their happiness knew no bounds when the authorization slips for huge amount of arrears of pay and allowances were received by them.

Govt.'s T.A. rules were considered to be complicated and difficult to decipher. Therefore, to avoid controversies, most of the staff in our office avoided doing properly the post-audit of T.A. bills. This attitude was not to my liking. I studied the rules and relevant instructions/clarifications issued from time to time and sort of acquired confidence to scrutinize the T.A. bills. My Accounts Officer who was very familiar with these rules helped me in this matter. After being armed with this confidence, I started conducting diligently the post-audit of T.A. and medical claims of Doctors, Ministers and MLAs who were in my charge. What started as a normal exercise based on norms prescribed in Audit Manual, turned out to an eye-opener? The audit revealed that there were huge over-payments. Therefore, a sort of campaign was launched in this behalf by me. This vigorous effort led to recovery of huge amounts of overpayments in spite of hue and cry by the concerned officers. This campaign had its positive side effect too. On the insistence of Heads of Dept., few clarificatory instructions were issued by us to all the controlling officers to take note of the wrong claims and to ensure that a proper care is taken to ensure T.A. claims being submitted correctly.

Not only that, a few instances of wrong interpretation of rules resulted in over-claim in T.A. bills of Chief Minister himself. As per standing instructions of HQs, i.e. Comptroller and Auditor General's office, the process of resolving the cases of Ministers and other politicians required the intervention of A.G himself before any communication was sent in this behalf. And because of the sensitive nature, audit of bills of politicians was rarely taken up. I did not stop at that and did scrutinize the TA claims of political figures also. As a result, after clarifications were provided by us, the General Administration dept. of the HP Govt. who was responsible for preparing bills of Ministers and MLAs agreed to accept the recoveries and also issued instructions within the dept. to ensure compliance of the rules in future. It was thrilling to rise to the higher level of performance by dealing with VIPs' claims scrupulously. And who knows, it satisfied my ego also. The support in this endeavor of my Accounts Officer, Mr. Narendar Kapur, is worthy of special mention. He induced me to continue to push ahead in this matter. All this hard-work made me known in the higher circles of office hierarchy and earned me high appreciation of my seniors including A.G. himself.

I had a really tough time performing the job of Confidential Assistant to Accounts Officer, Establishment. It was astonishing that every file that came to him was not only confidential but urgent and time-bound. There would be red-flags signifying the urgency. There used to be numerous meetings scheduled every day by different groups and each group would want their file to be given priority. A clash of dates and time would often ensue making my life miserable. Working late beyond office-hours was a routine for me. I would be totally exhausted and fatigued when I left office in the evening. I missed my friends, the Coffee House, the humor and gossips associated with all this. I pitied myself but to no excuse.

I still remember a most nerve-wrecking and harsh day (Sunday) I spent in office. It was mid-January. My boss asked if I could devote some time tomorrow and make a file ready for a very urgent and important meeting scheduled for Monday early morning. As usual with me I nodded my head in affirmative. And lo and behold, it started snowing heavily Saturday evening itself and by morning there was huge pile up of snow and there was power failure also. I still went to office, worked for few hours without any tea or food and without a heating stove or electric heater. I was virtually numb with cold and dead by the time I reached the Coffee House in the evening. Next morning when the boss saw that the file was ready, he couldn't believe it. He was deeply moved and embraced me signifying his love and affection.

In recognition of my services of exceptional order and commitment, I earned the highest reward an Auditor could aspire for; grant of an advance increment under FR 27 i.e. raise in salary to the extent of an increment though not due under normal rules. And this merit award was granted in few exceptional cases on specific recommendations of seniors and approval by the A.G. where after the proposal was sent to HQs for sanction.

Now, when I am recalling all this, I feel proud that all this could be accomplished. It is not that getting some award was my motto or I was working for it. Far from it; the guiding realty was 'you have no capital or seed money to invest in a venture and try to make a fortune. For a penniless person like you, getting a good job is the real option which, to begin with, would free you from the anxiety of next meals and secure a reasonable life of a middle-class guy.' At the same time, I was aware, that hard work and excellent performance was the only 'mantra' for growth and success. It was soothing for an ambitious person like me to visualize a career of high growth. I was not willing to accept status-quo or a slowly creeping growth which is normal in Govt. jobs.

Chapter 6
Meaning of meaningful work-life for me

My mother's oft-repeated advice was firmly settled in my psyche "Kisi ko tumhara cham pyara nahin, sirf kam pyara hota hai". This colloquial phrase full of real wisdom means, "No-body is enamored of your skin/your face. People care for and like your performance only." What I learnt from this pearl of wisdom always guided me in the journey of my eventful career. To me, it meant; "Identify what is expected of you and deliver more than what is expected. Be stead-fast in your commitment to the entrusted job and make sure it is visible to your seniors. Adopt and demonstrate a high degree result-oriented style of performance. Understand; it is the only way forward. You must deliver always and be seen to be doing that. There should be no looking back. Surpass your own expectations. Have your own yard-stick for evaluation of your performance critically. Look for and work on new ideas for further improvement. Be your own judge and hard task master. Be alert lest you fall into slumber or start gloating on your achievement. Always remember and remind your-self; avenues for growth are always wide-open for those who believe in self and their potential to excel. Remember, every new day offers a whole new promise. Believe in yourself and be rewarded."

Intrinsic strength of work-life; passion, ethics and sincere genuine commitment

Thanks to pertinent pearls of wisdom of my mother, giving my best to my job was not a burden to me. I enjoyed putting in my best. I loved my

154

job. Ethics in performance, being happily busy in work was the recipe I enjoyed. It enthrals me now, when my younger son, Ashish, who is a Doctor by profession, says I love my profession. It broadens my chest to listen to him say so. I didn't have to make any conscious efforts to do my job diligently, sincerely or to the best of my capability. It just always happened is all that I can say. In hind-sight, I believe the urge to give my best to the job was God's gift to me. I am sure; this urge lay embedded somewhere in my inner self waiting for a trigger to surface. I am happy, it always poured itself out un-consciously when the situation demanded. Being happily busy in my job has been a routine affair with me. Work stimulated me. It gave me energy. Even sitting idle at home was repulsive to me. If nothing else, I would just go for a walk or a small hitch-hiking spree. Nature and beautiful surroundings in the open in Shimla always attracted me. I never felt fatigued after a long walk.

A sacred faith for me; no loitering during office hours

Spending office time in indulging in gossips and other frivolities was far from me. Sticking to a responsible and sincere approach to work made me happy. I did enjoy the company of my friends in the canteen for tea etc. or in the 'Dhaba' for lunch but only during officially authorized breaks. I always remembered I had a job on my table to finish. Wasting office time in meaningless loitering was un-known to me. It was repulsive to see some of our office colleagues standing in groups here and there even after lunch-break. I wondered why they were there still and what it was that glued them together. May be they didn't have any pressure of work or they just ignored it. This is not to suggest that I was a loner or I didn't enjoy being with friends and indulging in gossips or enjoying their company. (I will come to this aspect of my life later in details. Right now, I am restricting myself to my office life only). In office, however, I and my friend, Raj Malhotra, whose table was next to mine, would indulge in innocently pleasant and humorous exchanges/slangs in low tones, while being seriously busy in our respective jobs. Paradoxical it may seem, but the fact is that this refreshed us but sometimes our other colleagues would feel disturbed and complain to the Accountant for the alleged distraction. And many a times, our senior would advise the complainant to enjoy the wit rather than getting disturbed. And the matter would end there.

When is being proud justified?

Being proud of one's great performance and achievements in work life is the music one should aspire to listen. Strive, work hard and deliver against odds even and only then feel proud. However, one has to take care to ensure that the pride is not misplaced and doesn't lead to perfunctory approach. I think; the context and accompanying circumstances would determine whether the pride is realistic, genuine and justifiable. If not, it may turn out to be a negative attribute of which one should be wary. But many people glamorize it and flaunt it indiscriminately. This is sure to lead to arrogance. And arrogance in any form or of any hue is nothing but very negation of the values. Therefore, it is right to conclude that self-pride is a positive attribute when it is accompanied by humbleness, has its genesis in achievements of positive nature like any recognition and awards. The sense of being proud of success in our endeavors is an elixir that is sweet and charming. It produces energy in abundance and propels us to give our more and more in this direction. It pushes us and gives a meaningful sense of direction to our initiatives. We feel motivated to excel and make attempts to beat our own past accomplishment.

One has always to remind oneself, 'BE POSITIVE, HUMBLE AND FOCUSSED. KEEP PUSHING AND MOVE FORWARD FOR THIS IS WHAT THE LIFE OUGHT TO BE. PRAY AND SOLICIT HIS PATH-BREAKING GUIDANCE IN ALL YOUR ENDEAVORS BEFORE MAKING A BEGINNING. SUCCESS FOLLOWS THEM WHO HAVE UNFLINCHING FAITH IN HIM, BELIEVE IN HIS GENEROSITY AND KINDNESS. LOOK TO HIM AND SEEK HIS GUIDANCE WHEN AT CROSS-ROADS. THOUGH HE IS NOT VISIBLE TO NAKED EYES, HE IS OMNI-PRESENT, HE IS OMNI-POTENT. HE IS HUMANITY'S HOPE, LAST RESORT'

When is being proud negative?

Being proud is negative when it is shallow, when it is rootless, when it is not based on actual performance but based on self-assumed success, when it is just arrogance; arrogance of self-assumed high pedigree and righteousness, arrogance of self-assumed high place and high status in society, arrogance of wealth, arrogance of one's manipulative capabilities and similar other negatives.

Some people believe being proud is itself the negation of virtues and is the anti-dote to being humble. In their opinion, being proud is poisonous, is always a negative attribute and therefore, despicable. There doesn't seem to be any rationale behind it. What is so bad about being proud of one's achievements if they are genuine and laudable? I believe; being justly proud stimulates. Only, a proud person can dream big for he/she is full of enthusiasm to do more and is keen to touch/conquer the new peaks. Success leads to pride and widens the horizon. Of course, it is important to be careful lest the pride takes the form of boorish vanity. Getting afflicted with vanity means the start of downward journey.

Chapter 7
Friends in Shimla; my real life-line

My first friend at Shimla

The first person who joined me as my room partner (through the good offices of a common colleague) first in the staff quarters of Cecil Hotel and later in 'Eleslie Cottage' was Ved as I addressed him though his full name is Ved Prakash Chugh. And we lived together for more than 5 years till I got married. That speaks volumes about our audacity to accommodate each other. It is my pleasure to recall with satisfaction that our association helped us pick up some valuable in-puts for healthy inter-personal relations and that too in a comparatively young age of early twenties when maturity in dealings is normally said to be far away. Unhesitatingly, I would describe Ved as a nice guy, plain and simple, true to what he professed about himself, had lot of wits and no pretentions, clear-headed about what he stood for and wanted out of this life, proud of his ancestors and his family's background, a knowledgeable person who loved reading books, believed in high morals, not given to profanity, always open-minded and willing to listen and accommodate others' view-point.

Over a period of time, we settled down to a mutually agreed work routine in house-hold chores. Broadly, procuring grocery and other eatables for the kitchen and preparing food was my assignment while cleaning the utensils and crockery/cutlery was his responsibility. Of-course, we would handle our personal chores ourselves. Depending upon our moods and forced by inclement cold weather, we were alternating between preparing food at home and eating out. We were maintaining proper accounts of money spent by each one of us on the common house-hold items and settle the accounts at the end of each month. This arrangement stood the test of time.

There were hardly any major differences or issues between us. That is not to say, we didn't differ on any matter at all. Quite frequently, we would have heated discussions on a variety of issues like interpretation of office rules, politics and political leaders and policies of the Govt., current affairs, movies and fashions, eateries of the town and relationship with common friends. Some pin-pricks here and there notwithstanding, we were comfortable and happy to be together. The essence of our relationship was mutual trust. We believed in each other. We hardly had any exclusive friends. Occasional serious arguments and heated exchanges alright but we had a very cozy, durable and 'envy of others like' true friendship which sustained us. We loved and heartily cherished it. Our relationship was our strength but others envy. We rarely talked to others about our differences which, if fact, were of minor significance and related to trivialities. It was amazing to many that for so many years we continued to be together. We enjoyed this amazement heartily. The understanding we had developed was effortless. It evolved over a period of time given our efforts and stead-fast commitment to the virtue of being true to each other.

The invaluable lessons that our association gave us

Our association of five years taught us both the importance of adjustment, mutual tolerance and patience so necessary for building a healthy and meaningful social relationship. It taught us to listen and talk to each other rather than talking at each other. Discuss and sort out the differences in time rather than carrying the heavy burden of differences and allow them to multiply. Another trait that evolved was, 'wait and allow the passage of time to cool down the heat'. Yet another interesting style that came handy many a times was, 'keep mum immediately after the discordant episode and let the other person realize the mistake'. Or just laugh away petty differences on the spot.

The foundation of inherent understanding/code of conduct was mutual trust. Both of us knew neither of us means any ill to the other. We were sure of the value of mutual regard for a healthy co-existence. Not that we planned any such efforts consciously. All this built up on its own. May be the underlying wisdom and maturity of approach was doing its bit.

Many a times Ved would say, "I am disenchanted with you. I do not want to live with you anymore. Find out a separate room for me." I would laugh it away saying," How funny? Why should I find? Do it yourself" And the matter would rest there. A few days pass and we both would be normal as before.

To nourish and enrich the relationship, each one of us would attempt to anticipate the mood of the other at a given time and suggest doing a thing of his purported liking like going to a movie and eating out or going to the Coffee House (which was our favorite haunt and a mood setter).

The conclusion- the association of over five years taught us both the virtue of being accommodative, tolerant and patient for developing and sustaining healthy and long lasting inter-personal relations.

The well-knit group of friends.

As is usual for a person of my age, I too was eager to build up friendships. With some efforts I was able, over a period of time, to be a part of an intimate group of few fellow colleagues of office. We came together gradually with some known colleagues taking the initiative and introducing us with each other. I think the desire for this association stemmed from each individual's urge to have some buddies whose likes, dislikes and temperament matched with his and who were willing and/ or eager to have the company of known and chosen guys. Not that some selection process was involved in it. It started with colleagues working together in a section and then covered their colleagues/room-mates working in other sections.

Of-course, the group comprised of those working in A. G. office only. The total number of friends in this well-knit group was seven; namely

Raj Malhotra (nick-name Ganja), S.P.Bhandari (Lamboo, he was tallest in the group), Sudarshan Khanna (Budhha, he was eldest in group and his mannerism was like that of an elder), Ved Chugh (padhakoo meaning an avid reader), SKS Mehta (carefree & easy going), VC Jauhri, a very talented and accomplished performer in office but a wonderful pal full of grace, decent etiquette and high manners and myself who probably had no nick-name except that my name was frequently mispronounced as 'neja' meaning the pine-tree fruit. On occasions, some others were joining us on invitation or otherwise of their own sweet-will but the core group was not expanded in true sense. There was no express decision about the composition of the group or the numbers but the tacit understanding was very clear; do not encourage others to get in.

I am proud to say that the group has remained intact in Chandigarh. We two, Ved and I, moved away on securing jobs elsewhere but we remained in touch with each other and even attended the marriages of some of us or as late as marriages of our children, when possible. I am happy to state that even now when we are not at one place and are in advanced age-bracket, we get in touch off and on and try to know each other's and family's welfare. Recently, the group got together with families at Chandigarh, thanks to the initiative of Mehta. I and my life-partner travelled to Chandigarh and had the pleasure of meeting Raj, Mehta and Jauhari on 14th October, 2012. This nostalgic reunion, even though for few hours enthralled each one of us with a promise to meet again.

It is truly sad and regretful for me and Mrs. Aneja that destiny snatched away Raj recently and we couldn't travel to Chandigarh to join in his last rites due to severe winter.

The dynamics and real strength of this informal group shall come out in the narration that follows. I am positive; it is going to be riveting and heart-warming, once real live details are chronicled. The depth of relations in the group was based on the pleasure of being together for mutual help and support when needed. Solidarity in difficult situations, a genuine desire of enjoying each other's company, sharing the bits of information frankly and consulting and counseling each other on personal matters was the rock foundation of the edifice.

Going on hitch-hiking trips, outings, picnics and other similar activities was group's passion. Pooling of resources and making best use of talent for the success of the planned event was a routine. The bond of attachment amongst the friends was unique. To me, any such bond doesn't seem to be conceivable now. 'Self' is the only norm that matters now. No-body seems to be aware of the eternal pleasure of 'sharing'. Youngsters don't mingle now frankly and openly like what we used to do in our times. Every-body seems to be carrying a personal agenda; well-concealed with motives of personal glory/success.

Group's basic Mantra; 'Freedom' (no running after girls)

Group's fundamental code of conduct liked by all and which came up without any conscious effort or any debate or formal discussions and whose genesis was voluntary evolution was 'no running after girls' i.e. 'Freedom' as we lovingly called it. Obnoxious it may seem that a bunch of young, single and eligible boys did not care to pursue any such aim. I have no answer because this issue was never a talking point between us. No-body ever mentioned it. That doesn't mean we didn't indulge in gossips as such or were not attracted towards fair sex. We did talk amongst ourselves about the movies and the charming beautiful heroines but didn't pursue it further. Talk about them, praise the beauty, debate their good acting etc. and leave it there. We were happy to be 'Free' and be our own masters rather than taking up the difficult task of wooing and pampering the fair sex. By present day standards, we were uncouth and cowards. Well, let it be so!

Shimla's population had the unique distinction of presence of pretty girls and women who knew how to maintain themselves well, behave gracefully and look pretty. 'Zero-figure' was unheard of in those days but the ladies seemed to be conscious of paying attention to it. As always and everywhere, the film heroines and heroes were the role-models for the fashion-conscious population. Shimla's gentry loved to dress well, looked eager to look well and knew how to conduct gracefully in the public. All this and other simple pleasures did influence us and kept the group away from distractions which could have had serious implications.

It sounds baffling that in such a wonderful scenario, none of us cared to hanker after girls. The reason probably was that we were too happy being busy in small pleasures in the group itself and believed this was the time for being really 'Free'; free from devoting time to a difficult task. Also, the concept of 'girlfriend' "boyfriend" was alien to the youngsters in India's middle-class then. Choosing one's own soul-mate was not an issue. It was thought that this was neither essential nor critical as is the case now. The overall impression seemed to be to follow the time-tested approach of leaving this to parents and seniors in the family. The seniors in the office also had a role in contributing to this nonchalant attitude. Often we would hear them saying, "Have nice time boys till you get married and start shouldering the responsibility of 'Grihast' (family life). Surely; the over-all environment in the society was suggestive of arranged marriages only.

Group's idea of being happy

Well then, what did we do in our free time? The answer is; we were happy in pursuing small pleasures in the group, namely:-

First and fore-most passion was going for outings, hitch-hiking, sight-seeing and visits to nearby historical places, buildings and beautiful picnic spots,

Enjoy coffee and the fare offered in the 'Coffee House',

A stroll on the 'Mall' in the evenings,

Time permitting, basking in the sun on the 'Ridge' in winters,

Going to movies,

Playing cards, of-course without any major stake, except payment for coffee etc. by the loser(s)

Indulge in cooking on Sundays especially some items of food which were normally not served in the 'Dhaba'; like 'Dal Makhni', 'Pea-pulao', 'Mutter Panir', 'Kheer'and Mutton/egg curry,

Visit a friend's native place in group to participate in his marriage.

163

Group's foremost passion; adventure trips in mountains

The passion of going on outings/picnics would get stronger during summers. Some of us in the group and I was in the forefront, who were crazy and always eager to go out; especially on Sundays and holidays. If nothing else, go for a small hiking in the neighborhood. The clean air, peaceful environment and long pine-trees were a wonderful attraction. I would just run down in the forest for some time and then stroll back leisurely unaware of the distance I had covered. The temptation to be away from hustle-bustle on a free day was too strong in me.

Going on an outing/picnic meant free-lance merry-making, enjoying nature's bounty of lush-green forests, flowers, cool breeze and indulging in a feast of assorted sweets, snacks and fruits etc. We would carry utensils, crockery/cutlery, the provisions, the pressure-stove and mats etc. All the members were assigned specific duties and most of us would do our part sincerely and in time. It had to be a collective effort. Each one, so to say, specialized and preferred a particular activity. Hence there was never a problem in finishing the cooking, laying the food, cleaning the utensils etc. and packing the ware. And, therefore, by the time it was over, everybody was happy having enjoyed the outing and be mentally prepared for the next one. I was always in the lead for cooking. I enjoyed doing it. The expectation of earning everybody's appreciation for the tasty food that I was confident of preparing was thrilling for me.

A chronicle of few adventure trips undertaken by the group

Kufri; a vast tract of hills at a height of about 8'000 feet and sharp deep slopes all around it was a must for us. In winters, the vast open hill-tops and slopes would get covered with thick layers of snow. Kufri was an eminently suitable location for winter-sports like skiing, sledge-rafting and free jumping etc. There used to be a winter-sports festival sometimes in the first fortnight of February. It attracted a large number of enthusiasts from across the country and abroad.

Kufri slopes were at a distance of about 10/12 kms from Shimla. No satisfactory local transport facility being available, we would walk down there; enjoy the thrill of watching professional players skiing and jumping on the tracks. Financial constraints didn't allow us to pay for the expenses of skiing etc. Therefore, we would enjoy jumping from the hill-top with all the woollens and gum-boots on and doing the body-skiing, get back to the top walking up and repeat it till totally exhausted. By evening, we would be dead tired and hungry and somehow manage to get back to our favorite haunt in the town, the "Coffee House" for rejuvenating ourselves with hot coffee and sizzling eatables available there. It was an event we always looked forward to and would not miss it, as far as possible.

Chail (at a distance of 35 kms by road from Shimla) is at a height of about 7'000 feet. It is a hamlet known for its world's highest cricket-ground and its serene surroundings, is thinly populated and known for the erotica associated with the king of Patiala. It is said that Chail, part of Patiala state, was built as a personal resort for the Maharaja after he was banished by the British from entering Shimla. Legend has it that the Maharaja abducted a British princess from the 'Mall' in day-light and the place where all this happened is still known as 'Scandal Point.'

Many other important hang-out places in and in near vicinity of Shimla were Mashobra, Glen, Tara Devi and Narkanda etc. I am not able to recall other names. My memory is not helping at the moment.

An ill-planned adventure trip

One day, I and my friend, Raj, decided to go to Chail. The decision was we do it on feet. One Saturday early morning we started walking loaded with some fruits, biscuits, boiled eggs, sugar and milk, butter and bread etc. in our back-pack. We also carried kerosene oil–filled pressure stove and a pot for making tea/coffee enroute. In our enthusiasm, we didn't look for any details about the logistics and terrain we had to cover during the journey. Therefore, when we left we didn't know that we had to cover three mountain ranges, going down and up every time and it was all deep reserve forest that lay before us.

For few hours in early morning, we had nice time running through valleys, watching flora and fauna, chatting with native passers bye and basking in the clear sky. Crystal clear blue sky-line and cool morning breeze were mesmerizing. Around 10 in the morning by when we had covered about 8/9 kms, we came to the shores of a rivulet. It wasn't very deep. Tempted by its clean waters and open space all around, we decided to halt there, have a bath in it. We had a wonderful time enjoying the nature and savoring the hot-steaming tea along with break-fast prepared on the spot. After a while, we packed up and started walking up the hill. By evening, we realized we were half-way through but there was no habitation. We were in deep forest not knowing which foot-track to follow for going to Chail. The danger of getting lost in the jungle loomed large before us. We were wondering what to do and which direction to take, when a group of persons passed nearby. Seeing the group we were thrilled at the prospect of knowing whether we were on right track and how far was our destination. Alas, the answers they gave to our query were difficult to follow being in their local dialect. However, their gestures seemed to convey that Chail was not far-off and they were not going there. Using our intuition and applying the sense of direction, we decided to follow a particular track.

After about an hour's walk, we were lucky. We touched the road leading to Chail. It was about 8'o clock and we were still three kms away from Chail. By now, we were dead tired and God only knows how we managed to cover this distance. Finally, we reached Chail at about 10' o clock in the night, by then all the shops were closed. With great difficulty, we saw some light in a shop and could manage to persuade the shop owner to give us shelter for the night. It was a 'Halwai's' shop but there was hardly any food available except some sweets etc. In the morning we went around, had a look at Patiala king's palace, the cricket-ground and other important buildings. Leaving behind the travails of yesterday, we enjoyed the surrounding lush-green forests and snow-capped peaks. At last, we were happy that we came here.

Summing up, we thought the trip could have been more enjoyable had we done some intelligent home-work before venturing out. We promised to ourselves, 'we shall not venture out again like this.'

'Tatta Paani'

Obsessed as we were with the passion for outings, we soon forgot our bitter experience of visit to Chail and the group embarked on a trip to a place called 'Tatta Pani', a distance of about 30kms from Shimla. Instead of going by bus, we opted for short-cut route on feet. The group started in the morning full of enthusiasm with some eatables in our bags.

This place was known for hot-water sulphur springs and cold water current flowing side by side in the river. The occasion was the annual 'Baisakhi Mela' there. A large number of people would descend on the hamlet from far and near for fun and a dip in the sulphur springs. It was believed that a dip there was a sure remedy for all skin ailments.

We all reached there by the evening but totally crippled with acute muscles pain except one of us; Bhandari, the Lamboo. With God's Grace, he was still mobile and did all the running looking for accommodation, food, tea and snacks etc. After few hours rest we were fresh again and enjoyed the evening in the 'Mela'. Yes, the return journey was undertaken the next day in a public transport bus. Notwithstanding the arduous journey and fatigue, the trip was enjoyed by all of us.

Genuine friendship; my foremost passion

Having friends, making friends and enjoying time in their company has been my favorite and an old passion since my childhood. The wonderful, cosy and heart-warming legacy of genuine friendship has been my life's real treasure. I was lucky enough to have the warmth of friends' company all along. Friends and their genuinely reliable support and affection have always been beside me. It sustained and nourished my life. I am sure the friendship runs in my blood. And lucky I have been that I had the good fortune of the company of friends starting from my days in school in Dehra Dun. It has been a constant phenomenon, an inseparable experience of my life thereafter. To many of my relatives and elders it was an ill-founded thought. But I persisted sincerely with this approach all along my life and I believe I have been lucky. I do not know why but it is a fact that hardly I ever faced an awkward situation, vis-à-vis my friends, individually and collectively both. Nay-Sayers have proved to be wrong so far.

I have fond memories of warm and comfortable relationships cultivated at Dehra Dun, Bareilly, Shimla, BS City and Dehra Dun yet again when I came back there in 1982 for taking up job in ONGC. I made efforts and could revive my contacts with two of my school mates, IP Dawar & Dr. VD Dang. This revival led to building up of deep cozy relations once again with them and their families. They are big support, as before; self-less, warm and like our real blood-relatives. The list of our friends and acquaintances is too long. Narrating all the names and warm experience with each one is worthwhile, no doubt, for their significance but it may stretch beyond reasonable limits. Therefore, I am refraining from it.

I believe; friendship is an important phenomenon in human life. We always cherish the sweet memories flowing out of our valuable mesmerizing experiences of love and affection of our coterie.

My lovely niece, Shashi (my eldest brother's daughter) and her husband, Surender Narula's presence in Dehra Dun is a big source of satisfaction to us. The loving couple is always too eager to help us when needed. Their worthy son, Gautam, is a gem of a person, brilliant, professionally qualified and highly competent as a successful Manager based in Gurgaon.

While recalling all this now, I am overwhelmed with nostalgia. The sweet smell of friendship is filling my bosom. This is how I am. I have had the satisfaction of cultivating and sustaining friendships throughout my life. I value these relations even more than close blood relations. I am aware, my friends were/are truly friends in need and friends indeed. I firmly believe; the friendship is friendship only if it is simply plain, without motives and is self-less. Genuinely warm, rooted in honestly deep mutual regards and concern for each other's happiness and welfare are the defining attributes of a self-less relationship. It is charming and attractive only when there is honest willingness to share, to reach out to each other and make sacrifice(s), when necessary. Otherwise it is a selfish phenomenon devoid of depth. It becomes a farce, is momentary and therefore lacks the warmth so necessary for adding value to it and making it lasting. It doesn't take long for discerning eyes to discover the truth and dump it.

My friend Ved & me in Elleslie Cottage (1962)   Me at Kufri Skiing Slopes 1962

Chapter 8
Shimla; the city beautiful of yore

Town planners' pride

It was a pleasure to see such a precisely planned city in the midst of hills at a height of about 7000 feet. It had complete basic infrastructure necessary for an urban dwelling. It had well-laid roads, water supply net-work supported by huge storage/ reservoir of water in the midst of town at the Ridge, had fire-hydrants spread to all corners of the city apart from the electricity distribution net-work along with street-light poles etc. Even the city's telephone exchange was equipped with latest technology i.e. auto-dialling. All these basic amenities had surplus in-built capacity. One could get telephone connection instantly. The water supply was 24 hours. Power-failure was unheard of. There were separate electricity lines for high–voltage connections in each building and tariff was low for high voltage gadgets like room-heaters, geysers and ovens etc. Shimla had its unique charm not seen anywhere else. Even Lutyen's New Delhi which was built around the same time seemed way behind it. It was obvious; the British had built it up with love and care.

The precision of planning is visible all around even now in the original core portion though Shimla has had planned and haphazard growth during the last 4/5 decades. The toy train that connects it with plains is a marvel of engineering expertise and skills. The 60 kms of railway track has 103 tunnels; the longest being about 2 ½ kms. The large number of office buildings, clubs and hotels etc. are spread in different corners of

170

the town to avoid congestion. The architectural innovations in designs and looks of the buildings are a treat for discernible eyes. The quality of construction, the structures and the materials used extensively for construction i.e. stones and steel seem to have been decided keeping in mind the geology, the terrain and climate of the region. It is a treat for eyes even now to watch these grand buildings standing in full glory even after more than 10 decades. The Viceroy's Lodge spread on a vast space in thick forests on the way to Summer Hill stands in its majestic glory even now. It was named as 'Rashtrapati Niwas' after independence but later, it was converted into Indian Institute of Advanced Studies during the tenure of Dr. S. Radhakrishnan as President of India.

Shimla known for the imperial grandeur of buildings that were once the institutions of power when the town served as the summer capital of British Raj reminds of the poignant stories of toil put in by hundreds of un-sung laborers and artisan who braved the harsh weather and built up the entire edifice. Of-course, the British created the entire infrastructure to meet their needs of office accommodation and a comfortable living for themselves like what they did elsewhere in the country. But what is unique and astonishing about Shimla are the length and breadth of the habitation and its location; the height of 7000'.

In the decade that I was there (1959 to 1969) its permanent population was about 40,000 but the infrastructure could conveniently cater to the influx of large number of tourists in summers.

Shimla shaped my future

During my stay of ten years I came into close contact with persons of high caliber and integrity. It made me understand the nitty-gritty of not only my professional life but it also contributed immensely in shaping my personal attributes also. The learning I picked up while inter-acting with and by observing closely the conduct and behavior of some of my colleagues and seniors in office helped me in firming up guiding principles, basic norms, mannerism and traits as a foundation stone of my approach to life. In other words, it surely helped me in shaping my view of life; the direction it was to take and put me into a horizon so likeable, worth chasing and living up-to.

Another important reason for my attachment to and love for this place is that I got married in 1965 to a wonderful woman called Krishna; my namesake; always bubbling with enthusiasm and extremely charming. I am conscious that it will be a herculean task when I sit down to pen down her.

Shimla's bounty for nature lovers; hang-out places in plenty

Apart from the natural beauty all over the place and its surrounding areas, Shimla of those days was a veritable mine of enticing natural beauty locations which one could go to. If nothing specific, just go out a little distance and spread your mat in a corner under the shady trees in some hillock, enjoy the surrounding scenic beauty and see it is an exclusive lovely picnic spot of your creation. Indulge freely in making merry in your own style or just lie-down and bask in the open sun on a wintry day, munch what you carry, enjoy cooking the way you like, lie-down and have that wonderful mid-day nap after sumptuous meals, (one has to do it to actually understand what it means for relaxation and getting ready for the busy days starting the very next day), lighten your emotional burdens and forget stresses, refuse to listen to anything other than enthralling music of your choice, carry cards and play games in the company of your mates. Take it easy, nobody is peeping around for there is no population pressure. Be free to share your emotions and anxieties with those whom you trust. Well, one can say, all this can possibly be done anywhere. Why a picnic spot or a Shimla. The answer is 'No' because the charm of being in the open in lovely surroundings is a magic of immense proportions. And when it is a sunny hot day (week-end) in a place like Shimla and the bounty of nature's munificence is in abundance around you, you are blessed. Even the God will not pardon you if you do not avail of His Largesse for the Mankind. I have no hesitation in confessing that I was always keen to avail of the opportunity to be away from home and office on Sundays/holidays and splurge freely in the open. And I never forgot that the window of free open warm skies was going to be short; only three months, April to June at the most.

Shimla's enchanting and lovable cosmopolitan hue

Egalitarian, truly cosmopolitan and epicenter of good living easily comes to mind while thinking of Shimla of our times. The vast majority of town's population comprised of educated Govt. employees, mostly of Central Govt. and Accountant General's office was the largest single employer. Its total strength was sizeable (about 2500). In a town whose total regular population was about 40,000, this number was considered to be large enough. A.G. office's bachelor 'boys' (as we were known in the town) were seen as a class by themselves, probably because we were thought to be better paid and had more disposal income. The 'boys' were visible everywhere and were the symbol of potential business for the trading community especially the 'Dhabas' because most of the 'boys' were eating out.

Shimla of those days had an aura of its own and there was a distinct mark of dignified behavior in public by vast majority of its population, especially those who were fond of having a walk in the evening on the 'Mall'. I believe; this probably had something to do with the legacy of old 'Raj' days. It was a treat for eyes to see such a charming crowd on the Mall in the evenings. Rain or snow, we hardly missed to go to the Mall and if some day we missed it, each one would rue it the most next morning. A leisurely stroll on the Mall in the evening was refreshing to mind and soul and filled the entire system with energy.

There was no population explosion then. You take a few steps out of the main town, so to say the down-town and a vast spread of open landscape, thick growth of pine and deodar trees welcome you. There was no traffic movement in the town except the cart road which was part of the highway connecting Shimla to plains and going out on to Hindustan-Tibet road, as it was known then. Except for few vehicles of the Army, no vehicles were permitted to ply on the Mall. Everybody would just take a walk to and fro office/residence.

Krishan Aneja

Shimla's pride; peaceful and crime-free environ

I can vouch-safe with all the strict sense of responsibility that Shimla of those days was 100 % crime-free; indeed a marvellous place for tension-free living. No thefts, no burglaries, no chain-snatching, no pick-pocketing and other similar petty crimes were ever reported. During my 10 years of stay there, I didn't hear of any murders or gun-shooting incidents. Molestation of women was unheard of. All these dirty things never showed their heads. It was a wonderful peaceful town. The windows in houses had glass-panes only. There were no grills or doors fabricated out of steel sections for safety. We were not aware of any security guards in residential areas. Lock the entrance door of the house and be sure nothing untoward will happen. A well-established system of home-delivery was available. Place your order either on phone or personally and be relieved. The shop-keeper and the porter will do rest of the job. The environment of peace was graceful. The citizenry apart from the authorities shared the credit for this in good measure. Shimla was a peace posting for officers of civil administration and Police. If I am not wrong, Ms. Kiran Bedi, the present fire-brand social activist was the first lady IPS officer of Punjab and was posted in Shimla for long. Ms. Sarla Khanna, IAS of Punjab cadre, was the Deputy Commissioner when I came to Shimla in 1959.

An interesting episode is worth recalling in this connection. In 1966, when Shimla became the capital of Himachal Pradesh after trifurcation of the state of Punjab, an incident of bag-snatching occurred. There was hue and cry. A feeling of insecurity gripped the town's residents. People started blaming it on HP police with rumors doing the rounds that with the departure of Punjab police, Shimla was no longer safe. The then district police chief, Mr. R R Verma, a young officer in his 20s, took urgent steps, introduced a strict system of checks/verification of credential of each individual on road after 8 PM and this restored confidence in public mind and within a week's time, the alleged snatcher of bag was apprehended. That was a fine response of the authorities which brought back the confidence of populace in the ability of District Administration.

Shimla, a real nightmare for singles during winters

The three months of December, January and February were most difficult for us, the singles. After sun-sets, the remnants of snow on the roads would turn into slippery patches of ice making it extremely difficult and risky to walk on. Howsoever careful one may be; the chances of getting hurt and/or fractures were always high. There was no easy escape for us from such hurdles as we had to go to town every evening for dinner. To save ourselves from such possible dangers, we would try to avoid being in the middle of the road which would mostly be slippery. Instead, we would take a detour and walk in the drain in the corner side which, normally, would have an undercurrent of water and hence comparatively safer to walk on. A little slip or carelessness here and there meant sliding down on the road and consequences are not difficult to imagine. Well, there was no escape for us. Going to town in the evening was a necessity for us since the alternative was more burden-some and full of hassles. Go to home just after office, have tea/coffee, sip it while sitting in the bed, stay in for some time for rest reading some newspaper/book/periodical and get out after some time to cook your food. Getting out of warm bed in severe winters by itself is easily said than done. You need a strong will to do so and chances are you will go hungry. This was no less troublesome. The result; either way it was painful and full of hassles. Choose the option you feel you are comfortable with. Life during these three months would be a test of nerves/patience, in any case.

Chapter 9
Shimla's hot spots

The Coffee House

The Coffee House at the Mall was the symbol of Shimla's liberal values. Apart from being the last resort of solace for poor bachelors like us who had an infectious attachment with it, Coffee House was the rendezvous by choice for the seniors comprising of high gentry/elite of the town, the literatures, senior civilian and army officers, the scribes, the politicians and others especially on Sunday mornings. People would throng it in large numbers and stay-put there for long hours unmindful of the ever-increasing gentry waiting in wings in the lounge. Visit to Coffee House in Sunday mornings had a unique temptation; the first concoction of the brew was always the best. I must confess; we also wished to be there on Sunday mornings, whenever possible, for no reason other than witnessing the charm of being there in the company of those gentlemen and women. Ladies' presence along with gents was customary in the social gatherings in the town. This, I believe, was a tribute to the ladies and reflected positively on the cultural ethos of the town. What is being hotly debated and demanded now, gender equality was already the norm here then. How sweet?

For us, the singles, the mention of the word Coffee House connoted multi-faceted attractions; hot soothing filter-coffee and a variety of snacks at prices we could afford, an escape from biting cold thanks to coal-fired stoves in its hall in winters, comfortable sofa/couches and a service with smile. The staff recognized the regular visitors like us and a warm smile

176

was writ large on their faces. When totally fatigued and yearning for rest, the Coffee House was our last resort. We would stretch our stay, leisurely eat food, take coffee and relax for some time before checking out without any reminder by the staff of our long stay. Of course, when there was rush and a bee-line of visitors were seen to be waiting, we ourselves took care not to unduly prolong our stay.

The 'Mall'; a gateway to unparalleled bliss

The 'Mall' with its heavenly exclusive ambience was an eternal ecstatic experience for those who cared for small pleasures. Being there in the evenings was enough to transport the otherwise busy looking people to a charming and soothing world of its kind. The amazing calmness of bunches of motely crowds and well-dressed gentry busy in their own exclusive worlds unmindful of going ons in their neighborhood was a treat for the eyes. Being there was a classic enchanting experience. What could be a better place than the 'Mall' for carefree exchanges in whisper like tones? You could smell freedom without frills, all around. It was a pleasure seeing youngsters, alone or in groups, small or big, strolling along, unmindful of the world. Everyone out there seemed to be on cloud 9; raving, chatting, humming or just talking. Nobody was aware of anybody in the vicinity. Isn't it surprising and a bit funny that the youngsters 50 years ago behaved and enjoyed free attitudes like what the present generation is supposed to be crazy about? Of-course, the difference is in the over-all behavior then which used to be sober and not splashy or flamboyant. Being sensitive to others and being within decent limits in public while enjoying a free inter-action within the group seemed to be the basic ingredient. On the whole, however, it is difficult to make out if the times have changed or they are the same as far as youngsters are concerned.

And let's remember that the vigilant police force didn't let you indulge in loose conduct. While on the Mall, "Keep moving and do not stop for a huddle" was the rule, which was followed more or less voluntarily. If, sometime, you forgot to follow it, the ubiquitous policeman will appear from nowhere and remind you "Keep moving or get down to middle bazar", where this restriction didn't apply. The only place on the Mall where you could stay for a while or get into a huddle was Scandal Point. It was quite wide with a traffic constable's post in the middle. He will keep an eye and ask you to disperse, when the place got crowded and the beauty is that nobody grumbled. For us, two rounds on the Mall were a routine in the evening to get freshened up before proceeding to our 'Dhaba' for dinner. Frankly, the nostalgia of prime youth days spent by us on the Mall, alone or in group is much deeper and fascinating than what I have been able to describe herein above. The Mall was Shimla's glorious identity; incomparable, unique and enriched by the graceful gentry.

The 'Sealed Portion' of the Mall

During British days, a designated tract of the Mall was earmarked as "Sealed Portion.' It would get converted into an exclusive territory for the ruling class. It is said that after evenings, Indians were not permitted to enter there. The personal attendants and the drivers etc. would accompany the gentlemen and ladies to the entry point and wait for a call for help and taking them back to their residences/hotels. The security staff and other service groups like those working in clubs and restaurants etc. were issued entry permits and allowed in to perform their assigned duties. These are the sketchy details I came to know through word of mouth. The actual situation must have been horrible knowing as we do about the attitude of the ruling class of those days. Full credit goes to gentle population of Shimla to continue to maintain the dignity of the "Mall" in true sense for many years to come. It is a pity that the Mall of present days is nowhere near its original 'avatar'. Blame it on population explosion and overall degradation of values.

The 'Mall's physical glory and its attractive vends

The 'Mall' had a unique distinction of being always spotlessly clean; no trash, no cigarette butts, no spitting, absolutely clean and very well-maintained toilets with a sweeper in attendance. The municipal set-up in the town was always alert to keep the 'Mall' clean adding to the joy of pedestrians.

Apart from the Coffee House, the Mall was known for its high end stores like 'Janki Das and Co's departmental store, which stocked almost everything that a consumer may need; consumables, durables, garments, shoes, crockery and cutlery, gift items and sports goods etc. all under one roof. There were few select restaurants known for serving a vast but select variety of fare. Davico's atop Janki Das's was the favorite jaunt of up-mobile Desis and foreigners who preferred western cuisine, jam sessions, liquor and loved to dance. X'mas and New Year Eve's functions and Beauty Contests were a regular feature in Davico's. Another popular restaurant during our times was 'Baljees'. It was known for its vast variety of delectable north Indian cuisine and was patronized by those who loved to enjoy the authentic Punjabi food. Its clientele was mostly from upper middle-class. It was being managed by the husband-wife team. It was known that Mrs. Baljee was keenly involved in supervising the kitchen along with the qualified team of Chefs and other staff. It was no surprise therefore that it was always heavily booked. Both these restaurants had a distinct ambience of their own and represented the cultural mix of Shimla's population. Of-course, the Coffee House was universally popular with everybody. The book-shops out there stocked books for general reading and periodicals to cater to different needs. The Geity Theatre was the hub for cultural activities. Except during winters, various cultural groups of the town and from outside used to perform there. The stores and other buildings on the Mall always appeared to be in good shape; maybe it was self-imposed code of maintenance and beautification of the prestigious shopping area. It surely reflected a good taste of the traders there.

The Ridge Maidan

Ridge Maidan, an enchanting vast open space in the middle of the town meets many utilitarian needs of the town. It is a flat vast open space atop a ridge, which was created by levelling the ridge top at the time of creating/building Shimla. It serves dual-purpose; a huge water-storage tank for storing and providing potable water to the inhabitants of the town, and a vast 'Maidan' for the benefit of residents; family-union spot for children to play freely, (no vehicular traffic is allowed), bask in the open sun, hold public meetings and enjoy in its vastness. The existence of such a vast open 'Maidan' in mountains at a height of 7'000 feet would almost seem to be impossible. There are no huge structures/buildings in its vicinity. Therefore, the last ray of sun warms up the Maidan. It was a virtual picnic spot for many. During winters and especially on Sundays, people would relax on the stands/benches lying there, open up their food baskets/tiffin boxes and enjoy their food, while the kids/children would enjoy running and playing games in the open. Basking in the open in the winters had a soothing healing effect for the body as also one's soul as though the dead were coming back to life. The added attraction on Sundays was the presence of army band in the "Band Stand'. The band would enchant the gathering while playing variety of tunes.

This Maidan also met a very crucial social need of Shimla's populace; sighting of moon by ladies of the town on 'Karva Chauth'. The Maidan was the right location for sighting the moon early in the evening. Ladies of the town would assemble there in the evening to perform the ritualistic 'puja' of the moon before breaking their fast. The festivities preceding the 'puja', the women in their best make over, attire and laden with loads of jewellery accompanied with their husbands and other family members was a real breath-taking event.

Like many other important land-marks and features, the Ridge Maidan is a master-stroke of futuristic vision for well-conceived town planning of the habitation called 'Shimla', the British's summer capital in India.

'Toy' train; the wonderful link with the plains

This wonderful stretch of about 60 kms of railway-track of 'narrow gauge' from Kalka in plains was indeed the life-line for keeping the town well-stocked with all essential goods and carrying of passengers. Travelling by train on this stretch was a unique experience; the speed of trains was slow being a hilly tract with lot of curves, culverts, bridges and a large number of tunnels (103 in all). The distance of 60 kms would be covered in about 6 hours which was exhausting and time-consuming no doubt but the green forests and paddy/corn fields etc. laid in steps were a treat for eyes with train chugging at the speed of a bicycle. It was not possible to take off your eyes from the green valleys, the rivulets/streams full of clean water running down the hills. The journey was truly enjoyable, if you were not in a hurry. Relax, enjoy the nature's beauty and you would land at Shimla a happy and relaxed person. On landing at the station, hand over your luggage-ticket to the licensed porter, write down your address on a piece of paper and soon he will be at your door with your luggage, secure and intact. It was a different experience; bewildering to some but satisfying to all. Along the entire route, catering facility was available at Barog station only. The eatables were hot and of good taste unlike what were normally available at stations in the plains. I was happy to have decided to travel by train when I went to Shimla for joining duty there.

This train was designed to keep Shimla well-stocked with supplies of steam-coal, grocery and other essential provisions from plains. Transporting huge stocks and bulk items like coal by road in those days was out of question and without adequate stock of critical items like coal; the life would grind to a halt. The steam-coal was an important fuel for kitchens and the heating of stoves in offices/stores and house-holds. During winters, the electric heaters were a help but not sufficient enough to heat up the rooms adequately.

The 'Hanumana 'temple atop Jakhoo hill

The Jakhoo hill in Shimla is a unique symbol of town's graceful identity. Standing majestically high in the middle of the town next to Ridge, its peak is about 8000 feet high and looks like a canopy full of lush green pine trees. During winters, the first showers of snow would grip its peak signalling the advent of difficult or charming days ahead for town's inhabitants; difficult for the old timers and charming for new comers like me. During the time I was in Shimla, no construction activity was allowed beyond a point on the Jakhoo hill to maintain ecological balance in the town. It is said that this hill is crucial in the topography of Shimla for its impact on town's climate. The 'Hanumana' temple on its top was a pilgrimage place for citizen especially on Tuesdays when people in hordes would slowly attempt to crawl up the steep trajectory of the hill and face the ferocious attempts of hundreds of monkeys wanting to pounce on the packets of 'prasada' in their hands.

Chapter 10
My social life in Shimla

An epoch-making phase

Ten years of prime youth spent in heaven-like place, Shimla, first six years as a free-lance bachelor and remaining four years as a newly-wed enthusiast, was a treasure of bliss that is ever-green in my sub-conscious. Well, any efforts, howsoever deep and sincere, are sure to fail to capture and genuinely portray the nuances that shaped it and colored it like a rain-bow. The enchanting memories of this miraculous period of life are fresh in my mind still. Describing them lucidly is a serious challenge before me. It would call for and demand a lot of diligence and competence to do justice to such a magical phase in our life. I truly lived and enjoyed each single day of my stay in Shimla notwithstanding the severe chill and its attendant difficulties especially during winters. My stay there was surely a trend-setter for the rest of my life. It shaped my future. Given the serious and substantive impact the events during this period had in shaping my approach to life, the narration has to be not only authentic but also interesting. It also needs to do justice not only to myself but also to the influencers i.e., my seniors and their families, my friends and my charming wife who entered my life on 8th May, 1965. I am aware, a harder task stares at me; bringing up in true form all what I lived through in the company of my select social circle. But more difficult is the dilemma; where do I begin? The answer seems to be that I start with myself being the lead actor in this narration followed by my coterie of close chums, my seniors and their families with whom I had the privilege of being their favorite youngster.

Satellite friends

We, the intimate group of pals, did also have some other common friends from amongst the office colleagues. One can say these were the satellite friends of the group. On occasions like birthdays, anniversaries etc. and some festivals we would join these friends and their families. And, during winters, when the families used to move down to their respective native places in plains, the group did indulge in some freak activities. This larger group's main engagement during winters would be playing cards with stakes in the evenings on week-ends. This used to put me into dilemma. Should I join in or stay away? To be honest, I was not keen being involved in the game of cards. But refusing it would invite ridicule. Therefore, most of the time, to escape from adverse comments, I would volunteer to take up the responsibility of doing cooking, getting snacks, making tea etc. or just helping in some other errands. So to say, I couldn't muster courage to disassociate myself completely and openly from these card sessions. Organizing and playing host to such gatherings was a challenge by itself. Only brave-hearts would offer to be the host. It involved making seating and heating arrangements which itself were a hard task considering the sub-zero temperatures. The host was also expected to make arrangements for drinks, snacks and other edibles. No doubt, all this was contributory but the hassles were challenging. The parties would start late in the evenings on Saturdays and continue till early Sunday morning. And who knew, somebody would gulp alcohol in excess, vomit it out or make a mess otherwise. The poor host had to handle the aftermath without any demur or fuss.

Even though the main activity would be gambling, sometimes with high stakes, yet there would be no tensions and pressures. Fun and frivolities were an inseparable part of the whole show. There were lighter moments in abundance comprising of funny, humorous and enjoyable interludes like singing, narrating jokes, folk tales and harmless exchanges full of sarcastic wit.

I had the pleasure of having close friendly relations on individual basis with some of my married colleagues. I used to visit them on weekends for a friendly chat and enjoying tasty home-made food which was a bonanza considering that we were always bored with 'Dhaba' food and any such opportunity was welcome. Many a times, I would stay for the night also, spend Sunday there, return in the evening and my dear roommate would complain of boring loneliness apart from being jealous of my good-luck. He too had some similar friends and I would have similar complaint against him whenever he ventured out alone.

My seniors and their families

(i)Mrs. and Mr. JR Pasricha.

Mr. Pasricha, my Accounts Officer and his wife were like my own elders. The relationship of intimate confidence and understanding grew up gradually over a period of time. Starting with office where Mr. Pasricha and I were quite at ease with each other, this extended to our personal relations also soon. Genuine warmth and deep affection sustained it. Not surprisingly, it was the envy of many. The mutually bonding oneness helped it grow stronger. They believed in me and I responded wholeheartedly to their gestures of affection and love. They welcomed my presence in their midst, invited me to share with them happy moments of leisure, treated me lavishly with exquisite food and made me feel as one of them in the family. It was my good luck and true privilege to be so close to a couple who were humane and wide open-hearted for those whom they loved. Lovable, always full of life, worthy of respect, they were far-above average human beings.

That was Mrs. Bimla and Mr. JR Pasricha (Yash as he used to address himself).Try hard as I may, I won't be able to do justice in describing as to what they meant to me. They had an abiding love for me and I respected them from the core of my heart. May be; we had a relationship/connection in our previous birth also. God forgive me for my inability to do justice to them in my narration!

Mrs. Pasricha, (I used to call her 'Bhabi ji') was a women of substance. Like scores of Indian life-partners, she always willingly and happily helped her husband in his daily chores and would smilingly adjust to his whimsical moods. After entering the bath-room, he would scream, 'where is my towel, my under-garments'. And after bath, he would want her to help him in locating and fixing his dress including tie and hand-kerchief etc. 'Give me some money. My wallet is empty' would be the next demand. And the last call would be, 'where are my shoes and brief-case?' After this entire hiccup, she would push him to the dinning-table and make sure he takes his break-fast alright. That was the magic of their love. She was a perfect host. Taking care of 40/50 guests in a party at home was no hassles for her and the beauty was that the food/snacks would be steaming hot for all guests even in winters. On such occasions, I used to help her, whatever I could. I knew; the art of hosting exquisitely planned and executed parties was perfected by her at New York when Mr. Pasricha was posted there in India's UN Mission. I, besides few others like me, were regular visitors to this house-hold, especially on Sundays, when Bhabi ji would treat us to un-common but highly sought after dishes; Indian (mostly South-Indian), continental, Chinese and variety of puddings. Many a times, I would hesitate to join them extending some excuse but to no use. They would politely rebuke me and persuade me to be not fussy. Their love and affection helped me a lot in getting away from my clumsy mood of shyness and face other friendly couples with confidence.

(ii)Mrs. and Mr. RL Dham.

Another kind couple who pampered me and some of our colleagues of the section was Mrs. Dham and Mr. RL Dham, who was our section officer in GAD 4 section. The dedicated team under his able leadership spared no efforts to clear the mess. This effort not only earned the appreciation of higher ups in our own office but also of the HP Govt. whose officers started getting their salaries and other entitlements in time.

The Dhams would often invite us for a treat at their residence on Sundays. Mrs. Dham was adept at giving an uncommon pleasant look and taste to the common Punjabi dishes. She had the knack of garnishing and presenting them exquisitely and the spread on the table would have a distinct aura. The lavish spread of tastefully cooked food would make us, the blushing invitees, rather nervous and introverts. Both Mrs. and Mr. Dham would prod us to help ourselves freely and seeing us blush, would try to reduce our embarrassment by diverting our attention to other topics, like movies and games etc. Most likely, this was the way in which the Dhams wanted to express their gratitude to us; the boys who helped him acquire the reputation of a successful performer and a competent leader.

Mrs. Dham essentially a supporting house-wife and devout mother of three, two boys and a lovely daughter, made all efforts to lighten the environment. She would encourage her children to join us and talk about studies, games and school to distract embarrassment writ large on our faces. Her mannerism would be subtle and homely; probably she was conscious of our uneasiness being face to face with such formal arrangement. After sumptuous meals, the sizzling hot coffee would provide the healing touch and make us feel relaxed. She knew; we were regulars at the Coffee House. 'Do come again' at parting time would convey it all.

Such heart-warming and touching homilies defined our personal relations with our seniors.

Two other senior colleagues whose association and bits of practical advice I enjoyed were BS Nayyar and SL Kumar. While I was highly enamored of the 'dabang' and frank attitude of Mr. Nayyar, Mr. Kumar was like my elder brother, always willing to provide some words of comfort now and then. I loved them both.

A rare opportunity that stoked my love for books

Mr. Pasricha was very fond of reading books. He was, in fact, a voracious reader and had a vast collection of books in his personal library at home. I used to borrow from him liberally and he encouraged me to indulge in this pleasure. I started buying books, thanks to his encouragement. To begin with, it was Agatha Christie and Perry Masson, the famous duo of those days for crime investigations and high court-room drama. It was a good beginning for me. The paper-backs cost only rupees two for each title. The official $/rupee exchange rate in those days was $/4.5 but the going market rate used to be 6.

Thanks to Mr. Pasricha, my passion for books was growing when consignments of variety of books selected personally by Mr. Pasricha started pouring in. The entire new arrivals were to be handled and kept in safe custody by me till these were properly accounted for, catalogued and handed over to the office Librarian. This turned out to be a personal advantage for me. Now, I had free access to this wonderful collection. And I indulged merrily in this pleasure. My illness and hospitalization for about four weeks meant the books remained in my official custody. Taking advantage of this God-sent opportunity I merrily indulged in reading variety of books on my hospital bed. I read Pearl S buck, Somerset Maugham, Shakespeare, Emily Sisters, Thomas Hardy to name a few. The collection of Hindi books also comprised of eminent scholars like Prem Chand, Sumitra Nandan Pant 'Nirala', Ram Dhari Singh 'Dinkar', Maha Devi Verma Amrit Lal Nagar and many others.

This experience was a unique contribution to my over-all development; 'an illiterate person turning a bit literate.'

Chapter 11
My mentor, my idol; Mr. JR Pasricha

Coming into contact with him just after joining duty in AG, Punjab's office was my good-luck indeed. He was my Accounts Officer for about 5 years. My sincere commitment to hard-work and delivering much more than expected pleased him beyond measure. Never let him down in the assignments given to me; rather outperformed and felt relieved. I knew; it would make him happy and proud of me. On many occasions, looking to the exigencies of work at a given time and before he explained it to me, I would decipher very quickly what the requirement was and make him smile even though the situation was grim. His meaningful smiles were my life-line. I was always happily willing to reduce his tensions, whenever and to whatever extent I could. In a way, it was my passion/ mission. I loved him too deeply. I can easily recollect his smiling face in different moods, different situations. I wish; I was an artist and could present him in his various enchanting hues.

Till I came into contact with him, I was a novice. I didn't have much knowledge or experience of how:-

to communicate with strangers with an alert attitude,

to avoid looking an odd man out in groups,

to be succinct and look confident while in meetings,

to face odd situations deftly,

to articulate views and carry conviction and

to listen attentively.

He was my guide, my philosopher and role-model. He was highly emotional like me. Strangely still, he would caution me about the pitfalls of being too deeply emotional. Try to be cool and balanced in facing the life.

He would often say, "Life is no bed of roses. To be happy, keep yourself busy and work hard. Make your own place in office and amongst people around you. Be compassionate and helpful. Basically, human beings are nice and believe in sharing love except some odd people here and there who are rather petty and conceited. Avoid them and reduce the chances of confrontation with them." Such conversations were common between us while walking together in the evenings after leaving the office.

His influence in shaping my life

When I landed in Shimla, I was virtually raw, had not picked up the skills of inter-action with my colleagues/seniors in office. I had not been exposed, till then, to the society like what it was at Shimla. I did have by then about 6 years of work experience but out there, the environment, the context and the pressures in office place and society at large were at a nascent and elementary level. At Shimla, I had entered a new phase in my life; a phase of learning and mastering skills for my balanced growth. I was keen to do it carefully but fast. A sort of make or break situation was staring at me. I badly needed a well-wishing, sympathetic and open-hearted mentor and that need was profoundly met by Mr. Pasricha. Within few days of my inter-action with him in the office and after a first visit to his house, I told myself, "Here is a person whom you can trust for guidance/help; self-less, enduring and genuinely true."

His role in honing my skills in work-place

The most critical learning for me turned out to be his art of making others believe in him. Carrying conviction with others in what he said or did was his forte. His mastery in communication skills and language would build up an environment of trust and hope. To impress others with his sincerity of purpose and dealings, he spared no efforts. Thanks to preparatory spade work done well and skillful articulation, his task in convincing others would become easy. His real asset/strength was his attitude of perfection. He would spend time in understanding the subject and issues involved in it. His approach used to be; master the facts/details and discuss important aspects with his subordinates before going for a meeting or when preparing to deliver a talk or make a presentation. Whatever he did, he would do it with passion. He would not compromise on basics and accept an argument for or against only if it is logical and relevant to the subject matter under consideration. He would often remind us, "Be sure; the details and facts being dished out by you are authentic and correct." Until satisfied, he would not accept them.

His skills of giving dictation to his stenographer were beyond compare. He was consistent in speed, clarity of voice, punctuation and over-all easy environment. The steno never got bored or sought any clarification in the course of dictation. His command on language was excellent. It was lucid, easily understandable and never deflective from the core subject. Just listening to him and watching him dictate was a great learning. His style of delivery reflected the mastery of the subject acquired after deep churning of ideas that was taking place in his mind. Often, in such moments, he would close his eyes to concentrate and get focus. Many a times, I would intervene and suggest a phrase or a word and earn his smile. He would be busy for hours with his steno and still look fresh.

Our relationship was an envy of many of my colleagues but who cared? I have no hesitation in vouchsafing that this learning helped me through and through in the art of effective dictation methodology. It actually helped me a lot in scaling new highs in my career subsequently.

Pasrichas; my role-model in personal life

In my personal life, his influence/contribution was stellar. Whereas I was a rustic small-town boy, they were well-groomed being from a well-educated family of Lahore and having lived in New York in elite society of diplomats for more than 4 years. My proximity with them was an opportunity of great learning. I would keenly observe and pick up what appealed to me. Primarily because of my close association with them I started being comfortable with other elders and seniors. One always learnt something new, worthwhile and tangible whenever one met them, either separately or in group.

Over a period of time, I became quite close and free with them. I could just drop in without any appointment or a formal invitation. There were no inhibitions about it either in my mind or with them. Of course, I was circumspect and judicious about the frequency and time of visits. I was always conscious of my position vis-à-vis theirs. Obviously, to be within reasonable limits and being dignified was essential for the relations to be stable.

When and where to take a pause while inter-acting with others, make proper gestures, avoid being seen silly, articulate well and emphasize a point cogently and many other traits necessary in groups, was another great learning for me. Not that, I became perfect or didn't commit clumsy mistakes or didn't make myself a laughing stock in a gathering, is not what I am boasting about. My deep gratitude and sincere thanks for what I learnt and gained from my association with them make me feel humble. After Mr. Pasricha's promotion and induction into Indian Audit & Accounts Service, and posting in Ranchi and Srinagar, we remained in touch with each other for many years. Later, we lost the touch which I always regretted. I was extremely sad when I learnt that he had met with a road accident on his way to Aligarh and lost his life. That was in early 70s.

Compassion and liberal disposition; their praiseworthy assets

Read the paragraph below for a reality check if you thought there is no element of luck in exams.

An episode of his liberal attitude and compassion, which his wife and daughter too had common with him is worthy of recall here. He was nominated as an evaluator of candidates' answer books of a paper of S.A.S exam. Another colleague of his was also similarly nominated. He would check a few answer books every day in the evening and leave them on his table. Next day, Mrs. Pasricha and their daughter together would spot the ones which were assessed by him as marginally lower than the qualifying mark. Seeing Mr. Pasricha in happy and free mood someday, they would together plead and urge him to take a kind view. On their insistence, he would review all those answer books again and modify the scores, where considered appropriate. And in this manner, a large number of candidates progressed to qualifying grade.

Mr. Pasricha's other colleague (I am refraining from disclosing his name though I still remember it) was known for his dry, stiff and arrogant attitude. In the normal circumstances even, the office people would rush out of his room immediately after finishing the discussions. We never saw this officer's wife with him either on the "Mall' or in the Coffee House. Therefore, there could be no chance of any pleading or a room for any clemency/leniency from him.

And that brings to fore the 'element' of luck in exams. Lucky were those who were part of Mr. Pasricha's packet and what to say of those who were in the other packet.

Shimla's social milieu

While discussing my work-life and social life in the preceding narrations, I have unveiled quite a bit about my personal life also. However, many more details/aspects still need attention. After all, a decade at Shimla and that too in the prime of my youth beckons many more details. I mentioned at one place, "When I thought I had arrived" This was in reference to my securing a job of my liking; as an Auditor in Audit & Accounts Dept. and "Arrived" meant "high surging expectations beckoned me to persevere and perform well to enable me to chase my dreams." This yearning for growth and craze for achieving sure success in life frequently overshadowed all other considerations. To me it meant a real challenge likely to impact my personal life.

The overall environment in the town was of high standard compared to what I had been used to till then. People looked more sophisticated and polished in their behavior. To be formal in conduct was the norm. It appeared, as if I had to pick up certain style to be comfortable in dealing with a section of the population. Improving my communication skills and English language came up as a first priority. To be careful in choosing the articles of my attire was the second consideration. Speak well, dress well, look well and behave well in public was the Mantra I gave to myself. What follows is the narration of how I attempted to strike a balance between work-life and personal life.

My comfort zone

After a few months in Shimla, I realized to my surprise, that I was quite capable of adjusting to the local environment and I need not be in a hurry to try to adopt certain contours of conduct of others blindly. And a major part of credit for this realization goes to Mr. Pasricha, with whom I developed a quick repo in the office. He had said, "Take off any such burden, if you have. Just be careful and circumspect in your attitude and disposition." The confidence to be my normal-self came back fast and the burden of hasty change vanished from my psych. Well, this also reminded me of my strengths:-

I was not prone to loose talk,

I always despised vulgar display of superiority,

It never occurred to me that I was the chosen one and hence entitled to showing off,

I am a normal person and have learnt to be as such through and through.

This was my comfort zone and I was quite happy being in the four walls of this zone.

Chapter 12
Eligible bachelor gets attention

The infatuation OR......that was not to be?

I turned 27 in 1963 and my relatives, especially my mother and elder sisters, were seriously busy trying to spot some suitable options/proposals for my marriage. One such girl with whom my elder sister at Hardwar was very intimate and liked her very much was her school teacher. After listening to the details about me, this girl showed an inclination to meet me. And, thanks to my sister's efforts, we were together in my other sister's place in Dehra Dun. That was Diwali, the first week of November, 1963, when we had the opportunity to spend time together and interact freely about the option. During the three days that we were there, we spent a lot of time together eating out, watching movies etc. We both realized that both of us were comfortable with each other. The unanimous opinion was we liked each other and both were happy about it. We concluded; we would welcome if the proposed relationship earned the approval of our parents.

It was not a norm then that the boy and girl meet directly and therefore, it was not surprising when her father took a different view. Of course, he had his other reasons for it too; my financial position and status in work place was not to his expectations. We two had also considered it but overcame this inhibition in our own way; (i) both will work and augment income and (ii) soon I could hope to clear my SAS exam which will be an entry into supervisory cadre and a reasonably good raise in salary

194

income as also place in the society. This didn't click with her father and the matter ended there.

Both of us were sorry for it but didn't have the courage to go ahead on our own. Looks silly now but this is what happened.

Mother accelerates efforts for my marriage

Coming to know of what happened in Hardwar, my mother was very unhappy. Though as a result of briefings by my sister from time to time, she had developed a fancy for the Hardwar girl but didn't pursue the matter further with her parents thinking it was against her dignity to seek a fresh dialogue with them. She redoubled her efforts now to find a suitable match herself. A well-wisher of our family brought up a proposal from a family in Bareilly. After protracted preliminary parleys through this common friend and finding the proposal satisfactory, my mother got in direct touch with the girl's parents to take the proposal forward. A few meetings between my elders, mother, sister and sister-in-law and girl's parents sealed the proposal in affirmation subject to o.k. by the boy and the girl. As was customary then, the respective parents sought their kids' consent by exchange of photos and furnishing of essential details and this happened in our case too. This ritual over, an auspicious day was fixed for formal meeting between the families to push the proposal forward. During this meeting, the boy and the girl exchanged meaningful glances and that was all. No formal opportunity was given to us to be together for a while and exchange pleasantries, if nothing else. The exchange of glances between us and a smile on our faces was thought to be our consent and that was that. Do you think; our refusal or seeking a separate meeting would have altered the plans? Not at all, a word of honor had already been given by both the sides.

I get engaged.

It was the auspicious day of Basant Panchmi, in January, 1965, when the formal approvals were exchanged between the families in the presence of some close relatives and friends. It was not customary then that the boy and the girl meet separately, inter-act and have some free time to exchange views about the proposed tie-up. It was thought that the spade-work done by families before fixing up a meeting was sufficient enough for going ahead with the proposal. Even not long ago, the custom was totally different. The mediators would inter-act, ascertain complete details of the boy and the girl, inter-act individually with both the sides, ascertain their consent and then only a formal meeting would take place between the respective parents to push the proposal forward. A meeting between the boy and the girl didn't figure anywhere. Being satisfied about the family was most important for both the sides.

I was told by my mother that during their times even such a limited ritual was not observed. The matrimony proposals were finalized by the elder members of the families after being satisfied about the status etc. of the families and no more. The women on both of the fence would be apprised/consulted about it with a view to find out if they had some inside information which may call for a re-look. The totally male-dominated society would not care to look beyond such a ritual. This reminds me of the rather funny details given by Mr. Pasricha, my boss, about his marriage solemnized in forties. He said, "My grand-mother met the bride's people through a mediator and after being satisfied about the family and its status went ahead and formally approved the proposal." On return from the bride's place, she happily conveyed her decision to all in the family. And when asked about the girl, her reply was, "She is a girl like any other girl. She knows embroidery, can do some stitching and can cook. What more are you looking for, Yash?" And an interesting aspect of this episode is that Bhabi ji was little less than 5' and our boss was 6'&4". But this glaring difference was immaterial for the grand-mother and nobody could ask her to re-consider it. And all this happened in Lahore, the supposedly elite, fashion-conscious and an advanced town of the country.

With the passage of time, the society and customs have kept on evolving. In our times, a formal meeting between parents in the presence of the boy and the girl was a normal necessity and it is what had happened with us. There was an environment of deja-vu and merry-making followed by exchange of nods of approval by both the sides. Everything was happening quite fast and I was wondering whether to ask for a one-on-one meeting with the girl when some senior person exclaimed, 'time for 'Ring Ceremony." And lo and behold the 'Pandit ji invited us to come forward and be ready for the ceremony. The Ring Ceremony took place to the enthusiastic applauds of those present. Both sides started exchanging greetings and gifts and a mini-party was hosted hurriedly by the girl's side for those of us present. And lo! We (the girl and I) were declared engaged where after feasts followed in both the house-holds and the boy and the girl happily returned to their respective work places.

Pre-marriage courtship, a rare phenomenon then

All said and done, a period of a formal courtship was not thought to be a necessity then. And even if one got such an urge, the tardy communication technology and lack of spread of facilities played the real spoil-sport. The only means for communicating with each other was exchange of letters, which again were totally unreliable. We did exchange few letters but the gap between sending a letter and getting a reply was too long. Ms. Chawla, the bride was posted in remote rural areas of Shahjahanpur district in U.P. and this added to serious delays. True to human nature, youngsters' did have similar urge as is today to be in touch with each other after engagement and the exchange of letters was as exciting as is the present day's love for free exchanges on mobiles. The pity was that you write the letter after summoning all the literary skills, post it in the mail-box and start looking forward eagerly to the response believing there would be no undue delay. But normally that wouldn't happen thanks to 'bullock-cart' speed of delivery of the Postal dept. No remedy, no other option and just pray to God for some miracle to happen. This is what I literally went through during the period of so-called courtship. My room-mate, Ved, was always adding to my misery. Being himself quite enthusiastic about the idea of exchanges, he would scold me if there was some delay from my side. As per him, the delay in reply from the girl's side could not be an excuse for me to not write the letter the same night and post it early next morning.

The D-Day is fixed

The exchanges gave fuel to the desire for an early marriage. I was not willing to wait for long. Quite naturally, I started looking forward anxiously to the announcement of our marriage date. After mutual consultations and study of Zodiac signs of the boy and the girl by a Panditji, 8th May, 1965, was fixed as the 'Day'. With this the preparations for the marriage ceremony started on both sides. I arrived in Bareilly on long leave and got busy with my elders in making preparations for the event. Even though the budget was not big but still doing shopping for the event as a whole and particularly bride's garments, jewellery and other necessary items became a daily routine. I was keen about choice of various items for her personal use and devoted full attention to proper selection particularly of the bag of decent cosmetics of high quality including imported items where possible. Many a times this keenness became the subject matter of jokes and lyrical comments by my Bhabbis. I enjoyed it all being overwhelmed by the care and full attention being paid. In Indian house-holds such an active and interesting positive role of Bhabbis is not so common. But it was opposite in my case since I enjoyed being their favorite 'Devar'.

I get married

As is usual in middle-class house-holds like ours, our marriage was solemnized in a traditional style like bride-groom leading the marriage party to bride's place sitting on a well-decorated horse/pony and band in attendance accompanied by the Baraties. The bride's place was well-decorated with lights, flowers and popular songs being played on the loud-speakers. This being a traditionally arranged marriage, Barat's and Groom's welcome at this stage assumed great significance. There are few ceremonies which are a must at this stage too which the bride's family profusely performed by following the traditional script. Aware that the 'Baraties' sometimes can be nasty, the bride's family were very attentive even to the minutest details. Their approach to make it memorable was palpable. There was big feast for the marriage party with varieties of dishes and sweets being served. It is customary to show-off on such occasions in an attempt to impress the groom's party and society at large and my in-laws too tried to fall in line.

After the feast was over and the guests dispersed, the Pandit ji took over and thus began the process of solemnizing our wedding. We both were made to sit on a make-shift dais, and necessary pooja for wedding started with chanting of shlokas from scriptures. This ceremony took about four hours and we were declared formally married after the last most important ceremony; seven phere around the fire-lit podium and exchange of 'Jai Mala' followed by applying 'Sindoor' in girl's hair. By then it was early morning and it was time for bride's departure (Vidai) in a ceremonial well-decorated palanquin (Doli as we call it). The bride's traditional welcome at groom's house by my mother and other relatives followed with fan-fare and the bride entered her new home. With this, the first phase of hectic activities ended but not exactly. Celebration followed for many days in our house to welcome the bride with my mother taking a leading part along with my brothers, bhabis, sisters and all our close relatives and friends but there was no splashy show-off. And, in any case, there was no such culture of vulgar display of wealth. Society at large was conservative. Being within limits was the common norm. Taking photos of different functions and making an album was not very common then. Being very religious-minded, our mother would take us to a temple or a gurdwara every day to seek blessings for the newlyweds. And of course we enjoyed it and tried to follow this holy tradition at the time of weddings of our sons.

Shimla (July 1965)

USA (May 2001)

Dehra Dun (August 2015)

Chapter 13
Our married life in Shimla

After vacation of a few weeks at Bareilly together, we came to Shimla, my work place. Going out on a honey-moon was not a common practice, one reason for which was the financial weakness of the middle-class then. And of-course, the infrastructure too was an impediment. In fact, the phrase 'middle class' was unknown then. Not as an alibi to justify this practice, I believe, this scenario had its own advantages relevant to the social milieu prevailing then. It enabled the young couples to enjoy their honey-moon longer; the bride waiting impatiently every day for months/years for her groom to return home from work and the husband always eager to rush home quickly. This fuelled/ignited the desire in both to be together infinitely. Working women was an exception rather than a rule and newly-wed brides indulged freely and willingly in cooking variety of food, keeping the house tidy and enjoy other favorite passions like singing, dancing, painting or whatever other fads like listening to songs on the radio or a gramophone. They would have sufficient free time for doing embroidery, knitting and similar other vocations. Such a life-style had its own charms. Looking forward eagerly to 'his' arrival in the evening and eagerness of rushing to home soon after close of office, is what added color and made life deeply rich. It meant enjoying freedom to be your own self even with lesser facilities and single source of income. I believe; life is richer, healthier and more enjoyable in the long run if there is less of rat-race and more of fantasy. I had such a vision for my married life. Alas, Mrs. Aneja's stay at Shimla was cut short for reasons of real life's compulsions. She had contractual obligation as per her bond of service with the employer to complete the remaining period as per contract.

Pangs of loneliness

I was miserable being alone so soon. I was not mentally prepared for it but that was what it was. I must confess this was the most stressful period in my life. How miserable I was and how I tolerated the separation is not worthy of mention. It irked me unbelievably harsh. The whole situation was disgusting to me because I had not been informed before marriage of this contractual obligation of hers. It was kept under wraps and that was really agonizing and painful. The few months that we had lived together were truly bliss. We wouldn't bind ourselves with a fixed or rigid routine. Go out on one pretext or the other any time was the sine qua non. Being together was the only thing that mattered. Get out of the house in the evening ostensibly for a small walk in the neighborhood, change your mind and go to a movie or eat out or spend time together aimlessly, conscious of the warmth oozing out of togetherness.

The first God Gift for us; birth of our lovely beautiful daughter

We were blessed with the birth of our darling daughter in Feb., 1966. She was a treasure of happiness for us from day one. Taking care of her with love and full dedication was the top priority for us. It was a scene watching Mrs. Aneja giving her a bath. Both would be happy beyond description with the mother holding her in the tub and poring slowly warm water on her head and she merrily dancing and enjoying the sprinkles of Luke warm current/flow of water. You take her out of the tub and she would start crying instantly. After the bath, Mrs. Aneja would chuckle, giggle and sing some couplet in her sweet voice while putting on her clothes. Feeding her and putting her to sleep was another passionate activity for Mrs. Aneja. In fact, she became the exclusive focus of her mother's attention making me envious, in a way. God's Grace, Sunita, our daughter, was an immense source of pleasure; always smilingly active while awake making the surroundings lively and soothing. She wouldn't want her mother to be away from her making her house-hold chores difficult. The good health that Sunita was gifted with won her top position in a children's health camp at the age of 6/7 months. In her small age of 8-10 months, Sunita could walk steadily on the Mall by herself and wouldn't allow us to pick her up thinking she must have got tired. These rich poignant scenes were our real assets over-shadowing our intimate personal relations. And when time came for them to leave for Bareilly, for enabling Mrs. Aneja to honor her contractual obligations, life became miserable once again for me. It was truly difficult reconciling myself with the prospect of having to live a poor lonely life once again.

I take a plunge, go for the S.A.S Exam and qualify it

The fantasy of living carefree in a make-believe world of my own dreams disappeared soon after marriage. The consequences of the delay in taking up this exam dawned on me. I realized that my salary income wasn't sufficient enough for the family now. The only option to increase the income was to qualify the SAS exam and look forward to promotion as an Accountant. Till then, I had believed that being able to deliver very well in the office was what mattered most. I always felt I could clear the exam any time I would want to. In the web of all these feelings, I overlooked the importance/necessity of passing this exam. Enjoying life in the company of friends was a contributory factor for this neglect. Another contributory factor was the negative refrain of many seniors. The loose talk used to be, 'cracking this exam was no child's play. Only five chances are available in all. You are doomed if you fail to qualify.' Such an environment was seriously disheartening for beginners like us. Despite all this negativity I always knew with confidence that once I jump into the fray I will clear both the parts one after the other. I was conscious that the main motivating factor for me to join this job was the prospect of growth after qualifying in this exam. That I must improve my financial position was obvious after marriage. But the arrival of our daughter added to my precarious financial condition and made me sit up and shed my neglect.

I took up this exam for the first time in Nov. 1966 but was unlucky. Horrified by the result, I went to my Accounts Officer, Mr. Narendar Kapoor, who too couldn't accept that it was a failure for me. Out of three Papers; two professional subjects and one English language, I had plucked in English. It was surprising to me and to him also. He knew I could handle the language well. The analysis of possible reasons for my failure revealed that I had erred in using my own phrases and language while making a précis of the given passage. He explained; the test is not meant to judge your command on the language but the ability to make a précis that captures the essentials of the subject covered by the passage. You are expected to make a précis by picking up the relevant paragraphs/phrases from the passage itself and present a coherent summary. I followed his advice next time and cleared the exam in January, 1967.

The real test of patience and nerves I lived through

The serious handicap of severely harsh and biting cold in Shimla during the three months of Nov. to January that I braved while preparing for second attempt of Part I exam is worthy of mention. Whole day's hard work in office notwithstanding, getting some food at home in the evenings was out of question. Mrs. Aneja was away to Bareilly and I was alone. Cooking the food by myself was beyond consideration for it would mean losing precious time. Hence there was no chance of getting any food at home. Make do with bread, eggs etc. whatever possible. Otherwise suffer the pangs of hunger. Even this seemed to be out of consideration many a times because of harsh winter. Cooking and eating would be possible only if you dare to come out of the warm shield of your quilt which was the only way to sit up and continue the studies. Determined to wash the blot of failure off my face, no sacrifice was too big for me. Desperate I used to be for all that sustains and rejuvenates life during icy winter nights; hot fresh food, an occasional cup of hot tea/coffee, warm room and a cosy bed but all this was not to be. I would keep reminding myself, "No excuses!

Don't falter now; you have had enough of laxity. Don't try to escape this time. You are on a mission! Remember, you have dear and near ones waiting anxiously and hoping to see you successful. Be courageous and try to live up to your own and family's expectations."

Many a times, I would go without any food even if some was lying in the kitchen shelf. The sub-zero temperatures and heaps of snow everywhere around played havoc both for personal physique and the psych. The falling snow, once an object of pleasure, was an object of scorn now. Achieving success in the exam was the only mantra that kept me going. Believe me; the odds were the harshest, I ever faced. And mind it, no one was around to feel and share my agony; an agony not only of loneliness, isolation and hardship but also of the fear of possibility of failure again. When you are alone, are under stress and full of anxieties and none of your own loved ones are around, the mirages encircle you making the already harsh world around more painful and this was what I went through in those three months.

A welcome new arrival in the family; Sandeep, our son

After a few months, Mrs. Aneja gave birth to a healthy baby boy on 21st Sept. 1968, in Shimla's prestigious women's hospital, Lady Reading. We were twice blessed; first for my promotion and now for God's Kind Gift of a son. It was a double whammy for us and both the parents' families. People from our families came to share our happiness. There were traditional 'pooja' rituals followed by celebrations. The newly born baby was the star attraction. Sunita, our daughter, was 2½ years now and she was excited to have such a lovely baby boy for a company. A learned Panditji declared after consulting the location of stars at the time of child's birth that Sandeep would be an auspicious name for the child. A new phase had started in our life. For support in house-hold affairs, Mrs. Aneja's younger sister joined us and stayed with us for some time when considering the incoming winters, Mrs Aneja and kids shifted to Bareilly once again in November. The pleasure of being happy with my family turned out to be short-lived. The high pressure of work in office due to trifurcation of A.G. Punjab's office into three offices; one each for the three states of Punjab, Haryana and Himachal Pradesh was crippling. I would come back from office very late every day, munch something quickly, enter the bed and try to get some sleep. Life had become difficult once again but there was hope that, come spring, the family will have nice time together and it really happened.

The spring of 1969 ushers in happiness

Happy days are here again. Come Spring and happy days returned with the arrival of Mrs. Aneja and children back to Shimla sometimes in March/April, 1969. The wheel of life entered into a usual routine; get up early, help Mrs. Aneja for some time, get ready and go to office, come back home in the evening sometime late sometime in time, sip a cup of tea, relax for a while, have nice time with kids and keep them busy enabling Mrs. Aneja to complete her chores in the kitchen, other household activities and finally be done for the day. Again follow the same routine the next day and move on. Days and nights started passing by in routine like this.

Sometimes, it made me wonder; is it what makes life meaningful? When alone, you yearned for the hustles and bustles of family life and suffered from the pangs of loneliness and its attendant miseries. And now when every-body who matters is around, it feels as if it is just a routine without any big excitement. The answer seemed to be then; lend a bigger helping hand to Mrs. Aneja in house-hold affairs and try to earn her little smile (she was always actually hard pressed for time for herself), sprinkle some salt and spice of change in whatever manner possible in spite of the pressures of daily routine. Pause and take a break. Move out of home with family on week-ends, go for a walk together, occasionally bring home in the evening some sweets and snacks and indulge in some light pranks with the kids. Life, sweet and charming, started rolling as a routine for the family now.

Chapter 14
Anxiety for further growth prods me to look for other options

Though very happy and excited after qualifying the SAS exam and subsequent promotion as an Accountant in A.G's office, an ache started pricking me. I was aware that the ladder of further growth in AG office comprised of one more step only. Under normal circumstances, the only avenue of promotion for an Accountant was that of Accounts Officer and that too after more than 10 years of service. For a person bitten by the worm of accelerated growth and high ambitions, this thought was discomforting with a nagging question, "what next and what could be the path for bigger growth in the profession?"

I was conscious that the SAS qualification was acceptable in Govt. sector only. That appeared to be a set-back no-doubt but there was a ray of hope. During that period in India's economic growth, the Govt. of India was making big investments in setting up huge industrial empires in almost all sectors. Though 100 % ownership of these entities vested in the Govt., these entities were being registered as closely-held Public Companies under the Companies Act. However, there was a huge gap in the 'Demand and Supply' chain of qualified professionals like Chartered Accountants and Cost Accountants. Hence, these Public Sector Companies were looking to induct SAS Accountants to man their vacant positions. The system that was in force for this purpose was unique; request the Accountant General to nominate suitable SAS Accountants of his office and allow the PSU (Public Sector Undertaking) concerned to screen them and pick up the suitable ones on deputation basis i.e. let these personnel work there for an agreed term with a possibility of absorption later, if found suitable by both after the expiry of the deputation period. This opportunity sounded as highly attractive. The immediate temptation was the deputation pay of 20% in addition to normal grade pay and allowances. Work there for a specified period on deputation basis and look forward to permanent absorption if interested, otherwise go back to your parent office. For those who had faith in their capacity to deliver stood a sure chance of absorption because there were large numbers of vacant positions. And after absorption, the avenues of growth were wide open. Keep performing well, pursue your ICWA course as a part-time candidate and look forward to a jump in status and un-hindered growth.

A longing that didn't materialize; settling down at Chandigarh; the city beautiful

Shimla's harsh winters always led to a strong urge, "get away as quickly as possible." And Chandigarh, always came up on horizon as a first preferable choice; feasible and within reach. Having visited it quite frequently, its manifold charms always attracted me. And my allocation to AG, Haryana's office in 1968 at the time of trifurcation of AG Punjab's office, gave a strong fillip to this urge. Like many others of my ilk, I too felt this is going to happen sooner than later. It was known that this office will surely be moved to Chandigarh considering the logistics; with Haryana govt. functioning at Chandigarh. However, that was not to be for me. My destiny had in store for me something bigger. The silent craze for making it big in life pushed me into different orbit; an orbit of growth which may not have been possible while being at Chandigarh. But notwithstanding this satisfaction the city beautiful again came up on horizon for permanent settlement when I superannuated in 1994. Yes, it didn't happen again. Shall we say, destiny again decided otherwise? However, being at Dehra Dun is no less charming and satisfying and we are quite happy being here.

I enter BHEL, Hardwar as a Senior Accountant

An opportunity on which I had pinned all my expectations for future growth came my way. I was selected, after due process, for deputation as a Senior Accountant to BHEL, Hardwar, a PSU of high repute. The management of BHEL, Haridwar, after due consideration and scrutiny of Annual Confidential Reports, had approved my candidature from amongst a few short-listed candidates of my office. I joined there in July, 1969 as a Senior Accountant, a step above Accountant. And the raise in salary on offer was about Rs. 100/month. Considering the inflation rate of those days, this raise was substantial. This was not the only gain that mattered. My selection in BHEL had opened up avenues for further growth for me. This was the first important step forward. God forbid, I never looked back thereafter. It was a dream come true situation. I was conscious that my entry in BHEL, a Co. of high repute and standing, was a first step for a bright career in Public Sector. I was conscious I had to perform well and deliver my best to carve out a respectable position for myself. And I am happy to say, I did perform quite well during my tenure there.

I realize; 'I can deliver in Public Sector'

After my joining there, Mr. VS Verma, the Dy. FA & CAO, thought of applying a quick check to be sure about my suitability for posting as in charge of Stores Finance Section; a very crucial section of the Finance Dept. He told me he was going to Bombay on tour for about four weeks and he wanted to be sure about my credentials to head such an important section. He told me cryptically, "Take these two files, scrutinize the proposals contained therein and meet me tomorrow morning with your observations." He didn't provide any clues as to how to go about for readying my observations. It was indeed baffling for me. I had not handled any such assignment in AG office. How to go about was a serious question. What added to my dilemma was that no other person, either a colleague or a senior was known to me there who could introduce me to the subject. My predecessor had gone back to his parent department about two weeks back. An assistant was posted in the section but he was on leave on that crucial day. An interaction with a junior clerk in the section whose duty was to receive and dispatch papers and maintain records thereof didn't reveal much. He was very candid, "Sir, I do not know much. The former Accountant and Mr. Negi, the Assistant, study these files, scribble notes on a sheet of paper, go to Mr. Verma and after approval by him, give that sheet to me and I type it on the file." That was a clue I thought I could work on. And I did scan the files, tried to understand the proposals contained therein and framed my comments/ response with regard to justification for the requirement and similar other relevant parameters and prepared my notes. Next morning, the interaction with Mr. Verma revealed that my observations were highly relevant and he liked them. He was happy and told his colleague, Mr. Jain, who was sharing room with him that he had found the right person for the job. That established my credentials of competence for the job. After Mr. Verma's transfer, I had had the opportunity to work with two other senior officers and it was a smooth going. I was happy; my seniors were satisfied with my performance. The experience of three years' working in BHEL turned out to be highly rewarding for my future in PSUs.

Hardwar; the holiest of holy abodes of Ganga

All of us, my wife and my children were quite happy on our being in holy city, Hardwar. Our relatives too were very happy on our leaving the far-off and extremely cold place, Shimla and coming closer to them. Our close blood relatives were in Bareilly, Dehra Dun and Hardwar itself. Being in Hardwar, the highly revered/sacred place in Hindu mythology was a great feeling. The family started nursing a hope of settling down here.

The holy river Ganga enters the plains here. The 'Har ki Pauri' here is thought to be the most sacred Ghat. It is believed; a dip here blesses the devotees, washes off all sins, and means salvation. Since times immemorial, elderly people have been flocking in hordes to this holy town with deep faith in what is written in scriptures.

The pilgrimage to Hardwar on 'Kumbh Mela' which is held after every twelve years is thought to be the ultimate life-time opportunity/option for attempting to purify the mind and soul. In old days when means of reliable transport were virtually non-existent, people would undertake the trip walking long distances on foot and by availing whatever means of transport available like bullock carts, horse-driven carts or trains etc. For those in far-off places, the trip could take months. Therefore, the individuals would be accorded a ceremonial bid-adieu by the family, relatives and friends in the town/village before they set out on journey. The pilgrims themselves and the family would be mentally prepared that they may not be able to come back. This was thought to be a final good-bye to the world behind. In those days, a trip to Hardwar was almost like a 'Haj'.

Mother Ganga's benign kind gift for us

A milestone of enduring happiness came our way in BHEL, Hardwar. We were blessed with our second son, Ahish, here. He was born on 3rd April, 1970, in main hospital of BHEL. We were too happy to have been blessed again with a son. There were feelings of great joy. The ceremonies of 'Name Giving" and 'Chola' were celebrated merrily in the company of relatives and friends. A loving, peaceful and healthy child, Ashish, endeared himself to all. Those days, two sons and a daughter were thought to be a complete family and Ashish's arrival delivered an ultimate satisfaction to us. Sunita, our daughter, was four years then and had started going to 'Nursery' class in the neighborhood. The name 'Ashish' and his family name 'Sonu' was given to him by Sunita. His arrival reinforced our desire to continue to be in BHEL on regular basis rather than on deputation. The place was good; the prospects of further growth were bright. Therefore, we and our relatives thought being nearer to our kith and kin was an added advantage. After all, we are a middle-class family and love to be closer to our near and dear ones. Our family's tradition of going for 'Mundan' of boys at Hardwar, if possible, was fulfilled in October, 1971. We celebrated it with gusto on Dussehra day in the presence of relatives and friends on the banks of Holy River Ganges, which was considered to be very auspicious. Thanks to such and similar other pleasures, life kept on rolling happily.

I decline the offer of absorption in BHEL

Considering all aspects, I got seriously inclined to get absorbed in BHEL, Hardwar, provided the terms offered by the management were attractive enough. Negotiations went on with the management team for some time but even after many rounds of discussions, the final outcome was dissatisfactory. The matter ended there finally. But my determination to stay focused on jobs in Public Sector Companies grew sharper. I was convinced by now that a bright future lay before me in PSUs. In addition, the work experience of more than two years in BHEL had by now given me the confidence to say good-bye to A.G's office and seek entry in a PSU of my liking. The hunt for new greener pastures began and with that, I convinced myself and my family to be ready to leave Hardwar, when an opportunity arose.

Start exploring options for job in some other PSU

My experience of three years as a Senior Accountant was my asset. It helped brighten up my chances for selection in a higher position in some other PSU. I started scanning newspapers for placement elsewhere after the terms of absorption offered by BHEL management were not found reasonable by me.

Bokaro Steel Ltd, a company registered in the state of Bihar for setting up an integrated steel plant of rated capacity of 4 MT in collaboration with the Govt. of USSR notified some vacancies of Accounts Executives in 1971. This was extremely tempting because, if successful, one would be entering the Executive Cadre and it was well known that an entry into executive cadre was essential for further growth in the Public Sector. However, there was a serious dilemma. Bokaro Steel Ltd. being located in Bihar was a big deterrent. Bihar was thought to be a badland then.

After discussing with Mrs. Aneja, my mother and my in-laws, I gave up the idea of jumping in.

However, destiny had wished it otherwise. Two of my colleagues in BHEL who had lived in Ranchi, a place nearer to Bokaro and in Bihar, had different opinion about the place. They insisted, all the three of us apply, appear for interview when called for and take a final call only after that. They recounted some of their happy experiences to mollify my misgivings. The argument was clear, applying doesn't entail any commitment. We applied, got interview calls and went to BS City. My friends also sought to project this trip as a chance for visiting few tourist and holy spots enroute, like Rajgir, Varanasi, and Allahabad besides Ranchi. BSL had promised to pay for our railway fare, making it more attractive.

The sum total; I applied, appeared for the interview and was selected as an Accounts Executive but not my friends. Of course, I was sorry for them. They had encouraged me, motivated me and led me to BS City.

Chapter 15
A significant breakthrough comes my way;
I get selected as an Executive in BSL

The news came that I was in the panel of successful candidates and should hope to get a call for joining the job sometimes in April/May. Now, I was face to face with a welcome opportunity for which I was anxiously waiting. I felt rumblings of joy within as though the good news had already encircled my vision. I was conscious that my dreams were no more dreams. These were within the realms of reality now. Everything around looked different; radiant, enchanting and colorful. I was deeply moved; a penniless migrant from Pakistan had spotted a bright star in the sky beckoning him to move forward. The choice seemed to be obvious; accept it and enter the twilight zone of satisfaction, happiness and endless prospects of a bright future and simultaneously make the first move to create a place of respect in society for self, for Mrs. Aneja, and our lovely kids. OR let it go considering the apprehensions about the place of posting and wait for the next opportunity but it could turn out to be a long wait.

Apprehensions about safety and security
in BS City are warded off

While at BS City for interview, I had met few candidates from Allahabad and Delhi who also had similar apprehensions of insecurity etc. To get a clear idea, we went to meet some senior officers working in F&A dept. who were from Punjab, Delhi, and U.P etc. and were there for many

214

years. We discussed with them our misgivings about Bihar in general and BS City in particular. Their response was very positive and highly encouraging. Each one of them was emphatic; come and join, if selected. There was no reason to be scared of about law & order position in BS City. Though happy and satisfied with this response, we decided to have a look and do a recce in the town ourselves i.e. we did a sort of an independent check on our own. We moved around in the town and found out it was a clean good city and whatever may be the reputation of Bihar, this town was secure, had good infrastructure and was very well maintained being a private township of BSL. The utilities like power and water supply were steady, being provided by captive facilities and were linked with the steel plant itself. Being a prestigious Public Sector Unit with huge investment by the Govt. of India, BSL and BS City were being given close extra attention by the security establishments, both of Bihar Govt. and Central Govt.

In nut-shell, this town was in much better shape than many of the big towns of north India. Apart from large number of Hindi-medium schools being run and managed by the Education Dept. of BSL, the town had a number of private English-medium public schools of repute. There was hardly any reason for us to decline the offer of appointment, if finally selected. I came back fully satisfied and started looking forward eagerly to getting an offer of appointment. When back home, I could conveniently convince Mrs. Aneja, with the help of details that I had about the suitability of the town and the potential of growth for me hereafter.

Chapter 16
I join BSL

The offer of appointment came in May, 1972. By then, considering all aspects, I had overcome the inhibitions and had decided to join BSL as and when the offer came. Therefore, after completing the formalities in BHEL, I joined BSL in June, 1972, as an Accounts Executive. With God's Grace, a new chapter began for us; a chapter that was full of promise for a bright future. I was sure; the highly encouraging Mantra of putting in my best with full sense of responsibility and commitment would help me equally in BSL too as it had done for me in my previous organizations. Do your best, give your 100% to your responsibilities and leave the outcome to Him. My interview pal, Mr. CL Suri had joined there two months back and had also made a stop-gap arrangement of accommodation for us. We arrived and quickly settled down in a living quarter in BS City, on a sharing basis, with an Engineer who was single. Got Sunita and Sandeep admitted in the school, fixed up ration/grocery for the house-hold and life started rolling on. The atmosphere in office was congenial. I was happy to have not faced any hassles and was able to complete the joining formalities quickly with full support from the HR staff. It was indeed a happy experience.

The first job assignment not to my liking

Upon completing the formalities, I was posted in Works A/Cs section, where my responsibility was to scrutinize and authorize payment of bills for service and maintenance of Company's large fleet of vehicles of all types. The system was simple. There were 'Rate Contracts' with the short-listed service providers detailing charges payable for each service component, consumables and spare parts. The bills were passed for payment by the authorized Auto Engineers with respect to work orders placed by different sections/units of BSL and then sent to Accounts for authorizing payment to the service providers. Thus the procedure of scrutiny and authorizing payment was a routine affair and, in my opinion, even an Accountant could handle it. However, it being my first posting in a new company, I dare not broach it with my Senior Accounts Officer. Days started passing by and my sense of discomfort and frustration at not being in a position to contribute significantly and showing my worth was growing.

I had a different perception of my role as an officer. Handling a routine job and being happy, easy going and lying low in one obscure corner of the office hierarchy was an anathema to me. A really challenging assignment was what I wanted. The vision in my mind for growth was, "Handle difficult assignments, meet the challenges, demonstrate skills of an able Finance and Accounts Executive and be noticed." I was confident, given a chance; I would be able to demonstrate my skills of a competent Accounts professional.

In my entire work life so far, I had performed very well, made the jobs I handled richer and had demonstrated distinctly my abilities to contribute and deliver in most challenging situations. And I had had a fair share of rewards/recognitions. Surprising it may seem to many, but all this negated a wide-spread belief that in Govt. jobs, it is narrow considerations of nepotism and favoritism that rule and that real merit is hardly recognized.

My dilemma about job assignment gets resolved

The dilemma I was facing was 'what to do' to get out of the situation of quagmire, i.e. my posting in an obscure section. Luckily, a way out surfaced in a chance meeting with one Mr. VR Chadha, who was my senior and was posted in Works Accounts Section. I had known him soon after arrival in BS City through Mr. Suri, my batch-mate. Hesitatingly, I broached my dilemma to him. He agreed that my concern was genuine and he would talk to seniors at an appropriate time. Mr. Chadha was a man of few words and was well-known for his balanced and fair approach in such matters and therefore, his inter-action had had a desired impact. I was given a patient hearing by my seniors, who promised to keep my concern in mind. As the good luck would have it, sometime later, the plant management conveyed that considering the commissioning of First Blast Furnace, Coke-Oven Battery and Bye-Product units in the near future, there was an urgent need to create a separate Operations Accounts wing in Finance and Accounts Dept. Thanks to the spade work done by Mr. Chadha, I was relieved of my assignment in Works Accounts section and posted in the newly created Operations Accounts section.

My new responsibility; a challenge of great magnitude

Upon my joining in Operations Accounts wing, I was given the responsibility of organizing two important sections; Sales Accounts and Raw Materials accounts section, ab-initio. This, no doubt, was a welcome opportunity and was surely in sync with my view of seeking challenges. I realized organizing two such important sections from beginning was a big challenge indeed and would call for big efforts but there was no going back. It was an opportunity which, if met successfully, would catapult me into a different league; league of real performers. And to be sure, BSL's Finance and Accounts dept. had lot of them already in its wings. What an idea, a young new face in the company of old-timer big-wigs? The only weakness that I could think of was my lack of experience in these sections and I knew; it was going to be a serious big constraint.

I must concede I was little scared. First of all, I was new to the job and two, none of either my colleagues or seniors in Accounts dept. had any such experience, and our FA and CAO, the Head of Dept., was not happy about this arrangement. He himself was a veteran of steel industry and was aware that the job of raising bills in steel industry was typically complicated and in his opinion it was necessary that an officer with past experience in Sales accounts be brought from one of the existing steel plants. However, the other seniors down the line who had taken the lead in getting me posted in Sales accounts section had their own reasons. Their apprehension was that once the doors for induction of officers from other steel plants were opened, there would be an inundating flood of officers being brought in large numbers at all levels on the same plea thus militating against the avenues of growth for themselves. My posting in Sales accounts was their tactical move to secure their own future. Till then, the policy being followed in BSL was to induct officers at initial executive level only i.e. Accounts Executives. They were, therefore, keen to uphold this policy. To resolve the issue, one Saturday afternoon all the officers walked into FA&CAO's chamber without any prior appointment. Later, I came to know this was a deliberate move of the seniors; a sort of mild confrontation with the FA&CAO. However, nothing untoward happened and discussions started though he was disturbed at such a sudden development. I felt insecure thinking it reflected negatively on me in a way. The long and short of the meeting; a compromise formula emerged. The FA&CAO who had wanted two officers to be brought from outside; one for Sales accounts and the other for Cost accounts ultimately agreed to get only one person for Cost Accounts from outside and leave the Sales Accounts section in my charge.

My resolve; face the challenge head on

The compromise arrived at in the meeting with the FA&CAO was that I hold the charge of Sales accounts for three months and depending upon my performance, the matter will be re-considered. Thus, my posting in Sales accounts got converted into a prestige issue. My seniors cautioned me to put in my best and come up to the expectations of the Head of Dept. This meant a lot of hard work for me. Not only the job was new but Sales accounts also lacked proper infrastructural base. I had with me a typist, a steno and two manually-operated type-writers, one for my steno and the other for the typist for typing of invoices. Disturbing though it was but not hopeless considering that the real work of dispatches of finished products was few months away and by the time the production began, additional hands would be provided.

I now started concentrating on how and from where to secure help necessary for getting familiar with the basic working of the section. The first window of hope for me was a group of officers in the plant responsible for dispatches of finished products. They had joined from Rourkela Steel Plant and were quite familiar with documentation etc. I held consultations/meetings with them to broadly get familiar with documentation job and pricing of products. With their help, I built up a data-base of sale prices of pig iron and bye-products of Coke-Oven battery which were the Units of production to be commissioned in about three months' time. I also visited and met Accounts Officers of Sales accounts section at Bhillai and Rourkela steel plants, gained valuable insight into the working of this important section and collected Price Lists of items BSL was going to produce with the commissioning of Blast Furnace etc. Having thus equipped myself with confidence, I got into self-actualization mode. I got busy in creating the Price Master and other inputs necessary for preparing the invoices. Well, before the commencement of sale and dispatch of products of Blast Furnace and Coke-Oven-Battery from the plant, I was ready with a clear blue-print for handling the job. The Senior Accounts Officer of Operations accounts section, Mr. P.Chatterjee, my boss, was a great support.

Mrs. Indira Gandhi, the then Prime Minister, inaugurated the first Blast Furnace on 2nd October, 1972 and with that the dispatches of Pig Iron and bye-products of Coke-Oven Battery started. We had done our spade-work well and there were no hiccups or delays. It became a smooth affair sooner than anticipated. The feed-back I received conveyed that the FA&CAO was satisfied with our progress till then but still had misgivings about future when the Rolling Mills would start rolling finished products. He called me once, tried to gauge my capacity to handle the job well but I don't think I was happy with his facial expressions. I was unhappy since he did not let me know anything about his misgivings, if any. I ignored his nonchalant attitude and felt determined even more now to push ahead as I was doing. By then, I had satisfied myself that I can do it and will do it, come what may.

Challenges associated with
Sales Accounts section start unfolding

It was an open secret by then that the real problems lay in pricing of rolled-products. The pricing formulae of these products were fairly complicated and determining correct price for each product was cumbersome. However, the silver lining was that the Rolling Mills were due for commissioning after more than three years. So we had time available for planning and creating appropriate procedures for billing of these products and maintaining detailed accounts for the sales, as a whole. But there was no room for complacency. By now, it became known that the scope and contents of job in Sales accounts was very vast. It started unfolding itself, one by one, with all its varied dimensions every day. Anybody with a determined mind could grasp it and handle it, no doubt, but the journey ahead was obviously a serious challenge. At the same time, it satisfied my strong urge to perform and demonstrate I can deliver.

Briefly, my job meant:-

Raise Invoices in time and push them to the concerned Branch Sales Office without delay enabling it to present the shipping documents to customers' Bankers for realization of the sale proceeds expeditiously,

Coordinate with Branch Sales Offices for transfer of realized funds to BSL's Bank accounts and reconciliation thereof with my office records,

Maintain Party Ledgers and generate analytical reports of outstanding dues against customers called Sundry Debtors and many more reports for use by various offices within BSL and regulatory authority for the Sector, the JPC (Joint Plant Committee).

Invoicing of Rolling Mills products; a complex process

The invoicing of Pig Iron and bye-products was just a beginning and didn't involve any complications. We were able to handle it without any hassles. The complexities associated with invoicing of finished products of Rolling Mills were little away yet but not far off. It was obvious after my confabulations with Sales Accounts Officers of Rourkela Steel Plant that this was a massive and a voluminous effort. It had to be done with the help of EDP Branch and in close coordination with various agencies in the Plant involved in shipping, documentation, testing of finished products, issuing of test certificates for the finished products and the Traffic Dept. responsible for obtaining RRs from railways. Clearly, it was unthinkable, if not impossible, to manage it manually. This called for total computerization of the jobs/activities of my section. And total computerization was a major project necessitating collaboration and day to day co-ordination between Sales Accounts, EDP and various agencies/sections in the Plant. And this project was to run concurrently with the current work in the section which was increasing by the day and was being done manually.

A welcome change in my job portfolio

A few days after I had taken charge of Raw Materials Accounts section, a terrible picture of the state of its working unveiled before me. A scrutiny of few of this dept.'s bills for payments to contractors revealed a manipulated approach to the tendering process. A composite job would be split into many small jobs thus making it fall within the powers of Head of Dept. to award the work on a single-tender basis. This was a serious violation of the tendering procedure and was malafide. I was scared and felt incapable of handling it. I brought it to the notice of my seniors and requested that I be relieved of this responsibility arguing that the Sales accounts being at a nascent stage needed more attention. Luckily, this plea of mine was accepted and the charge of this section was given to my colleague who was holding the charge of Cost Accounts. I had taken a plea that since raw materials constituted a very large segment of costs in steel making, it was appropriate that these two sections are with one officer and my plea was accepted as logical. In its place, I was given the charge of making payments of miscellaneous contingent bills of Operations group. This was a welcome relief enabling me to pay full attention to Sales accounts.

Chapter 17
Organizing Sales Accounts Section; a mixed bag of big challenges and opportunities

Having been put into the position of a pivot for sound functioning of Sales Accounts section, I had no option but to get to the bottom and begin from beginning. It was a challenge I had to meet successfully for it had the potential to make or mar my future in BSL. Very early I realized that full computerization of section's work was the real challenge and that it should be organised in such a way that it is able to handle the increasing load of invoicing and accounting in its entirety i.e. maintenance of accounts of sales, realization and accounting of revenue, party ledgers, sundry debtors, analysis thereof and sundry reports for management information system etc.

Broadly, the task of computerization meant:-

(i)   explore and learn the essential requirements of the integrated job of invoicing and accounts maintenance on the computer,

(ii) develop and sharpen skills, own and staff's, necessary for the job,

(iii) co-ordinate with and secure co-operation of concerned in-house agencies like EDP Section, Sales Co-ordination wing in the Plant called PPC, Shipping and Traffic sections of the Plant, Sales & Marketing office of HSL at Kolkata, and Central Excise dept. of GOI

(iv) take the lead and stay put there till the gigantic Computerised System is created and gets stabilized

(v) be always in lead actor's role to overcome bottlenecks/delays, if any, during the development phase of the system

(vi) be sensitive to the concerns of own staff about computerisation as such and handle their misgivings about loss/reduction of job opportunities

(vii) apprise and keep briefing the Seniors in the dept. about the progress of the Project and ask for guidance and help when required

(viii) develop rapport and build warm personal relations with concerned Officers and Engineers of sections involved in it.

Accounts Dept., which in effect meant I, had the sole responsibility for system's development being the user and system's ultimate beneficiary. Other agencies had a supporting role only. And in the beginning itself it became evident that plant people especially PPC were wary and aware of the fact that the system would not benefit either them or other groups in the plant. And this apprehension came true very soon.

The initial resistance by EDP section

The key role for developing the computerized system was that of EDP Group. Their initial response for taking up the work of developing it was discouraging citing constraint of man-power and non-availability of computer capacity. This was sorted out after some time after discussions at the level of Heads of Depts. It was decided that soon after induction of some Programmers in EDP, this project shall be taken up with the start of 2nd shift in EDP. And it happened soon since not much complications/ steps were involved for invoicing of Pig Iron etc. At that stage EDP agreed to take up only invoicing of Pig Iron and bye-products. It was explained that the existing machine (IBM 1401) couldn't take any other job for our section due to capacity and technology constraints. The proposal to buy a main-frame machine along with terminals to augment capacity was under way for giving a major push to computerization efforts in the Co. We were assured that Sales Accounts' additional requirements of computerization of invoicing for rolled products and accounting jobs would be taken care of after the arrival and commissioning of new machine and its terminals

Need of the hour; be original and create an innovative computerized system

The realization that total computerization of all the jobs of my section was going to be a long-drawn affair became clear after few meetings with the EDP Managers and software professionals. At the same time, it was also evident that there was no escape either for them or for me. I realized that being a new project, I had the pleasure to innovate and conceive a structure of my preference in line with the anticipated flow of inputs/documents from the Plant and also the outputs I would need to accomplish the goals of an efficient invoicing, accounting, reporting and monitoring system. My visits to other steel plants had revealed a nagging state of accounts where both the functions i.e. invoicing and accounting were not taken up simultaneously. Therefore, it strengthened my resolve that accounting function must also be computerized simultaneous to invoicing. The long-term benefits of simultaneous implementation of computerization of invoices and accounts were over-whelming. I reckoned; this was the time/an opportunity for putting to test my ingenuity to try to usher in a system with a difference; a system that would be easy to work with and enable natural flow of data from invoicing system to accounting system.

Staff's misgivings about computerization handled to their satisfaction

Most of the staff in my section were first-timers in a job, were from a rural and small-town back-ground and computerization was a mystery for them. Another apprehension floating around was that computerization means squeeze in job positions and lack of growth opportunities for the staff. We, therefore decided to (i) educate the staff about the benefits of computerization, how it would lessen their physical fatigue of preparing large number of invoices manually on the type-writers and preparing various reports manually, and how the staff being not 100% sure and familiar with the complex pricing structure of rolled-products would lead to either under or over-invoicing resulting in customer dis-satisfaction and also adversely affecting Sales Accounts section's reputation.

We decided to (i) involve the leading and influential staff members in discussions with EDP group and Plant people, (ii) take them to the EDP/Plant to familiarize them with the flow of finished products and handling of dispatch documents at various levels and sections in the Plant, (iii) hold free discussions in our staff's meetings with concerned staff, Engineers and Officers in the Plant to give them a feel of the quantum of the work to drive home the point that such huge volumes would require more staff/officers to handle it with speed with computerized system only and not manually. We also assured them of the introduction of system of incentives, in due course, on meeting of the targets. These efforts yielded the results; the resistance, if any, was largely wiped off. Not only that, my section's staff was able to handle, on their own, the union leaders effectively.

Leaving behind this hurdle, we (EDP group and myself) started on our mission; create a system that is simple, free of jargons, easy to follow and user-friendly, is comprehensive and capable of handling the entire product-line of BSL, is supplemented with in-built checks to ensure correct pricing and takes care of accounting with its vast and complex dimensions. We were satisfied we had made a good start on a journey with deep implications for holding intact the top-line of BSL's finances.

The dual challenge for me

By now, it had fired my imagination that the computerization was going to be a long-drawn affair, it could be introduced in phases only and in the interim period, the work would have to be handled manually. The redeeming aspect was that our HR section was helpful and we were getting additional staff in phases. Thus the wheel kept on moving and increase in staff strength kept pace with the growing work load. But there were certain limitations though. BSL had no system of Accountants or supervisory staff. There were two categories of staff, the Executive

Assistants who were quite experienced and Assistants who were fresh from colleges. Each individual whether EA or Assistant handled his own jobs and reported directly to the Accounts Executive. This system turned out to be a big constraint for me since I was hard-pressed for time being busy in day-long meetings in EDP and/or in the Plant

The result was that I had to be in office till late in the evening almost every day. There was no escape. The invoices had to be pushed out to Sales Office in Calcutta every evening through a staff courier who would travel by train in the night from Dhanbad, and hand over the packets early morning to staff in HSL's Sales Office there who would in turn push them to respective Branch Sales Offices by air.

Being late in office meant neglect of my responsibilities for the family. How much I suffered emotionally, as a result of this, can be a matter of conjecture for others but for me and my family, it meant a great deal of stress and deprivation of happy moments of togetherness.

Chapter 18
Mammoth Computerization Project; team's proud achievement

Three major entities involved in the development of this system were: (i) Sales Accounts section, (ii) EDP group and (iii) a chain of entities in the plant. PPC (Production Planning and Control) section under the direct control of GM (Works) was the nodal agency for our inter-face with Plant. The number of agencies in the Plant whose co-operation was essential for development of the project and codification of in-put documents was large and they were physically far-away from each other. This triangular approach i.e. inter-action through PPC turned out to be time-consuming and cumbersome resulting in zero progress or very little progress for long. It was fairly clear that waiting for PPC's involvement was going to lead us nowhere. Therefore, we the EDP and Sales Accounts, decided to do the job of designing the computer savvy formats of various documents ourselves and then request the Plant authorities to suggest modifications/changes, if any. But this approach too was getting rigged at the hands of PPC who turned out to be a stumbling block. Soon we reached the dead-end without taking a single step forward.

The senior most officer who was incharge of PPC and who reported to GM (Works) had his own opinion about the system, "Do it manually or whatever but do not load plant people with additional work". His main plank was that in other steel plants, the job was taken care by EDP and Accounts. This matter remained un-resolved for some time but with the intervention of my boss, Deputy Controller of Accounts, and his one-on-one meeting with the GM (Works), it was agreed that the plant people will help in designing the formats etc. but codification job shall be handled by Sales Accounts. They may seek help from two officers of PPC who were nominated for this purpose. Virtually, therefore, the entire burden of developing the system and making it ready before the commencement of dispatches of rolled products devolved on our shoulders.

The path-finder idiom that helped; 'be original and innovate'

The stark painful reality; non-cooperation by PPC, couldn't deter the team comprising of Accounts & EDP from moving ahead. Rather, it made us determined more to keep pushing even though the road ahead was really difficult. To wade through the currents of negativity encountered till now, we were expected to devise an off-beat and an innovative approach to the subject. Mr. AC Jain, Senior System Analyst in EDP, who had just returned from the USA and who was responsible for execution of this prestigious project, came out with a brilliant idea, "Let's get closer to those who matter directly through personal inter-face." At his instance, our seniors, Mr. K. Ramaswamy, Chief of EDP and Mr. BG Joshi, Deputy Controller of Accounts agreed to the idea. The strategy agreed to was, 'invite them to Seminars/expositions in EDP and Training Institute and educate them about the veracity of computerized working.' Both Mr. Ramaswamy and Mr. Joshi took a leading part not only in the first symposium but also delivered talks on some subsequent occasions also.

We had realized by now that we needed to be patient for the results to flow. The long-term vision for arranging these get-togethers was to (i) develop a personal rapport with individual officers and staff in the plant with a view to motivate them, (ii) also try to enthuse them with the prospects of reduction in paper work for them and (iii) faster movement of wagons with the help of a computerized system.

Mr. Budhiraja, Head, Training Institute, turned out to be a big support for this project. The Institute provided full support in organizing these meetings. Mr. Jain was in the lead supported ably by his team of Programmers, Bijon Chattopadhyay, Mittal and Rangarajan. Mr. N Sarkar the Administrative head of EDP and I worked behind the scenes and also on the Dias to keep the pitch of involvement high; pay personal attention to each one of them and take good care to make them comfortable.

This was the first such unique attempt in BSL. The plant people especially the clerical staff had never been invited to such an important gathering before and treated so nicely. This strategy started working well. The resistance of PPC notwithstanding, these people who were actually responsible for handling/creating the input documents etc. got motivated enough to devote time with us. Most of these staff members/officers, who were experienced in their jobs, having joined from other steel plants, started joining us freely in our deliberations and freely exchanged information critical for the smooth functioning of the system.

Now we knew, we had created an asset of critical significance; a bouquet of talent and experience for providing us with tips/information; viable, dependable and practical for our project. A real significant hurdle had been crossed. Now was the time to get going; rather than chasing those who were determined, for reasons whatever, to stall the project or delay it. In the mean-time, the main-frame computer along with its terminals (30 in all) for capturing the data on-line had been received. BSL was the first Public Sector Unit in the country to have acquired such a big machine with peripherals and latest technology for its computing and data-processing needs. The phase of constraints of capacity (machine) and data-processing (card-punching process) were over. The new machine had huge capacity and it was very re-assuring for me; the Sales Accounts system would be free from any limitations of capacity or technology. I was happy I was getting familiar with computer hardware also.

My morale booster; the buck-up support and encouragement of seniors

My immediate senior in Sales Accounts, Mr. Chakraborty, ACA, was miles away from this project. Mr. Joshi had briefed me, "He is there for name-sake. Management is aware of your capability to handle the affairs of the section by yourself. He is in Sales Accounts for administrative reasons." It was an intelligent ploy; pampering my ego while getting rid of the real problem, "Where to dump this old guy?" In fact Mr. Joshi would often console me saying, "It is good. He doesn't interfere and this freedom gives you unfettered choice to decide the lay-out/final shape of various components of the computerization project. You can concentrate un-interruptedly on this very important project."

It was a significant message loaded with far-reaching implications for me, "You are the master, and you have full support of higher ups. You will not be disturbed, give your best and make a success of it." The message was unambiguous and encouraging, "Keep toiling with zeal and unimpeachable courage. Top Management is happy with you." Seriously speaking, this liberty was a double-edged weapon; you succeed and the management is happy but if you falter, your future is at stake.

This was a big challenge indeed. But it is also a fact that such an unassailable position strengthened my hands vis-à-vis EDP team. Though I was just at E-1 level in hierarchy and my counter-part in EDP, Mr. Jain was at E-5 level, a very vast gap in bureaucratic hierarchy but I was his equal, so to say. With regard to authority for taking a final view for deciding contours of an input or output document or a report, my stand was final. I didn't have to say, "I will come back after consulting my seniors."

The EDP team and I had developed excellent working relationship in the interest of mutual advantage. In fact, there was a real convergence of interest for both; making a mark in the organization by creating successfully an innovative system, easy to work on, user-friendly, not requiring extraordinary skills. It was going to be in the hands of junior staff for working in shifts on day in day out basis.

Team's recipe for success of the mission

The self-given mantra for the team was, "Be open, frank and sensitive in interaction in the team to derive maximum satisfaction and quick high-yielding results."

In line with this theme it was a pleasure to work in close coordination and there were hardly any differences in team's basic approach to the project. I and EDP team would avoid ruffling each other's feathers. In a situation of difference of opinion, we would disperse saying, "Let's agree to disagree for the present." We knew, passions would calm down by next meeting and a solution acceptable to both would emerge. An additional important reason for the bon-homie was the vastness of the scope of work and anticipated long duration of project's completion. We had to live together in an atmosphere of mutual goodwill and convergence.

It was known that the system for preparing of invoices of all the rolled products would be completed before the Rolling Mills start rolling the products. And the development of vast tract of accounting system followed by development of an efficient MIS would be on the agenda next. Both these systems had far-reaching implications for the introduction of an efficient and effective control system for the Management at different levels. It was envisaged that the system would cater to the requirement of making available various detailed reports for the people at working level, some consolidated reports for middle-level management and summary presentations of critical importance for top-management. Therefore, each component of the project was critical for integration into one stream. The more we discussed the details, the more it emerged that peaceful confabulations in the group were the real way out for its successful completion. And the tacit understanding of the top management that this team shall not be disturbed till the completion of the project was easily visible on the horizon though no such formal orders existed on record.

Many other depts. of BSL and some other steel plants were keenly watching the outcome/progress of this prestigious project of its own kind. My exploratory educational visits to Rourkela, Bhillai and Durgapur steel plants had impacted their vision to think of developing an integrated system like what we had envisaged and were working on in BSL.

Team rationalizes its efforts and persists till success

The responsibility that our group was entrusted with demanded that we give our best in creativity, originality and competence to make BSL proud at the end of the day; proud of having successfully completed an integrated system of Order-processing, Dispatches, Sales Invoicing and Accounting system. With this a new era of On-line use and functioning of computer applications on the Main-frame Computer began in BSL.

And I should not forget to mention that Mr. K. Ramaswamy, our EDP Chief, was truly a visionary. How else can one explain his leading role and services to the IT sector? Thanks to his vision and serious coordination efforts, BSL was the first Company in Public Sector and probably second in India to have got clearances from multitudes of Govt. agencies for the import of Main-frame computer with 30 terminals and that too in an era of controls and licenses. Not only that, Mr. Ramaswamy provided guidance and support to the group through meetings and inter-action with his counterparts in other depts.

Our strength was we were under direct focus of the top-management thus making us acutely conscious of our role and were not contract-hired professionals whom you don't expect to put in their heart and soul into their assignment. We were a team of committed in-house professionals led by a competent leader, Mr. AC Jain; a leader with a vision inspiring confidence amongst the team members. He was at ease in building bridges and developing strong inter-personal relationships within the group as also with other depts.

There was well-defined distribution of assignments to each member of the group:-

Mr. Jain was the coordinator and his personal responsibility was designing the overall structure of the project with component-wise and stage-wise break-down.

(i) Bijon Chattopadyay's responsibility was to write programs, designing of format and codification of critical documents; Sales Order and Dispatch Advice.

(ii) Mittal and Rangarajan to handle designing of formats, structure and lay-out of different Masters Files in computerized format, and install the Masters in the system,

Operating the existing programs and generating various output reports was to be handled in rotation by (i) and (ii).

As a user, Aneja to co-ordinate with each one of them separately as well as in the group till end.

My involvement with each one of them separately put me into embarrassing situation many a times; not able to spare time for one or other of them. Time management turned out to be extremely critical for my own sake as well as for speedy progress of the project. No doubt, each one of them was a genius par-excellence but none, either them or me, had any prior experience of handling such a system and this made our jobs really challenging. And there was nothing to fall back upon for help in our assignments because none of the other steel plants had attempted any such an innovative computerized system so far. The only hope was Tata Steel who, it was believed, had similar system in operation but nobody was sure if any support could be expected from there. Tata Steel was our customer for Pig Iron and I had had a chance earlier of visiting their office in Jamshedpur in connection with outstanding sales dues. I offered to lead Mittal, our Programmer, to Tata Steel office to explore the possibility of some meaningful interaction. But the visit was of no use. Their EDP group declined our request and we were back to the time-tested realization, "Self-help is the best option."

The great motivation for each member was being part of such an important group. Each member of the EDP team was earnestly busy and it was always a pleasure to be with them for exploring newer territories and discussing various options including wild new ideas. These exercises were lengthy, time-consuming and tiring. We had nothing before us which we were to copy-cat.

The first basic critical input document which we picked up for redesigning was the Dispatch Advice. As its name suggests the customer's name, address, destination station, full description and weight of material dispatched etc. were the vital inputs to be given in it for raising of invoices. We felt it would be appropriate to have a look on the DA format of Rourkela Steel Plant whose product-line was the same as ours. Giving a totally new format to our DA was out of question. If we suggested any major changes, it would raise the hackles of operations group in the plant which was the last thing we could think of doing given that their co-operation was not only vital but also the game-changer.

After few meetings, we were successful in redesigning of separate formats of DA for different products keeping in mind the nature of the product and its pricing structure. In the next phase the group took up designing of (i) Price Masters for each product separately, (ii) Sale Order Masters, (iii)Customer Master, (iv) Destination Master by codifying all the rail-heads in the country and many other permanent files on the computer. At that stage, we were concentrating on Invoicing Project only. The accounting package was equally big but was not being considered at that stage.

The gin of ambitions keeps pushing me

I was the only representative of Sales Accounts in the joint team. Mr. Jain and each one of his Programmers were go-getters, always in hurry. And, on behalf of Sales Accounts, I was the only one to inter-act with them. Considering the pressure from each one of them, it was but natural that there would be heated exchanges about my presence at a given time. Nobody in the group was bothered about my plight or my constraints or limitations. And to whom could I blame about all this pressure? Of-course myself for this was the flip-side of being over-ambitious. And I knew; there was no escape. I had to live with it having exhumed the gin with its vast tentacles. Of course, at the initial stages the real magnitude of project's vast fangs couldn't have been known, due to our inexperience and also the pressure of zeal to accept the challenge, come what may! I was deeply in the mud, having to ignore my family and myself for the sake of this project. My working day began at 9.30 but the end was always un-predictable. Usually, my day was of 12 hours, almost as a routine.

A shock of intense severity that couldn't demoralize the team

For developing the computerized 'Price Master' for the rolled products to be produced in BSL, complete list and details of size and grades etc. were required. PPC, the nodal agency, was responsible for furnishing these details. But securing them from PPC proved to be a herculean task.. Their reluctance and diversionary tactics sent shivers down our spine at the initial stages of discussions but when they actually furnished the details, we were shocked. The list contained all grades and sizes of the rolled products which a rolling mill can produce and not the ones which were approved by the Management of BSL. It was a huge list. One of the engineers in PPC, with whom I had developed close personal relations, told me about the gravity of the mischief planted at the instance of seniors. We were perplexed; what to do. At that stage, I turned to my friend, Mr. SG Tudekar, Head of Research and Control Lab. Looking to our dilemma, he promised to furnish complete and correct details of the rolled products which were slated to be produced in BSL as per the approved DPR (Detailed Project Report). And, pity on us, he kept his promise and after clearance from GM (Works), furnished it to us. I wonder now, what would have happened had it not been for Mr. Tudekar to come to our rescue. The saying "friend in need is the friend indeed" overwhelms me even now for his invaluable support. But for him, we couldn't have escaped the blame of failure.

Designing, finalizing and installing 'Price Masters' in the system; a real test of resilience

The pricing structure of steel products was very complex. Starting with base price, separately for each product and grade of steel, the final price for the customers included umpteen number of extra charges; like length extra, width extra, additives extra, yield-strength extra, tensile extra, packing extra and many more. Having known that Rourkela Steel Plant which was the only other steel plant producing flat products like us were determining the final price manually for each item and for each Dispatch Advice, the team resolved that we must avoid this pitfall. It was obvious that this procedure was not only time-consuming but was also fraught with sure possibility of irregularities and malpractices at the stage of invoicing. In real sense, it was nothing but using the computer as a printing machine. The essence of computerized working was missing in this approach.

All of us, the EDP (Service provider) and Sales Accounts, (the user) were ill at ease with this system. We decided to evolve a fool-proof and a steady system for overcoming these pitfalls. The solution was "Price Master" built up as part of the computerized system and which would have in-built details of base price and extras to be charged for each dispatch. The dealing hand in Sales Accounts would put the product code against each entry in the Dispatch Advice and the system would pick up the price chargeable for it from the Price Master. The resultant satisfaction would be for the customer and the supplier both but keeping the Price Master updated always was also a challenge by itself. Every change in base price or extra(s) would need to be fed into the Price Master before the real invoicing job was taken up. We realized thatthe process was time-consuming but there was no other choice. We went ahead and built up a comprehensive frame-work in the system; the 'Price Master' being embedded in it. Well, this effort took the team of three, two from EDP and one from Accounts, more than a year to complete.

Thank God, the other Masters were not as complicated or volatile as the Price Master. We had broad idea of time-frame of commissioning of various units in the plant and were scheduling our codification etc. work accordingly. The commissioning of first unit of Hot Rolling Mills was important and before this Mill started rolling out its first product, Hot Rolled Coils, we had to make sure our system was fully operational. We did few trial runs and found to our satisfaction that all was o.k. And when the first lot of this product was dispatched, we were dot on time in getting the invoices printed without any hassles or a re-run. The top Managers in EDP and Accounts profusely facilitated the team. Even the then GM (Works), Mr. Mehta, conveyed his appreciation. A land-mark milestone of commissioning of a fully computerized integrated system of Order processing and Invoicing had been established.

This was a big morale-booster for us. And we continued with our efforts fully satisfied that our seniors' support was 100 % with us. In the process, all of us had become addicts and workaholics to the core. Nothing could under-mine either our enthusiasm or commitment to the project. That all this happened in Govt. sector would appear to be unbelievable. I know, even in Private sector, such a high level of motivation, team-work, camaraderie and sincere commitment is rare.

A glimpse of team's sincere commitment to job

The team loved its job. Each one of us believed; the team was on a mission. Project's successful completion was what really mattered. It was a team effort in true sense of the word. Believe me, in my chequered career of about four decades I never faced such a subtle enthusiasm again in a group. None of us ever felt the project was mighty difficult. We will do it and in time was our target. While designing and finalizing the contours of soft-ware and computer files etc. we would be silently busy. A peep into our office room would suggest we were sitting idle; no-body talking, just sitting and smoking and by implication wasting time. But, as is natural in such groups, we, in fact, would be busy scratching our brains to find an answer to apparently mundane question(s). Even the exchanges in the group would apparently be suggestive of a drift. The old-time famous tale of opium-addicts in huddle would appear to be unfolding itself in the group. Bijon, the genius of a Programmer, would address me, "Dada, ami bolchhi" and go into silence and I would be waiting for him to come out with real issue. The matter of fact would be we both were seized of a problem to which a solution was not in sight. And when the solution emerged we would laugh violently loud and relieve ourselves saying, "I told you so already." Bijon was gem of a person and an invaluable support for the group. Innovation and out-of-box thinking was his forte. As a user of the system, I would explain broad contours of our existing manual working and also spell out my requirements of computerized out-puts.

Thereafter, he would pick-up threads from there; examine the inputs needed for compliance of our needs and get busy in programming effort. Such heartening and smoothening memories are ensconced deep somewhere in my inner-self. It is ecstatic to recall them and be deeply happy as if you are back to the same era and are living them once again and enjoying the thrill.

A golden Era of seamless contribution and accomplishment by the team

Every committed and ambitious individual (like me) propelled by self-zeal to perform and deliver his/her best looks forward to recognition of his/her labor and contribution upon achievement of the target. Some such expectation did catch our fancy upon reaching the fruition stage now and we were happy that the task assigned to the team had been completed well and in time. My reward was the development and successful completion of the computerization project for Sales Accounts. It was my golden moment. My un-relenting and untiring efforts of many years had borne fruit. The long spell of my silent hard work of about 8 years (1973 to 1981) was, un-doubtedly a landmark phase of my career; a performance achieved at the cost of my own and family's neglect. The zeal to deliver the best and usher in a system of its kind, a system that on its successful implementation was to bring glory not only to the team but also to BSL as a corporate entity, was there for everyone to see and appreciate. We, my friends in EDP and I, had done it in spite of umpteen hurdles on the way. Our strength was team's single-minded pursuit of our common goal; to create an integrated system par-excellence. None of us had any individual agenda. It was a miracle that each one of us was deeply motivated. I am conscious His Benevolence was around!! And to cap it all, the change of team's leader mid-way, had had no impact. Mr. Jain had quit BSL and joined BHEL Corporate Office in New Delhi and in-came L. Rajen Babu, a young Systems and Programming Expert from within BSL. God's Mercy for the system that this gentle-man was equally if not more keen about the success of the project!! A new vision, a new strength and the team kept up its efforts without any rumblings.

The next phase of the project, namely development of computerized sales accounting system, was equally challenging. The team got going enthusiastically on this system under the able leadership of new leader, L Rajen Babu. Team members long, personal and healthy association had helped create an environment of camaraderie and synergy amongst the members. And it reflected not only in office but also gave fillip to warm social relations between the families.

Chapter 19
My Glorious Moments in BSL

The fruits of my achievement in Sales Accounts section were very well reflected in senior managers' favorable bias for me. As per policy in vogue, the officers at our level were shifted after every 3 years' stay in a section. It was a routine that was religiously followed every year in May/June. And every year my name would be at the top of the list but no action would be taken; reason being the reluctance of my current senior manager to let me go. The refrain "He is needed there; he cannot be spared yet in office's interest. I shall not take a position to the disadvantage of smooth working of such an important section." And the matter would rest there. But truly speaking, apart from office's interest which was a genuine concern, this was also a ploy to keep themselves free of anxieties about this section. They were aware that this man was taking adequate pains, was handling the critical job of computerization well, was putting in sincere efforts and running such an important section to their entire satisfaction. And no hassles or problems were coming up for them to handle. They knew, the computerized system was critical for section's smooth functioning as also for a sound financial health of the Co. And dislocation of the key figure could mean problems of accountability if the successor was not competent enough to handle the job well. Thus, I continued in Sales Accounts for almost 9 years.

Me, an object of jealousy?

This situation made me an object of jealousy for many of my colleagues who were keen to enter Sales Accounts for their own reasons. And I became the 'bête noire' of many eyes. A particular group in Accounts Dept. with a regional bias remained always active to uproot me from there. Believe me; I neither paid any attention to this nuisance nor confronted anybody. "Let them do what they feel is right. Why should I divert my attention to an issue which is a non-issue as far as I am concerned? Happily, I will go when management decides." At the bottom of this attitude was the satisfaction that my beloved system had entered a stage of no return and surely, a person of an average capability would also be able to handle it. In any case, other officers in the section and the old experienced staff were Sales Accounts section's real strength. Now, I was happily ready to get detached. The baby had grown up now. Its canine teeth were strong enough to face any challenge.

With a heavy heart, I bid adieu to my beloved section in June, 1981 and took charge of Operations Accounts which was also under Mr. R Jambunathan, my boss. He consulted me before he agreed to this change.

The big temptation I overcame

An amusing happening (amusing to me but not actually) occurred soon after I assumed charge of this section. One fine morning, a person (not advisable to disclose his name) came to meet me at my residence. I was aware that he was running a small eatery in the neighborhood market offering south Indian fare. Therefore, his coming to my house was surprising. But all the same, I invited him in and asked him for the purpose of his visit. He informed that he was working as a contractor in maintenance wing of a zone and had submitted his bid. He was desperate to get that job, at any cost, because his labor force of about 20 persons was idle. Offering to me the brief-case that he had brought with him, he mentioned, "Sir, this is 2 %. This is as per past practice. I am willing to do more, if you so desire, but this work must be allotted to me." After seeing the tender papers which were in his hands, I recalled that a final decision to award this work to this gentleman had already been taken last evening since his offer was the lowest and I had also signed the final minutes of the tender committee meeting. Nothing more was required to be done now. The work was going to be allotted to him in the normal course and no out of way favor was required to be done to help him.

If I wished, I could have retained the money which, as per his explanation of 2 % should have been about rupees sixty six thousand. This was substantial amount considering the inflation rate and the salary structures of those days. I politely declined his offer and gave the brief case back to him. That was the first and the last time that any contractor made any such offer to me. The word spread in the contractors' fraternity, 'This man is different. 'I was happy I had done a courageous act. I have always believed; the ill-gotten money surely spoils the future generations.

A chronicle of some thrilling moments for me

Mr. A Ramchandra Rao, joined BSL as its GM (F&A), sometimes in 1973, on transfer from Durgapur Steel Plant. He was known to be well-versed with the working of Sales Accounts. One afternoon, he walked into my room and politely said, "How are you, Mr. Aneja." Seeing him there, I was flabbergasted. "Sir, I am honored but you should have sent for me." I have come to see your work-place, meet your staff and have a look at some of the records. He asked me what checks and controls I was exercising on critical documents like RRs, Test Certificates and Dispatch Advices. We explained to him the details and also showed our control registers etc. Believe me; he was more than 100% satisfied, hugged me and promised to shift my section to a more suitable exclusive-type rooms rather than being located in one part of a big hall. "Complete security of documents in your section has wider bearings for revenue generation and its proper accounting." That was a big compliment for us though our section was at a nascent stage then. And from then on I was asked to attend periodical meetings of Sectional Heads though I had an officer of the rank of ACA (E4) as my boss and I was still at junior most level (E1).

Sometimes in early 1973, Mrs. Aneja was admitted and operated upon in BSL's Main Hospital. Even after a reasonable period, her wound was not healing and she got fever also. My repeated meetings and requests with the Doctor concerned didn't have much impact. Rather, her condition was deteriorating. I rushed to Mr. BG Joshi, our DCA and explained my problem. Immediately, he contacted the Chief Medical Officer and asked him to summon the doctor concerned and also visit the patient himself. Thereafter, he went with me to the Hospital in his car and on reaching there we found Mrs. Aneja had been shifted to the Operation Theatre. God's Mercy, she was saved.

In 1975, I along with my batch-mates was due for promotion to next level as per the policy in vogue. Though we were anxious about it but none of us raised it with our seniors. And suddenly one day the news came that orders had been issued. Before I could convey this news to my staff, PA to GM (F&A) told me to come. Reaching in our Sir's chamber I was taken aback. Sweets were there on his table and he offered them to me, hugged me and conveyed his blessings. Over-whelmed by this lavish spread of sweets and love, I ran out; my eyes flooded with tears of joy.

Well another incident that choked me with emotions occurred in 1975. One afternoon, the PA asked me to come and meet the GM. It was hot sultry mid-day of June when mercury was at its glorious peak. Seeing me in his chamber, Mr. Rao, my GM, called his PA in and shouted at him, "Do you know where his office is? I will tell you, it is ½ a mile away from Main Admn. Building. How pathetic, you made him walk in blistering mid-day sun. Don't ever call him here. Connect him to me on phone unless I give specific instructions to the contrary."

As per promotion policy, our batch was due for promotion as Dy. Managers in 1978. However, due to certain critical reasons, not concerned with us, our promotion was getting delayed. Our

GM and other senior managers were keen about it but helpless. Therefore, we the concerned officers sought a meeting, met the MD and received from him a positive assurance. It was decided to create the required number of positions in the cadre. However, at this stage, there was an in-advertant faux-pass and I got left out of the promotion list. When I went to meet my GM to convey my anguish, he was profusely apologetic. It was he who was responsible for wrong assumptions about promotion policy which led to my exclusion from the list of promotees. He repeated his regrets many times but there was no going back on it. Going to MD again was not possible. A few days later, our Chief met us in Officers' Club and it was pathetic to see him seeking forgiveness of Mrs. Aneja for this omission.

Every year on teachers' day (5th Sept.), few meritorious teachers were given awards based on the recommendations of a joint committee of two officers of Education Dept. and one officer from some other Dept. But every year, there would be protests blaming the committee for its allegedly biased and unfair recommendations. It would turn out to be an embarrassment for the Management. Rather than creating goodwill, the awards would result in bitter criticism. To bring fairness and objectivity into play in the process of selection, the Management decided to include an impartial member into the committee. The criterion was, (i) he should be an outsider i.e. not from the state of Bihar, (ii) should be from F&A Dept. and (iii) none of his children should be in BSL's own schools. And my Dept.'s choice zeroed in on me. In selection committee's meeting next year, the members (those from Education Dept. and natives of the state), frankly told me a story which ran like this, "In Bihar, when it comes to distributing favors, the order of priorities is (i) your own kith and kin if available followed by (ii) somebody from your own caste (iii) or somebody from your village and (iv) last of all somebody from your own district. And our foresight doesn't go beyond this. Therefore, this year the entire burden of selecting candidates is on your shoulders. Tell us the criteria you want to follow and we will help you in getting the inputs." The committee evolved a criterion for selection, got it approved from the Head of Dept., worked on it objectively and made the recommendations. Happily, this year there were no murmurs or protests.

A poignant episode that moved me deeply at the time of my leaving BSL for joining in ONGC in May/June, 1982, amply reflects the then GM(F&A), Mr. Ghosh's soft belly for persons like me, notwithstanding his apparent harsh exterior. After getting the offer of appointment from ONGC, I went to meet him next morning. Sitting opposite to him I conveyed the news to him. He got up from his seat, called me to his side, grabbed me and hugged me, patted my back for few minutes before he uttered compliments and congratulated me. For few minutes, I was in a different world. His PA was surprised to see his Boss showering love and affection on somebody for what he had seen and known so far was contrary to all this.

The service rules stipulated that I serve three months' severance notice or pay an amount equal to my three months' salary in lieu thereof. However, I couldn't delay my departure for so long because of the start of schools' new sessions in June/July. I was not inclined to pay for the notice period for obvious reasons. Mr. Ghosh immediately called the Senior Manager (HR) who informed that MD could waive the stipulated condition. "You make preparations for departure in June itself. I'll talk to MD and obtain his approval", he told me. And it was done. I was in ONGC, Dehra Dun on 30th June to be within the deadline.

In the cinema theatre in Officers' Club, two cane chairs were always kept vacant in the middle row. They were meant for MD and his Spouse. When and if they came, they would be seated there. One evening, we happened to occupy the bench adjacent to these chairs. After sometime, the MD and his wife came and sat there. During intermission, I introduced myself to him. And lo! His response was extremely flattering. "I have seen you on files. You are doing very well. Keep it up. I am happy I saw you today."

Sales Accounts section gave me professional competence

In Sales Accounts section of any commercial business organization, two functions are critical for organization's fiscal health; (i) preparing and presenting bills/invoices to the customers at the earliest to expect to get the dues in time and (ii) to keep a tab on defaulting customers through an efficient system of analysis of sundry debtors and follow up at speed. We in Sales Accounts met these targets efficiently thanks to dedicated team work and an efficient and user-friendly computerized system.

Starting with about 35 invoices/day in the beginning in 1972, we reached a tally of 350/400 invoices/day after the commissioning of Rolling Mills. Notwithstanding such a heavy load, our invoicing team made sure that all dispatches are accounted for and invoices raised and pushed out within 24 hours. As for realization of dues in time, the system of presenting documents through customer's bank helped in realization of dues from most of the customers in time except the Govt. depts. to which the documents were presented directly. The realization of dues from govt. entities was always a matter of concern. We persisted and followed up the matter with the concerned entities regularly through correspondence and set up a team exclusively for follow up through personal visits.

To conclude; it is appropriate to say that the rigorous efforts made in the first 8 ½ -9 years that I spent in Sales Accounts which were devoted to creating/setting up of a model monolith; the integrated computerized system of invoicing and accounting and keeping our team well-motivated and enthusiastic about their jobs brought our section to glory. By introducing schemes of incentives to keep staff motivated as also personal attention by the officers we could achieve what was difficult, to say the least.

A very efficient use of technology and dedicated team work did the trick, as they say.

Krishan Aneja

Thanks Sales Accounts; you gave me the thrills of personal development

Sales Accounts in BSL was my first major achievement in Public Sector. To a person who was shy by nature, not given to sticking his neck out easily and taking the lead, was hesitant to communicate well in formal groups like official gatherings/meetings, was neither highly educated nor exposed to any formal training etc., the posting in this section turned out for him to be a boon, rather God's Gift. It gave him not only unparalleled job satisfaction but also enabled him to hone his skills at team-building and learn to concentrate on the core activity without neglecting the daily routine work. The varied assignments I handled during the development stage of this section not only put a great responsibility on my shoulders but also forced me to be innovative and give my best along with my team of officers and staff. The long spell of about 9 years was instrumental in my personal growth also along with that of the section. We were continuously under focus alright but the involvement of seniors at every crucial stage of computerized system's development was a big morale booster. There was full freedom of planning, action and execution. There was no interference from the top except when we sought it. We were free to organize symposiums, hold meetings, visit other steel plants for help when felt necessary. But let's not confuse freedom with license to do what we pleased. The freedom entailed great responsibility for there was no space for excuses in such an environment.

The quid-pro-quo for freedom in official parlance; "the fruits of freedom are onerous liability and heavy responsibility; you are bound to deliver to the satisfaction of seniors or be ready to face consequences."

Because of necessity and also out of feeling of sort of gratitude for my whole-hearted devotion to the seamless growth of the section, none of my seniors was ever willing to release me from the section though there were objections for violation of the principle of rotation in job for officers. In July, 1972, when I started this section, we were in all three persons; myself, one staff member and one Steno and when I left it in 1981, there were five officers and about forty-five members of the staff. The entire

248

work of the section had been computerized and Invoicing Wing of the section was working in three shifts of 8 hours each, a sort of first of its kind in any office's history. Even no other steel plant could do it. The miracle of shift-working was achieved thanks to successful culmination of a settlement with the staff unions. Who did it or how it happened, is not important but what is rewarding is that it happened and it set in motion an era of understanding between the employees and the management.

Chapter 20
A scintillating and memorable rendezvous of wits in our Accounts Deptt

The busy work schedules hardly gave me any respite except on Saturdays when the office was closed for staff in the afternoon but open for Officers. We would join in a free-lance huddle in some senior officer's chamber when exchange of sarcastic wits, humorous notes, some light couplets and jokes etc. would flow freely in the closed environs of the room along with rounds of tea/coffee and snacks. It was Mr. Srivastava, the brilliant officer in charge of the key section of Central Accounts who would welcome all of us for this unique and unparalleled gathering. Each one of us waited anxiously for this miraculously happy conclave wherein a few selected personal friends of Mr. Srivastava from other depts. also used to join. Listening to bouts of witty exchanges and scintillating deliveries in this gathering meant washing off of tensions and stresses of the week and you would be ready to face the coming new week with a light mood. It was an entertainment par excellence; thrilling, healthy, above-board and non-personal. Mr. Jauhri, Company Secretary, was a regular visitor and he was one of the main contributors with his trendy one-liners and any endeavor/attempt to counter him meant inviting trouble. He out-witted most of others except Mr. Srivastava himself and Mr. RG Singh, both of whom would often join hands to outwit Mr. Jauhri.

Believe me, the excitement in my mind while recalling this extravaganza is palpable as if I am re-living it. I am thrilled to the brim while narrating it and trying to present it in its true colors. The whole scenario is oozing out with its sweet lingering memories. In my entire work life I have not had any chance to witness such an enjoyable feat either before or after it. God's Praise be to those who made it happen!

The collegium of open-minded competent Managers in F&A Dept. of BSL

It can be said proudly that inter-personal relations between officers in F&A dept. were absolutely healthy. The entire credit for such a clean environment rested mainly with few seniors, namely Mr. SC Gupta, the ACA, Mr. GS Grewal and Mr. Srivastava, Senior Accounts Officers who occupied a prominent position and were the leading stalwarts in the dept. Mr. Gupta was extremely helpful by nature and his personal rapport with each new comer like us was a source of big relief. He would always encourage other officers to feel free with regard to official as well as personal issues. There was an acute shortage of accommodation when we joined duty but he pursued vigorously with Town Administration dept. and got allotted to us hostel accommodation as a stop-gap arrangement. In personal matters too, he was of a liberal disposition. Bringing all the new appointees to a social get together for tea and a game of cards was a routine for him. There was no air of superiority in his approach and dealings. Such a bon-homie amongst officers of F&A Dept. was a source of envy to many other depts. To be fair, I must confess, I didn't witness such a clean and healthy environment at any work-place during my long spell of work-life. We enjoyed it the most since it made us free to devote single-mindedly to our jobs. Being mentally free was a unique help in giving our best to the Organization.

Mr. BG Joshi, Deputy Controller of Accounts; an inspiring leader

Thanks to this computerization project, which was not only prestigious but also very essential for smooth functioning of Sales Accounts section, I got opportunities to get closer to him. Based on the feedback he was getting, he was happy that I was handling it well with fore-sight and competence. One after-noon I went to him for explaining to him my problem of not getting support from a section in the Plant at the instance of a very senior officer in the Plant. He assured me of his support and to relieve me of the tension, he sat down for a chat with me. Alluding to the computerization project, he quipped, "A Math student only can do justice to such a complex assignment requiring analytical skills and a long-term vision." And when I told him I was a Commerce student, he exclaimed, "I can't believe it. Aneja, you are giving me a shock of my life" And the reason for this comment was that he was a great lover and an enthusiast of Math and believed that a scientific brain with analysing skills only could handle such a complex and vast computerization project.

My gratitude and thanks where they are due the most

Through this attempt at memorabilia of recalling the golden period in my work life in BSL, I wish to place on record and convey my sincere gratitude to all those who made it possible; my senior officers, my colleagues and staff in Sales Accounts, my able and committed associates in EDP and Plant and yes, top of all, my family who patiently endured my absence and the neglect, especially my life-partner Mrs. Aneja, who tolerated me and my erratic responses at times. She handsomely made up for kids what I was expected to do; a loving and caressing attention which was their due.

Bravo! 'Salam' to all of them!!

Chapter 21
BS City; a charming well-planned & executed township

Our stay of ten years in BS City was a wonderful experience for all. The ten years spent in BS City during the prime of life in the well-planned township with all the facilities well-provided there brings back the sweet lingering memories that are ensconced deep in our inner-self. It was the most happening phase for the entire family indeed; I was fresh with the dose of excitement on having entered the executive cadre and both of us (I and Mrs. Aneja) were happily looking forward to a new chapter of good days ahead for the family. It was a fateful turn for the better in family's fortunes. These 10 years gave to the family more than what seemed apparent and within our reach; all-round growth of children, eventful work-life for me and a richly happy carefree social life for all of us. It generated a refreshing sense of total fulfilment what with still more bright future on the horizon. A sense of upbeat feeling to put in our best and keep pushing ahead happily in the right direction had taken deep roots. This phase can easily be described as the foundation, solid and deep, on which each member of the family later built up his/her own magnificent edifice. This crucial decade still rings bells of happiness in the ears of each member of the family. Ask any one of the family even today about Bokaro and the response would be uniform: it was the most memorable golden period replete with 100 % satisfaction.

It was a phase, which each one would want to grasp and re-live, if possible. I know, I wouldn't be able to do full justice to the narration (which I am attempting now) about this phase; a phase that spurred our hopes and aspirations, boosted our spirits, let us live freely and merrily, gave new meaning to the charm of openness in approaching life, indulge in the pleasures of happy social life and be happy in spite of some problems, big, small and petty, off and on, here and there.

Huge infrastructure and facilities provided in BS City

The prime consideration that seemed to have weighed with the authorities to locate the steel plant at Bokaro was availability of huge reserves of coking-coal and iron-ore in its vicinity and freely available land for the plant and the township. Accordingly, the Detailed Project Report (DPR) of Bokaro Steel Plant did include a separate detailed plan for an integrated township apart from the infrastructure for the plant. Considering the size of planned work-force, the proposed township's lay-out was huge. It was divided into separate sectors for:- (i) living quarters with each sector supported by neighbourhood shopping complex, schools, play grounds, parks, well-laid roads and adjacent walk-ways, (ii) a separate sector for schools and colleges (iii) a big fully developed 'City Park' located near the main highway in the town, (iv) Hindi medium High Schools and Middle Schools managed and funded by Education Dept. of BSL, separately in each sector (v) an OPD Dispensary in each sector and a centrally located Main Hospital of 600 beds capacity, and (vi) a City Centre comprising of a major shopping area and Cinema Theatres etc.

All these facilities were planned to come up in a phased manner in tune with the growth of the Plant and growth in number of employees. In the interim period, the nearby town 'Chas' was developing fast to cater to the shopping needs of the residents. BS City being the private township of BSL, there was no interference of Govt. authorities. BSL's Town Administration dept. was responsible for its upkeep, maintenance, cleanliness, hygiene and development. In fact, this TA dept. was a sort of local municipal authority for the township. And it was a nodal agency for co-ordination with local civil authorities for maintaining law and order and ensuring safety and security of the residents and house-holds.

A meaningful effort by Town Administration
to hold the price-line

Keeping a vigilant eye and ensuring reasonable price levels of essential commodities like vegetables and fruits, grocery, milk and milk products and poultry products was one of TA's crucial responsibilities amongst others. A time-tested approach was adopted by the dept. to keep under check high price level of these items. Weekly 'Haat', a sort of Farmers' Market, on Sundays was the answer, in which villagers from nearby areas, whole-sale traders and vendors would bring and sell their produce/goods without the involvement of middle-men. Naturally, therefore, their rates were rock-bottom and this was a big relief for the residents. The vegetables/fruits/poultry would be fresh and people would buy the items in bulk and store them at home for the week. We, the north Indians had a special advantage as far as fruits are concerned. Since we were the major consumers, the vendors would happily open up fresh boxes for us and allow us to pick the pieces/bunches of our choice. It was indeed a great advantage and we were able to get good bargains along with the benefit of choice.

On the whole, the town was a nice, fully integrated habitat and its infrastructure and facilities fully met the basic needs of the residents.

High-end English-medium public schools in BS City

A long term policy initiative of BSL's management helped in setting up of English-medium schools by known and well established trusts/societies of long standing. Broad contours of the policy were two-fold; provide land on lease at a nominal rent and give a fixed amount as subsidy for creating the infrastructure with a rider that fee-structure would be fixed appropriately in consultation with BSL Management. In hind-sight, I believe, it was not only a virtue but also a necessity to attract well-known and established bodies to open a branch in BS City. This benevolent policy initiative helped to create the environment of trust ensuring availability of reputed schools in BS City. It was a big attraction by itself; it assured persons like me to know that the basic requirement of children's education was not a concern.

The outcome of the brilliant policy initiative was on expected lines. Well-established English-medium schools of long standing came forward from all over the country to establish their schools in BS City. The first major school to start classes was St. Xavier's and over a period of time many others like Holy Child, Chinmaya Mission, DAV, Kendriya Vidyalaya, to name a few, opened their branches.

This initiative proved to be a boon for the parents and their children. This facility was not only economical but also avoided the need to keep children in far off places in hostels. These schools vied with each other for maintaining high standards of education, co-curricular activities and sports. Therefore, it is not surprising that children of BS City, even now, have an edge in securing admissions in colleges of high standing, IITs, IIMs, Medical Colleges and other professional programs. Throughout our long stay of ten years in BSL, children's education never bothered us. Thanks to good schools and a healthy competitive environment, our children were a happy lot and performed very well then and afterwards.

The policy makers of those days were probably a different breed; far-sighted, visionaries, honest to the core, clear-headed and fully committed to the broad social-objectives of far-reaching implications. Such initiatives not only reflected the concern of policy makers to look after the welfare of the employees and their families but also served a broader social objective of far-reaching consequences for the good of the country; encourage development of human-resources of high calibre on merit. But for the policy decision of providing land and subsidy, no institution of repute would have ventured to start a school in an isolated place like BS City in the tribal belt. And the implications were obvious; without proper facility of children's education, BSL couldn't have attracted the talent it actually did. I for myself can vouchsafe that I would have declined the offer even though it was a great breakthrough for me.

Cosmopolitan composition of Officers' Cadre

The work force at officers' level was cosmopolitan in character with inductions having been done on the basis of an open all India selection process. There was no regional bias. This made work life free of avoidable bickering in the Plant and in Office and this happy trend percolated down to community life as well. One had to see its charm unfolding in the Officers Club where families not only enjoyed the movies and other facilities available there but also built up social equations irrespective of any inhibiting consideration.

Bokaro Kala Kendra, the apex cultural organization

Another important factor for healthy congenial social scene was comfortable cultural kinship amongst people. The Bokaro Kala Kendra set up by the Management served as an apex body for promoting cultural and socio-religious activities under its aegis. The Kendra built up a huge complex where apart from a centrally air-conditioned Auditorium with full facilities, there were separate mini-halls/rooms etc. for different cultural associations to enable them to hold meetings and conduct practice sessions. With the setting up of BKK, various ethnic, linguistic and cultural and social organizations received a boost. In turn, this brought people together, gave fillip to their urge for creative and cultural activities of their choice and liking. The Kendra also used to organize an annual festival of inter-association competitive presentations where each group would participate, earn accolades of the art lovers and also win awards. The result was super cultural fusion and free exchanges amongst people of different states of the country.

Management's positive role in enriching cultural environment

A thoughtful action by the Management to organize rich traditional cultural events to celebrate the commissioning of major units of production in the plant added charm to the festivities. Leading artistes of performing arts were invited to perform on such occasions. These shows were a feast for hungry souls of art lovers. It was our good fortune that thanks to discerning choice of organizers, we had the privilege of watching dance recitals of legendry Sitara Devi, Sonal Man Singh, Raja Radha Reddy, Birjoo Maharaj and many more artists of repute of Bharat Natyam and Mohini Attam (Sorry for the slippage of names in my mind). The Music concerts included performance by legendry Ravi Shankar (Sitar), Amjad Ali Khan (Sarod), Jagjit Singh, Pankaj Udhas, Runa Laila (Light Music), Ruma Thakurta Guha (Kishore Kumar's first wife) and many more legends. I must confess we neither had any such mesmerizing opportunity either before or after we left BS City. Our good luck that in a short spell of ten years we savored such memorable events one after the other almost every year. Let it not be understood that hereafter we didn't have any such opportunity. What distinguished the spell in BS City was the regularity of the shows and convenience of enjoying the shows in the exclusive environs of our Officers' Club/Russian Club. And for mass entertainment of general public, Qawwali, Mushaira and Kavi Sammelan etc. were organized in the Community Centre in the township.

Healthy Contribution of socio-religious groups of the town

Apart from the cultural endeavors of identity-based cultural groups, some social groups associated with states/regions used to organize socio-religious events like 'Jhankies' of Krishna Leela on Janmashtami festival, Dussehra celebrations including 'Rama-Ravan' yudh, burning of effigies of demon king and his kin/associates followed by a massive show of fireworks. Durga Pooja festivities including cultural shows and magnificent Pandals dotted each important location of the town. Public functions on the occasion of Kali Pooja, illuminations and fire-works on Deepawali festival and 'Kavi Sammelan' on Sarawati Pooja day were held regularly. In short, such a varied and vast social milieu/canvas was a big contributor in developing harmonious environment amongst the fraternity.

Identity based social groups' role in enriching social life

'Mil-vartan' was the name of social group set up by people of Punjabi origin. As the name suggested, its members believed in and practiced 'sharing together' concept. The group used to organize picnics/outings for families, celebrate functions of Punjabi flavor like 'Lohri', 'Baisakhi',

'Guru Nanak's Birthday' in appropriate formats. The member families would join in these celebrations enthusiastically when the children would be exposed to native religious/cultural ethos and women would feel free to communicate with each other in Punjabi language. Such groupings built up satisfaction among members of being supported closely by their own people. A thread of closeness; trustworthy and dependable, seemed to bind them together. Away from their homes and blood relations, the members felt they were not alone and were part of a big family.

Our well-knit social circle that sustained us

Apart from such identity-based social groups, we developed kinship with some other residents at individual level for varied reasons; families of children's class-mates, own colleagues and their families, neighbourhood friends, acquaintances acquired in club etc. and later developed into friendship and other occasional inter-action groups etc. Indeed, this phase of our stay in BS City was such when there is natural urge in young couples like us with growing children and away from own relations, to want to have friends around. And it is mutual between similarly placed people to look for the comfort of sharing and enjoying happy moments in each other's company. While on the one hand, these gatherings would let the children and women feel free, participate in the programs/get-togethers on birth days, social events and festivals etc., the men-folk indulged in their own favourite pastimes.

Those were the days, when it was indeed a pleasure for women to prepare and serve a variety of their best home-made food, snacks and beverages. They eagerly looked forward to comments of praise and appreciation of their culinary skills. And who would not want to be complimented, "Bhabiji, this is the best 'Dahi-Bada' or cake I have ever had in my life." In addition, the pleasure of sharing/exchanging recipe with their friends would keep them happily engrossed for hours. The best part is that the women would not complain of fatigue after hosting such an event. On such occasions, it was normal for ladies to pool their talent, provide physical support to each other and help in service when the function was on and after it also. Having done it, they would feel happy. I wonder; why the ladies of our times were not scared of organizing and hosting such meets. Probably, the nostalgia that lingered on for weeks after successful hosting of such marathon events was compensation par excellence. And the additional charm would be a whisper, "when can we have a repeat session, please?" The sweet memories of this wonderful phase in our life are so fresh that I am feeling as if we are in the midst of it. Compared to what I see today in youngsters/couples' gatherings, the era gone bye was a superlative phase of high class social life. Self-interest did weigh with individuals but it was not pre-dominant.

A well-knit, very intimate small informal group of friends

Our informal circle of close friends too was big. It got built up over a period of time and many factors contributed to its birth/existence. In this group, it was normal to pay visits or receive friends unannounced on weekends or on working days even. There need not be any specific occasion for such visits. Your child or wife may have something to talk about; some problem in home-work or some recipe or some similar other small or non-issue. No problems, just walk in, have chat, relax and come back chattering after a cup of tea. In any case, when you have reached such a stage in inter-personal equation, the formality of fixing prior appointments does not matter. Such a closeness and freedom is really rare but we were lucky, we had it and we loved it. Informal groups in our times were afflicted with this malaise, so to say. Such groups were a wonderful addiction; you loved to indulge in it.

Officers' Club; the jewel of BS City

Considering all aspects, this key entity can be said to have weaved the fabric of social integration and served as a genuine abode offering entertainment, relaxation, happiness, peace of mind and satisfaction all under one roof. Officers' Club was a sort of an oasis in the desert of lonely habitation, BS City. It had facilities and infrastructure necessary for it to render service to the members. While the building, equipment and other facilities were provided by the Company, its management was in the hands of an executive committee whose members, President and other office bearers were elected by the members through an open process. The nearest town of some significance was Ranchi but reaching there, if at all somebody ventured, was a nightmarish experience of sorts. Therefore, the club had a unique position in social circuits of the town. A major attraction for almost everybody were the movies (Hindi and English) which were screened regularly in Club's open theatre of about 3000 capacity. People would enjoy the movies and also avail the occasion to come closer to each other. Other facilities in the Club like Swimming Pool, Library and Reading Room, Cards lounge, Bar and Eateries and facilities for indoor and outdoor games were the hang-out points where people would create their exclusive domains along with enjoying the facilities.

New Year Eve celebrations in the club

The most keenly awaited function in the Club used to be New Year eve's celebrations preparation for which would start in early December itself. A massive build-up of stop-gap auditorium, huge stage, dance floor, lighting and seating arrangement for about 10,000 people, public-address system and decorating the venue used to take about four weeks. A separate enclosure was earmarked for Eateries to cater to the taste-buds with variety of snacks, beverages and food. There used to be plenty of variety entertainment programs but the real attraction would be the dance floor. The youngsters would merrily dance in high spirits to the sounds of drum-beats, bands and solo/group performers on the stage and wouldn't want to vacate the floor for elders to let them dance and jostle to the slow numbers of yester-years. (There were no DJs then.)The function would start at 8 pm and continue late till past midnight or rather early next morning. Starting with light entertainment programs and followed by programs of invited professional artists; singers, dance troupes and solo performers, the evening would reach its zenith at zero hour when lights would be switched off for two minutes and people greeted each other in whatever manner they liked.

It used to take lot of efforts for the organizers and security staff to control the mobs of enthusiasts who would be too keen to jump on to the stage and indulge in revelries. One can appreciate this frenzy more when told that the huge stocks of liquor would exhaust well before midnight and one would hear people running to market or homes to fetch some more of it. Just not to miss such an elegant entertainment program, people used to delay/postpone their winter vacations.

My idea, in brief, of what a Club ought to be

Our Club was what a club ought to be; a facilitator for people to come together, socialize and relax in its precincts while enjoying their favorite choices; movies/games/sports/ avocations of sorts. It was a place for pampering yourself freely with the hobbies of your choice like borrowing books, reading newspapers/magazines, playing cards, relaxing in the Bar and enjoying a drink, listening to soulful numbers and watching light professional entertainment programs. Above all; an institution loved by all and a place where each member of the family could have choice to indulge in his/her favourite activity either together or separately. Our club fully met this criterion. The club was always full of life and people of all age groups looked forward to going there in the evenings, whenever convenient. If nothing else, just move around, rewind down the memory lane with friends, enter the cinema theatre when you feel like and come out when getting bored, go to the "Panwala" and have the pleasure of picking up a 'Pan' of your choice or a cigarette or go to reading room and relax. Well, this was my way of getting refreshed while in the club.

An unbelievable non-bureaucratic code of conduct in Club

A few very important, un-written but meaningful traditions in the club were, "(i) No talk about office or Plant and (ii) no formal salutation to the seniors when in club." and people loved to adhere to these codes of conduct. The only time there was a violation of the code would be an announcement on the PA system advising a Doctor about an emergency in the hospital or an Engineer about some breakdown in the Plant.

The message was loud and clear, "All members are equal in club." The GM (Works), Mr. Mehta, was fond of movies but he would be late, usually. It was a fun and pity both, watching him struggling for 3/4 seats vacant and together for the family to be seated together. The code of conduct wouldn't allow any junior officer to vacate own seats or help him. It was left to the Manager of the club to help the family. Many a times I was left wondering, "Is it same Mr. Mehta who was synonymous for shivers in his review meetings?"

Chapter 22
BSL; the cradle of professional work ethics

BSL's core strengths for effective management control

Apart from the well-thought out policy decisions for employees, BSL, a monolith of a company, had the advantage of having in place well-defined and well-scripted procedures, codes and manuals for regulating its business of running the company in a most professional way. The procedures for selection of vendors and placing final orders for supply of materials, equipment, services and award of contracts for construction, erection and commissioning of various units in the plant were in place duly codified and approved by the Board. The Book of Delegated powers was elaborate and unambiguous to enable functionaries at different levels to take decisions within the frame-work of policy paradigm. The role of various depts.' representatives in the collective decision making process of Tender Committees was clearly defined. In nut-shell, the entire policy frame-work was focused on one thing; help the functionaries in quick decision making. Apart from the written words in the manuals and codes, the informal working processes too were biased towards speed in decision making and were intended to help avoid conflicts in the committees e.g. the presenting officer in a tender committee was required to fill in the basic information like tender no., quantities, items to be supplied and other details of the tender document in the prescribed format before the committee. And when after due deliberations the committee arrived at a decision, the presiding officer of the committee would dictate committee's

264

final decision to his stenographer in the presence of other members and members of the committee would disperse only after signing the minutes of the meeting. The un-written understanding/instructions for committee members were clear; deliberate till a final decision is arrived at. As far as I am concerned, being in Sales Accounts from 1972 to 1981, I didn't have to participate in tender committees during this period. My association with tender committees was for about a year after I took charge of Operations Accounts section. But nonetheless it was a happy experience. The pressure, as explained above, on the members to finalize their recommendations was welcome. It gelled very well with my attitude as it reduced the opportunity for outside interference and any undue pressure on members. In fact, by not accepting the brief-case from a contractor in the first few days of my joining Operation Accounts section, a clear message 'no none-sense man 'was delivered to the contractors' community and the Management's diktat of finalizing the committees' proceedings quickly, came in handy and added to my comfort. And I was equally happy in Operations Accounts section as I was in Sales Accounts section where I didn't have to handle public dealings.

A master-stroke management style of GM (Works); his 'first thing in the morning review meeting'

For a young budding Executive like me, it was thrilling to watch our GM (Works), Mr. MF Mehta, conducting his review meetings. Luckily, I had few opportunities to attend some of these meetings as a Finance Representative. It was a scene seeing even otherwise boldest souls looking like sheep when cornered. Indeed, he was a very hard task-master but very kind-hearted too when it came to somebody facing genuine difficulties, either in work-place or personal life.

His 'first thing in the morning' tele-conference review meeting would start sharp at 8 am when a review of previous day's performance of various units of the plant would be taken up. Mr. Mehta would be his wittiest and sharpest best and the volley of his questions would pertinent on unit's performance in the last 24 hours. He would have before him the review data compiled by PPC giving salient details of performance of each unit with analysis of short-falls or losses in output, delays or major break-down, if any, in each unit. The sequence of units to be taken up for review was pre-determined and would be the same every day. And Heads of Units including Service/Maintenance Heads would be seated in their own chambers with details of their unit's performance ready to handle the salvos of the Chief. As can be expected in such review meetings, the chief would be sarcastic, shout and demand instant response for the shortfall/sudden break-down etc. No arguments or alibi would be acceptable. The meeting would take about 90 minutes after which the critical issues highlighted by the unit head(s) would be taken up for detailed review in the chamber of GM.

Balance Sheet of my performance for 10 years in BSL

Summing up my work life of ten years in BSL, I would say it was the most satisfying decade of my entire work life of about forty years. No doubt, my performance and achievements during ten years in Shimla were equally good; the only difference being my position in the office hierarchy. While in Shimla, I was at the bottom i.e. a class III employee, in BSL I was at an Executive level and was expected to take initiative and decide the course of action on my own. That's why; I believe my role in BSL was really more demanding. There were challenges, obstacles and lack of experience and guidance when I was asked to create and establish Sales Accounts section. I neglected myself, my family, and my comforts and whole-heartedly gave my best to my job. I indulged in enjoying and meeting the challenges; I received and enjoyed the patronage, love and affection of my seniors arising out of my dedication and super sincere commitment to my job and commendable performance. The words of appreciation I received from time to time boosted my morale, gave me energy and reinforced my resolve to surprise everyone every time by delivering more than what was expected. And I am happy and proud that I did it. Of-course, it became possible thanks to the whole-hearted cooperation and support of my colleagues, my staff members and the officers/engineers in EDP, and the plant without whose cooperation, Sales Accounts couldn't have achieved the position it did acquire; a fully blossoming commercial arm of the Company, an entity capable of safe-guarding the commercial interests of the company. It was known that unless the invoices were raised regularly every day in time, the cycle of realization of dues would be delayed and it would hamper the process of collection of revenue and thus adversely affecting the top-line of the Company. The computerized system that was created by us was not only original in concept but also its design and structure was unique; starting with ensuring raising of invoices with speed, it ended with establishing a MIS (Management Information system) of a wide spectrum; generating different reports for different levels of Management. The big satisfaction was that the system met its lofty objectives and in a way induced other steel plants to take a leaf out of it. In inter-plant meetings in Sales Office in Calcutta, BSL representatives were the envy of others being always ready with detailed analysis etc.

Chapter 23
Reminiscing the golden phase of
our life in BS City (1972-82)

My tale of sweet and sour plight

Upon entering the coveted Executive Cadre in BSL, I was full of enthusiasm and was keen to excel. Therefore, true to my style, I spared no efforts to outperform and earned the well-deserved appreciation of my seniors throughout these ten years. Not surprising, therefore, that the time I spent in BSL was the most happening phase in my life. It was the most exciting spell by all counts indeed. My sincere hard work and salutary contribution delivered what I wished; a smooth raise in position after every 3 years besides loads of appreciation by Management from time to time in various manifestations and hues either tacitly or openly. It was a reward worth struggling for.

Let it not be assumed that all this came my way just like that. I ignored myself almost completely during the first 5 years, couldn't give to my children in full measure what was their due, and loaded Mrs. Aneja with heavy responsibility to be my substitute in my absence. I was always conscious that being a nuclear family and being far away from our elders, I was expected to spend more time with my family. Making up for the loss of sane advice of elders and others back home was a nagging worry. And I did seriously attempt to make up for my absence in some other ways; bringing high quality general reading books/magazines which children liked the most, apart from sweets and other goodies. As soon as I would reach home, holding back the temptation of sweets and other gifts, the three of them would pounce on books/magazines to have a look on the titles and would struggle hard to pick up their favorite ones. The search and scuffle that ensued would make them busy and happy forgetting the anguish of my absence. As for Mrs. Aneja, my frequent absence meant difficult times in managing the affairs of the household; hence her serious un-happiness.

The long duty hours or my visits to outstations on official business were a critical link of my assignments. I abhorred getting late in the evenings or going out unless really necessary and would rush back as soon as the assignment was completed even if it meant travelling in discomfort without reservation or in a public transport.

On the whole, the ten years in BSL/BS City were highly satisfying and fulfilling. I would love to relive it. I know it is not going to happen but recalling it and making attempts to capture this wonderful spell now is by itself a rejuvenating experience. The incumbent ever-lasting nostalgia flowing out in the process is a big treasure of immense value. The contentment of having lived such a fulfilling life is so refreshing and blissful even today to me.

Children's happily significant grooming

Not only me, the children too had a completely fulfilling happy times during our stay in BS City. Ask any one of them even now and each one would happily describe this phase as the most cherishing. They had their own reasons; (i) they were happy being in prestigious schools, (ii) had opportunities for wholesome development, (iii) had the company of nice friends in the school, in the neighbourhood as also in our close circle of select few friends, (iv) had access to various facilities like swimming, indoor games etc. besides movies, in English and Hindi, of high standard in the Officers Club and free inter-action with friends, (v) were free to indulge in games and sports of their liking (vi) enjoyed merry making in picnics and outings in the company of near and dear ones and (vii) were getting close attention/support of parents in routine matters also. In fact, thanks to their mother, they were and even now are a pampered lot. Mrs.

Aneja wouldn't burden them with any household chores even if it was just fetchinga bread from the nearby neighbourhood outlet/kiosk. The overall environment was most conducive for their complete development. The healthy long spell of ten years in their formative years easily contributed to development of their rounded personalities.

Ten long aromatic years in BS City; bliss for children's sound growth

Sunita was 6, Sandeep was three and a half years and Ashish was just 2 when we landed in BS City. Add to this the ten years and you realize that our stay there combined childhood and adolescence for them. These formative years in BS City proved to be a bed-rock of balanced growth for them. And this reflected very well later when both Sandeep and Ashish entered in senior classes in Dehra Dun's prestigious day school; St. Joseph's Academy and Sunita got admission in Delhi's prestigious exclusive girls' college; Lady Irwin College. And when the time came for Sandeep and Ashish to seek entry into professional undergraduate programs, there was absolutely no difficulty. While Sandeep succeeded in qualifying in Indian Railways' most prestigious and country's one of the most hotly contested competitions; SCRA, Ashish was successful in qualifying the All India Competitive entrance test and got admission in prestigious and India's top ranking medical college; King George's Medical College, Lucknow. In fact, he had qualified for admission in four prestigious colleges and we had tough time deciding which ones to ignore. And icing on the cake; no capitation fee to be paid. Children's meritorious performance had done us proud. But for their personal achievements on merit, all this wouldn't have been possible. It was impossible for us to support them and pay the heavy capitation fees. The sound foundation in schools in BS City and Dehra Dun made them the really deserving proud siblings in their own right.

Children grasp the meaning of 'value for money'

It indeed was a phase of double satisfaction; we were satisfied on being able to provide them well within our means and they learnt to respond happily to the financial limitations faced by a middle-class educated

270

family aspiring to live a healthy clean life. The communication channel, though tacit, between us and them was clear; there would be no let-up from our side in making sure that you get due attention and support, but would make serious attempts to excel in studies with a view to secure admissions in professional colleges in due course on your own initiative and merit. The satisfaction for us was that they shared our concerns very well and put in sincere efforts in their studies; securing high grades and getting merit certificates apart from high ranks in their class. In a way, the principle 'value for money' got ingrained in their minds in their formative years in BS City. God's Grace, there couldn't be anything more to aspire for!

The proud mother; tale of Mrs. Aneja's happiness

The ten years in BS City were a spell of great significance for Mrs. Aneja too. It was the most creative phase in her life. She had the privilege of doing her part of our responsibility of looking after the material needs and well-being of our children during a most important phase of their life; childhood immediately followed by adolescence, the phases that had the potential to mould their future. To look after children well is a God given privilege for women. And for a woman of substance like Mrs. Aneja, it was a dream come-true. She conveyed unambiguously many a times that her first and foremost duty was towards children and that I stood no chance of getting same attention. In her wisdom and rightly so, there could be no more important and more satisfying responsibility for a mother than to (i) watch them grow happy and healthy, (ii) take good care of all their needs, (iii) feed them well and provide them with healthy nourishing food with good focus on quality and variety, (iv) help them in their home-work starting with alphabets and keep helping them at least till primary classes, if not beyond, (v) be attentive and listen to their problems, small and big, and help them overcome them, (vi) keep the channels of dialogue open to enter into healthy conversation with them, aim being to be their close and dependable confidant; the underlying idea being providing impetus to development of a rounded personality and assimilation of high and healthy values in them. For her, this was and is the most satisfying single act. She would not compromise when the matter concerned her children. No sacrifice is too big for her if it brings cheers to them. The truth is that she is like her mother who too was hysterically crazy about the well-being of her children.

A mammoth contribution made by my in-laws in our children's growth

The story of our children's healthy growth is incomplete without bringing up the sterling positive contribution made by my in-laws during this phase. Almost every year during summer vacations, the children would be in Bareilly in their Nani's place. The phrase 'Nani's place' is loaded with all that stands for freedom and even now it is commonly referred to as the most-sought after resort especially during long vacations. The affectionate care, love and close attention that they received there made them a pampered lot; enjoy variety of food of their particular choice, receive careful attention of each member of the family and in particular story telling sessions with 'Lala ji' their grand-father. It didn't matter whether the story/tale was authentic or was a fabricated one. What was important was sharing together the lighter moments and anecdotes of practical wisdom. They were intelligent enough to realize immediately that the story was not a genuine stuff or had been told earlier umpteen times but would still listen to it pretending to be attentive punctuated with a meaningful smile to let him know the reality. Poor 'Lala ji' would smile too to let them know that he agreed with them. After all, how can one remember and narrate endless number of genuine stuff day in day out? Being in his company in the evenings and indulging in all sorts of pranks or not listening to his words of caution gave them a sense of mischievous pleasure; a pleasure beyond compare. They knew his rebukes were nothing but a show only. Also, another charm for them was the company of their cousins in the town when they would be free to indulge in plays and games in their company and get opportunities to show off in any manner they liked.

Every year during summer vacations, we would board the train in First Class coupe at Dhanbad for Bareilly and thus would start children's picnic of free and boisterous merry making in the train. In a way, this used to be a grand opening for the wonderful rendezvous at Bareilly during their stay there. The pampered lot that they were would feel absolutely free there it being their maternal grand-mother's (Nani) place. They would relax all the time, follow no discipline of waking up in time in the morning or going to bed late in the night, spend as much time in the bath room as they liked, demand the food, snacks and other eatables of their choice, indulge in dangerous tricks while playing, not paying attention to words of caution and generally behaving like free birds.

The children would also receive pampering attention from their mother's brothers and sisters, Mukand, Manohar, Tilak, Sulochana, and Vijay Luxmi during their stay there. It was total freedom and happy times in the company of all. Do what you want to, play as long as possible and have fun telling tales of BS City and listening to local fantasies from all those around.

My mother-in-law, very intelligent, soft-spoken, a great listener, a true human being full of compassion, a repository of deep emotions and pure love would spare no efforts to make them happy even if it meant a lot of rigor and hard work for her and would shower her benign love in abundance. Being her eldest child's children, they had special attraction for her and she would let it be known openly even if it didn't go down well with her other grand-children. Finding time from her nerve-racking routine, she would insist they should tell stories of their achievements in studies. With pleasure, she would listen to their demands for preparing different varieties of food, would try to accommodate their choices but many a times would succeed in persuading them to agree to the normal stuff; a sort of intelligent give and take approach.

At the time of our children's departure from Bareilly after vacations were over, she would be most unhappy of all. This free and open environment of love and affection truly impacted our children. They recall all this with great fervor even now when they are together.

My tribute to a devote Indian Mother

Dear mother, thy name is synonymous with generosity, sacrifice, affectionate love, compassion and un-ending struggles for your children even till your last breath. My personal experience tells me that a loving Indian mother is destined to be blessed with real substance for her family and especially her own children. Really lucky and blessed mothers are those who are equipped with vision of substance, depth and who inspire and motivate their children to help them pick up a healthy value-system; learn to be happy, secure and confident about their present and their future. A mother's influence on her children and in shaping their future is the greatest. They internalize and imbibe what they pick up in her company. A mother's attitude to her own life is the subtle learning curve for children especially at the tender age of kids. Her role is critical because she is seen to be the provider of all their needs (Annpurna as is known in India), is closest to them and is softer in her dealings with them being blessed with higher emotional quotient. Usually, mothers are lenient, prone to forgetting and forgiving easily, do not mind overlooking the shortcomings in children, are protective by nature and pamper them with a conviction that in due course they will start shouldering their responsibilities successfully. By instinct, the mothers are compulsive defenders for their children in the belief that they are poised to make amends later when they grow. Most of them are willingly inclined to think, "Let them grow up with love. Hopefully all will be well ultimately." They do all this and more in earnest hope of seeing them grow before their eyes physically healthy, mentally mature, sober in disposition and conduct, endowed with a balanced and healthy value-system and capable of facing/overcoming the odds in life with confidence as they grow and become worldly wise. "Hope sustains life while losing hope is suicidal." The phrase in Hindi, "Asha mein hai jeevan, maran nirasha mein hai, uthhan manush jeevan ka bus abhilasha mein hai" conveys/reflects more cogently this approach of "All will be well. Let's not worry." Well, Mrs. Aneja surely is closer to this attitude for her children and has happily lived by it. I would say, "She is blessed. Our children have not belied her hopes. God's Mercy and Benevolence, they have proved worthy of her hopes and confidence in them!"

The enlightened mothers like Mrs. Aneja are blindly in love with their children and wouldn't countenance any adverse opinion about them.

They are eternally positive about their great future and live by a blissful expectation of their meritorious performance in their larger life. And to top it all, such an expectation is self-less. Children's happiness in their larger role as head of a family of their own is the greatest satisfaction for a devote mother.

A happening decade concludes leaving a trail of scintillating memories

I would say BSL/BS City was a great experience. The ten years spent there put the family on an unbelievably satisfying trajectory of growth. The initial negative feelings in our minds about insecure law and order position associated with the place and apprehensions about shortages of essentials of life soon gave way to optimism for whatever may have been true about Bihar in general was untrue for BS City. There was neither any law and order problem nor there was any scarcity of essential items. It was a secure place and necessities were generally available freely. Ofcourse the price level was high and some shortages now and then did create difficulties but this would be true of any upcoming new habitation in a remote and under-developed area coming regularly under pressure of ever-growing population. Sooner than expected, we got happily busy with our routines. The free atmosphere in office and in the town enabled each one of us to be happily busy in our pursuits. And this peaceful and congenial environment proved to be a potential contributor in our growth in future. It was here that we made a real beginning in family life and thanks to His Benevolence, we pushed ahead happily thereafter. Indeed, it was family's good luck that all that potentially matters for a happy living and growth was in place; (i) conducive environment for work life for me, (ii) potential for Mrs. Aneja to fulfil her domestic obligations without hassles and aspire simultaneously for personal growth, (iii) decent facilities for education for children, (iv)reasonably good infrastructure/ facilities for a comfortable living, (v) avenues for pushing ahead for each member in his/her respective domain and above all an overall congenial atmosphere and a vibrant social circle for a healthy and blossoming relationship.

And when time came for saying good-bye to BS City, we were sad; sad to get up-rooted and disconnect with the place we loved so much, a place that became synonymous with our growth, a place that was instrumental in shaping our lives and a place that had truly become our home. BSL gave us our future and shaped our destiny. Besides, it was painful and harsh to say good-bye to our close friends with whom we had shared closely our happy and moments of sorrow. I have no hesitation in acknowledging that every minute of the social life that we embraced in BS City was our best experience. It is to the credit of the place and our friends there that after saying good-bye to it some 30 years ago, we are still in love and emotionally attached to it so deeply. The fragrance of sweet memories of ten years in BS City is simply enchanting and is still fresh in our senses. Thanks to Lord Almighty for this wonderful gift!!
Bye-Bye, BS City, 29th June, 1982.

The soul stirring love of friends at the time of our final departure from BS City

The real magnitude, depth and spread of our social circle came to light at the time of our final departure from BS City for joining ONGC in 1982. For days together, when we were busy doing packing etc., our kitchen was virtually closed. Except for occasional tea and warming up milk etc. for children, nothing was prepared in-house. Our friends/colleagues overwhelmed us with their gestures/acts of love and support. Even on the day of our departure, tiffin-loads of food were given to us, duly packed. Hysterical sobs and wet eyes all around moved us deeply while bidding good-bye. It sank deeply in our psych, "Well this is the real treasure/ wealth earned during the last ten years."
Money does matter in life but this was an invaluable treasure; the treasure of love that was going to be ours for rest of our life. I am indebted even today to some of our friends who accompanied us to Dhanbad from where we were to board the train for Dehra Dun and helped in completing the formalities for transportation of our luggage in the same train. But for them and their efforts, we and our luggage would have been stranded at Dhanbad railway station in the midst of night with terrible consequences.

In BSL, I had accumulated in my bag a huge load of goodwill and appreciation in work life and this was my real treasure; a source of proud critical self-appreciation. Knowing about my desire to seek avenues of employment elsewhere, one of my senior colleagues for whom I had deep regards commented, "Why do you want to leave now? It is time for you to enjoy the fruits of your contribution to the Organization? Relax and be here. A great future awaits you." He was Mr. GS Grewal, a very tall person in stature as a competent Manager who not only loved his profession and job but also enjoyed the reputation of a kind-hearted individual always helpful and considerate to others.

Chapter 24

What Prompted Us To Think Of Leaving BSL?

BSL and BS City shaped entire family's life and fulfilled our dreams. Still we thought of saying good bye to both. Why? The primary consideration for such a decision was children's future.

In 1982, Sunita entered class twelve and Sandeep, Ashish were in class 7th and 6th respectively. Irrespective of family's deep bond of attachment with the place, we had no intention of settling down there. No doubt, the place had an array of plus points and they were compelling enough for a permanent settlement but let's not forget; BS City was in Bihar, a state too well known in the country for all the wrong reasons. The very idea of spending all our life in a far off and secluded place was painful, to say the least. That we will have to leave BS City at an opportune time was a settled conclusion. Apart from the sense of mental discomfort, the anxiety for children's higher education was the prime concern now. Being aware that the procedure for admission in professional colleges was skewed, it was necessary for me to look out for a job somewhere in North India. We being domiciled in Bihar for long, our children would be eligible to seek admission in colleges in Bihar only if they fail to succeed in All India open tests which were not too many. And considering the uncomfortable environment in colleges there the very thought of sending children to colleges there sent shivers down our spine. Yet another reason for thinking of getting out of BS City was the long distance from our native place and its poor connectivity.

To sum up, we believed, it was pertinent and high time that we looked seriously at options to move to a place in north India like Delhi, Chandigarh or any other big city in west UP keeping in mind children's need for proper higher education and also to plan for our post-retirement dwelling. I was already in mid-forties and a house of our own was also equally high on our radar; a real top-most priority. I earnestly started looking for options outside.

I join ONGC as a Manager

Luckily, I succeeded in early 1982 in getting selected in ONGC, Dehra Dun and that was a dream come true. In the back of my mind, I still had sweet memories of my stay there of three years in 1949-52 and the added charm was the higher position of a Manager (Joint Director as they called it in ONGC) which was on offer. The place had always attracted me and everybody in the family too shared the vision of happy days ahead. The excitement was palpable; not only in my mind but also the entire family. All our relatives and friends were happy too and felt relieved at the prospects of our getting out of Bihar. 'Welcome home' was the refrain on the lips of our dear and near ones. It touched us deeply and kept reverberating in my mind for long time to come.

Chapter 25
An overall view about ONGC

ONGC, Oil and Natural Gas Commission then, was set up in 1959 by an Act of Parliament by converting Oil and Gas Directorate of Geological Survey of India as an autonomous body; the idea being to remove the bureaucratic shackles and accelerate efforts for exploration of hydro-carbons in the country. It was the vision of the then worthy Prime Minister of India, Shri Jawahar Lal Nehru who was ably supported by the visionary Petroleum Minister, Shri Keshav Dev Malviya. At that stage, India was at a nascent stage in its efforts in Oil and Gas sector, being challenged by constraints of non-availability of high technology in this field. The act of setting up of an independent body by the Govt was loaded with high expectations. And this meant a phase of struggles and challenges for ONGC in the beginning itself.

Under the dynamic leadership of the Minister, Shri KD Malviya and full support of the Govt., ONGC entered into agreements with foreign countries, especially Romania and Soviet Union to seek technology and support for exploration. In due course, the efforts started yielding results with discovery of hydro-carbons in Cambay basin in Gujrat and Sibsagar in Assam. ONGC intensified its efforts in other prospects like Shivalik ranges in Kangra and Indo-gangetic basin in UP, Bihar and West Bengal but not with any significant discovery. In the meantime, the development drilling in Ankleshwar basin and other adjacent areas in Gujrat, and Assam helped in making a beginning in indigenous production of hydro-carbons. Exploration efforts in other basins continued but without any significant discovery.

As the good luck would have it, the seismic survey done with the help and support of Soviet Union in west coast off Mumbai indicated existence of rich hydro-carbon prospects in the area. This was followed by exploratory drilling there again with Soviet Union's help which ultimately led to discovery of huge reservoir of hydro-carbons which was later named as 'Bombay High'. This discovery changed the scene dramatically and now was the time to draw development plans for harnessing the potential of huge reservoir. Encouraged by positive outcome in western off-shore, efforts were intensified in other basins in the East Coast. With support from World Bank and other multi-lateral agencies, development of Bombay High started earnestly and oil and gas started flowing out in 1977. This altered the whole scene. ONGC was now the focus of attention globally. The exploration efforts in East Coast in KG basin also proved the existence of huge reservoir of natural gas there. ONGC continued to push ahead with intensive efforts which resulted in more discoveries and growing production of oil and gas but the baggage of bureaucratic work-culture which it inherited from its origin as a Directorate of GSI continued to afflict somewhat its work-culture.

The picture has changed for the better after ONGC's new avatar as a Corporation in 1994 though some traces of the bureaucratic approach are still visible. It is painful that as in other PSUs, operations and activities in ONGC, a heavy weight prestigious national oil co. known for its robust financial health, continues to be influenced by the system of undue control by various Govt. agencies, the top most being the Ministry of Petroleum & Natural Gas. Yes, of-late, the Govt. has brought about big changes and has given autonomy to successful PSUs like ONGC and it is showing results.

The ascendance now of young Managers, Scientists, Engineers and Technocrats to Senior Management positions in ONGC's top-management has brought about visible dynamic changes in the work culture. Management's emphasis on making greater use of technology, a professional approach to big-ticket acquisitions of oil and gas assets abroad by its highly successful subsidiary, ONGC Videsh Limited, introduction of a dynamic process of planning and introduction of the policy of Asset Management has already changed the scene for the better. I earnestly hope and wish good luck to ONGC in its endeavours for its all-round growth and great performance especially in its exploration efforts. I am proud to have served this great organization in the last lap of my work-life for twelve years. It was an opportunity for me to contribute my mite richly in my areas of responsibility. It is a matter of satisfaction that ONGC recognized my sincere efforts and rewarded me with good growth.

Chapter 26
A welcome phase begins

With dreams of a wonderful life ahead, our mind loaded with lingering sweet memories and nostalgic feelings of getting so close to our blood relatives, we arrived in Dehra Dun in mid-1982.

After arrival, we stayed in my sister's house in Railway colony for few weeks followed by some temporary make-shift arrangement in a house for few months. It was a really difficult phase but we had to accept it till a reasonable house was arranged on rent. After initial struggle, we were able to find a reasonably good living accommodation in Rajender Nagar, a very well developed locality near Tel Bhavan, my office. Life started rolling out smoothly for the family at this stage.

Our dream project, own house, starts taking a shape

We had left BS City with a vision; build a house of our own in Dehra Dun as quickly as possible. There were three important considerations, (i) we liked the city and were enthusiastic about our own house here (ii) I was already past 46 and we believed it was high time that we had a shelter of our own quickly and (iii) there was a strong possibility of myself being moved out of Dehra Dun within the next 2/3 years.

I earnestly started looking for a plot of land in a good locality but within my budget. After sometime, we were able to find a parcel of land, we thought was o.k. and the price was within our budget. The deal was done in Dec, 1982, and hectic activity started for firming up the plan, design and lay-out of the proposed house and getting the plan approved by the local civic authority. Our architect presented to the family a few lay-out plans and it took us few months to finalize one. Securing approval of the plan proved to be tricky due to lack of clarity in policies. It meant lot of delay and lot of running around in different offices before the plan was approved. Sometimes in early 1984, the construction started after 'Bhoomi Pooja', an auspicious activity for soliciting blessings of deities for the proposed habitat.

I confess, building the house proved to be much more difficult than what I had thought. It was a phase of controls, permits and shortages of critical building materials like cement and steel. Add to it my difficulty in being not able to find sufficient time being hard-pressed in office work. It was indeed a challenge of great proportions but there was no escape. Both the office and house construction were urgent and top-priority. The only option was, 'face the situation adroitly'.

I had no past experience of house construction nor fully comprehended or anticipated what was to follow. The initial preparatory work which comprised of following took a lot of time to complete:-

Fix up a good architect, competent contractors for undertaking different activities like levelling the site, digging of trenches and most critical work; civil engineering,

Secure from concerned Govt. Depts. The permits for controlled items like steel and cement,

Fix up agencies after due diligence for supply of other building materials of standard quality. Of all the required materials, finding and selecting building-quality timber was a herculean task.

Similar exercise to be done for fixing up carpenters' team, electricians, plumbers and specialist stone masons,

Make sure to find and devote own time for proper supervision, and

Make sure the availability of funds in time.

After fixing various agencies, attention shifted to arranging materials, ensuring coordination between different workers' groups, finding time for proper supervision and arranging funds. But thanks to support provided by some friends and despite all hiccups, challenges and delays the construction of the house was completed in about twelve months' time. God's Grace, we entered our house on 31st Dec, 1984.

Friends extend helping hand

The support, guidance and physical help provided by stalwarts of Dawar family, Mr. TC Dawar, IP Dawar and OP Dawar will always be remembered with gratitude by my family. Each one of them stood by me like my own people during this difficult phase and extended a helping hand for procuring very critical items like timber, electric cables and fittings etc. Mr. TC Dawar's help in arranging high quality timber logs and getting them ready for use after sawing to required sizes in his own presence was a unique kind gesture which I always admire from the core of my heart. His guidance and visits to the site during the construction phase helped me a lot. Inder was intimately involved at every stage of construction and was always too ready to extend a helping hand. He travelled with me to Delhi/Faridabad for buying electric cables and electrical fittings. The Dawar brothers are helpful by nature. The youngest of them, OP Dawar was equally helpful and would provide critical tips and suggestions at different stages including finalizing the lay out.

We get a roof of our own!

There were problems galore of varying nature during the construction phase but Thanks to His Kindness, at the end of the day, we were extremely happy. Happily, we entered our own house on 31st. December, 1984. We were now proud owners of a house we built with so much love and care. Now we had a roof of our own and that was a big satisfaction. It is no use narrating all the problems and hassles faced then. 'All is well that ends well' is what ultimately matters. Of course, it is worth mentioning that soon after this, I was posted at Jammu as Head of Finance wing in Northern Region and thanks to successful completion of this project the family continued to be in Dehra Dun comfortably and Sandeep, Ashish could complete their 10+2 program from St. Joseph's, Dehra Dun undisturbed.

Krishan Aneja

Re-union with old school buddies; a wish come true

Anybody going to a new place has some anxieties about the place, its society and concerns for adjustments and developing relationships there. Naturally, a palpable thought kept on lingering in mind that I was better placed in this respect and should be able to meet some of my old school-time friends and renew my old bonds. A wonderful opportunity came my way soon when one of my colleagues in ONGC took me along for introduction to a joint family comprising of three brothers, married and having grown-up children living under one roof. On arrival there, one of the three brothers kept on looking at me intently for some time, recognized me, brought out a group-photo and pointing his finger at a photo asked me, "Isn't it you?" He was right that was me, the group photo was our farewell photo of high school and he was Inder (IP Dawar) my old pal standing next to me. I just can't describe how happy we both were on this re-union after a gap of thirty years. This re-union paved the way for development, in due course, of very warm, intimate and genuinely deep loving relations between us.

Inder was gem of a person; a true friend indeed. A very loving, soft-natured, considerate and helpful, highly reliable and dependable and kind-hearted were his sterling attributes. He was like my own brother and the two families always looked around to meet and enjoy each other's company; occasion or no occasion. He breathed his last on 5th October, 2006. A massive cardiac arrest had snatched him away. His smiling face is ever present in my mind. Truly speaking, his going away has jolted me and has left a void.

I also have the pleasure of renewing my friendly contacts with another school-mate, Dr. VD Dang. The school-time memories of our joint struggles in coping with the studies have blossomed into a bond of close relationship between the families. The two ladies, our wives, have developed very intimate and warm bonds of friendship. Given an opportunity, the families join each other happily in family functions apart from normal social visits.

Chapter 27
Glorious phase of growth in Corporate Cadre in ONGC

As has been usual with me, I handled different job assignments with distinction in different locations, contributed my mite in bringing about improvements, where necessary and added value and speed in execution of various responsibilities. I brought about systemic changes, created and installed new computer systems and established new transparent procedures in the interest of bringing about improvements. Nothing else mattered even if it meant facing some difficult situation here and there some times. The basic approach that I adopted was; spot talent amongst my junior colleagues, build up core teams of competent professionals and guide them effectively. The result was all round improvement with the introduction of streamlined and efficient work culture and lesser hassles in execution of the jobs; much to the liking of those involved in them. Not surprising that this added to the success of such endeavours.

Thanks to such initiatives, I could implement what was in the best interest of Organization. It also satisfied my urge and helped in demonstrating my competence as a professional zealot.

Some broad details of my contributions

CPF Trust

A casual scrutiny revealed that the accounts of trust were in real bad shape. I got them thoroughly checked and recast by engaging a Chartered

Accountants' firm. It also transpired that the corpus of the trust was also not being invested effectively. Few meetings with our Bankers, SBI, and a visit to Mumbai office of the Bank helped in putting in place an effective procedure for maximizing the ROI.

Central Payments section

This was one of the main assignments for me on joining in Stores Finance wing in 1982. There were frequent complaints from the Stores & Purchase officers about delays in the issue of Letters of Credits by the bank in favour of suppliers of goods & services in different countries. It meant delays in procurements since the foreign supplier's delivery schedule would commence only after the receipt by him of a valid Letter of Credit. On discussions with the Bank Manager it was revealed that a very minor weakness was resulting in delay at Bank; non-availability of adequate number of typists. The Bank Manager was un-aware of it since nobody from ONGC had brought up this issue with him. Thus ended the hassles and LCs started flowing in in time.

Instant collateral benefit for me out of above exercises

The honest commitment with which I worked to improve the financials of the Trust stood me in good stead later at the time of my interview for promotion as AD (F&A). On being asked by Member (F) about my job profile at the time of interview in 1985, I mentioned, "In addition to charge of JD (F&A) in Stores Finance, CPF Trust is also my responsibility." Hearing this, his focus shifted to the working of Trust.

"Tell me, is it permissible to grant non-refundable advance to a member for the marriage of his/her daughter?"

I replied "No Sir, the rules do not permit such a transaction."

To be certain that I was sure about the correctness of the answer, he emphasized it was ridiculous that for daughter's marriage one could not get a non-refundable advance and again my reply was an emphatic no.

He reinforced his question saying, "What would you tell the Chairman, ONGC, if he insists for the grant of such an advance to one of his personal staff members?"

I replied "I will carry the Rule Book and politely draw his attention to the relevant rule."

"What, if he still doesn't agree and insists for it?"

Mustering courage and invoking all my wits, I replied, "I will rush to you and seek your support saying 'trahi mam, trahi mam' which means 'save me, protect me'.

And this frank and bold response which confirmed that I knew Trust's rules well yielded for me success. I was selected and placed on the top of the panel though as JD I was at the bottom in my batch.

The moral of the story is "Keep working hard and be sincere. Clutch on to your wits in difficult situations. Be firm in your conviction. It pays."

Vigilant attitude and due diligence resulted in huge savings for ONGC

Another incident related to opening of LCs reinforced my conviction that all was not o.k. An innocuous proposal was received from Purchase Dept. for opening of a LC in US $. On surface, it appeared to be normal like any other proposal and my staff had processed it accordingly and put up to me for approval. On scrutiny, I found that the original offer made by the bidder about a year back was to cover this transaction under the line of credit offered by French Govt. and accordingly the payment was to be made in FF. By a recent amendment to the Purchase Order, it had been changed to US $. This gave rise to some doubts since the FF had greatly devalued in the last one year which meant substantially fewer outgo of Rupees for opening of LC in FF. Since full details were not available in the proposal papers, I declined to process it further. Accordingly, at my insistence, this case was taken up for detailed scrutiny. A committee at a very senior level determined that the proposal to open LC in US $ was malafide. After protracted negotiations and exchange of correspondence with French embassy in India, the bidder agreed to receive payment in FFs. And this resulted in huge savings to ONGC. I was happy though there was no word of appreciation for me by the seniors.

NORTHERN REGIONAL OFFICE

A new beginning, a new role for me at Jammu

A new phase began for me in early 1985. On promotion as Additional Director (F), I was posted to a newly carved Region, namely, Northern Region, as its Finance Head. This was welcome for it recognized tacitly my capability to handle the affairs of a Region. This region was created to give boost to ONGC's efforts for discovering hydrocarbon reserves in Himalayan foot-hills and Shivalik Ranges with focus on exploration activities in the states of J&K and HP.

For me, it was not only an opportunity to create a new set-up of Finance & Accounts in the Region but also a unique opportunity to get to know the technical aspects of ONGC's core activities of exploration and drilling. I whole-heartedly availed of this opportunity and got involved in depth in field activities. This experience was wholesome and I tried hard to pick up in some details the preparatory work of creating appropriate infrastructure for drilling like land acquisition, constructing approach roads, getting ready the drill-site and the foundation for installation of Rig, environment clearance by the state govt. etc. All this helped me a lot in getting educated about the core operations and in turn this enabled me to carry out detailed scrutiny of proposals for expenditure.

Summing up my stay in Northern Region

To sum up; my stay of two and a half years (1985-87) in NR was educative, thrilling and adventurous all at the same time. I gained good working knowledge of various wings/disciplines, contributed extensively in deliberations for completing various tasks, and joined the RD and other senior officers' team in site visits with a view to generating consensus on the spot for scope, necessity and quantum of the proposed job. The civil engineering jobs like widening and strengthening of existing state govt. roads to enable smooth movement of heavy trailers loaded with Rigs and Accessories, construction of new approach roads from state highway to drill-sites, storage facilities/

godowns and other infrastructure always led to difference of opinion between Civil Engineering Dept. and Project Manager on one side and Finance Section on the other. The entire expenses for these works were to be borne totally by ONGC which were very substantial. Thus, instead of spending time in table discussions in a cosy conference room in the office when normally a consensus is elusive and the execution gets delayed, the decision making group led by RD himself with Finance Head in tow could take a final decision on the spot and expedite the process of execution. This approach yielded dividends as it avoided endless arguments between different sections. The practice of Finance Head being present at site and agreeing broadly to the proposal in principle on the spot after being satisfied with the need was not heard of earlier. This was an innovative concept in decision making in a Govt. Co. Of course, agreeing in principle to the proposal on the spot didn't mean doing away with detailed scrutiny of the estimates or ignoring prudence or giving up other salient checks.

A young Executive who helped me in organising professionally the work in Finance wing of the Region was Mr. SK Sharma. He was the pick of the then GGM (F) for Northern Region. He had told me, "This young officer is most suitable for a new Region like yours. You will be happy to have him there." He was absolutely right. Quite energetic, committed to delivering his very best and handling the big load of work single-handedly comes to mind easily while thinking of SK Sharma. A big satisfaction to me was the confidence that this young officer would handle the section's work efficiently during my absence from Jammu on official trips. About eight years later when I was given the additional charge of PIB section in Dehra Dun, this gentleman proved his professional skills of analysing critically the big-ticket investments in projects of critical importance for ONGC. And now in ONGC Videsh as GM (F), he is a leading member of the Corporate Team which is busy playing his role of a prudent financial analyst in determining the viability of Oil & Gas assets which ONGC Videsh is acquiring in other countries. The task this subsidiary of ONGC is doing is critical to India's energy security.

My fundamental approach to my job as a Finance Executive

I believe; such an experience for a Finance Executive is thrilling for it enables him/her to observe and appreciate the ground reality, offers an opportunity to contribute effectively by suggesting alternatives, makes Finance Rep. to believe that he/she is actively involved in decision making and in hastening the process of execution. Even otherwise also, getting familiar with the operations/processes of the Organization and site visits enlarges the knowledge base. This awareness builds up confidence about the need and quantum of the proposed job/activity/assets. It inhibits the Finance people from making routine comments on the proposals before them. My personal experience suggests that comments of Finance Section which are based on facts and actual ground position result in their acceptance or at least create environment for discussions to be held in the spirit of give and take rather than confrontation. That Finance Section is an adversary and its observations are a hindrance is a commonly held view amongst Line Managers' fraternity. The approach of cultivating harmonious relations, lending listening ears during debates, putting forth views and comments on the basis of working knowledge of operations picked up during spot visits or otherwise and attempting to build up rapport through personal discussions is what I have been practicing with satisfaction throughout my career. I always believed; confrontation, refusing to heed others' view-point and insistence on acceptance of own suggestions neither helps the organization nor creates bridges of mutual respect. When there is no malice, ill-will or personal interest to be served, consensus is inevitable and it makes life easy. Practice it and be happy. Of-course, all this is possible only if there is no hidden agenda or personal interest.

I get elevated as DGM (F)

An interview for selection as Deputy General Manager was to be held at Dehra Dun and I had made bookings and finalized my travel plan for going there accordingly. However, a message received from HQ informing of Chairman's visit to Jammu for a Review Meeting indicated that it was to be held just a day before my date of my interview at Dehra Dun. I was perplexed and felt sorry for being not able to participate in it. The RD surprised me and asked me to stay back for the meeting. He assured he would see to it that I reach Dehra Dun in time for my interview. He further asked me to present Region's man-power plan also in addition to Finance Section's presentation. In fact, this man-power plan had been firmed up by us after review of Region's requirements of staff for the next two years taking into account the approved operational activity plan. The review had confirmed our apprehension that the Region was over-staffed and accordingly we finalized the draft of a communication to be sent to HQs indicating the numbers and names of the surplus personnel to be transferred out of the Region. Accordingly, in the Review Meeting I presented the man-power projections plan highlighting the surpluses which were a drag for the Region. The presentation was received well. After the meeting, the RD explained my situation and requested Chairman to permit me to travel to Dehra Dun along with him in his airplane and thus I reached Dehra Dun in the evening and was in time for interview the next day.

In the interview meeting next day, the Member (Personnel) raised the issue of surplus manpower in NR and started blaming the Region for inflating its requirements thus resulting in huge surplus. This was contrary to factual position. The postings had been done by HQs on their own without consulting the Region. Therefore, Member (P) raising the issue of surplus manpower in NR at the time of my interview was a clear indication that he was hostile to me for reasons best known to him. I maintained my calm and explained the Region's position and requested him to consult his own staff but it resulted in a rebuke for me. It ignited a heated controversy and much against my wish I had to counter him forcefully. Seeing the surcharged atmosphere, I told my-self, "Your chance is gone. You should have controlled your temper but the arrow was out of the quiver now." However, it was my good luck that Providence had wished it otherwise. 'Fruits of hard and sincere work are always sweet' proved true for me at this crucial juncture. The Chairman

Krishan Aneja

was observing the exchanges between me and Member (P) and seeing the situation taking an awkward turn, intervened and confirmed my statement referring to the presentation made by me at Jammu a day before. With this, Member (P)'s umbrage at me proved to be un-called for. I was successful and promoted as DGM in due course and posted at Mumbai as Head of Finance in EBG. I left Jammu in November, 1987 to join in my new posting. Bye, Jammu!

BOMBAY REGIONAL BUSINESS CENTRE

Business-like and professional work ethics in Bombay office
The first impression I got in Bombay office was comforting. The atmosphere was business-like and professional. It was a big change compared to Dehra Dun and Jammu. Every office activity was streamlined and one didn't have to waste time in sorting out daily routines. Most of the services had been out-sourced and the quality of jobs being handled by service-providers was satisfactory. The office premises were taken care of well. The standard of cleanliness, hygiene and up-keep was likeable. Staff coming to office in time and getting busy soon in their jobs was a refreshing scene.

Soon after joining there, my Secretary asked me to hand over my personal papers to her to enable her to ensure that insurance premiums or other similar periodical payments were made in time. She noted down the names and addresses, phone numbers, dates of birth, anniversary dates of my close relatives and would remind me in time for action. This is called professional work ethics. And the surprise was that this was her first job after finishing her college. Tell her a job to do and forget it. She would do it or get it done, as advised. The reason, she was committed and sincere by nature and was professionally trained as PS. That was Manisha. Similarly disposed by nature were section's other staff and officers.

"Love thy job, devote your 100% and forget. Rewards will follow"

In my entire work-life, I had handled enormous and challenging jobs which kept me happily busy, forced me to innovate, tested my nerves,

294

challenged me to simplify and re-write the rules to wipe-off drudgery and reduce the load without compromising on fundamentals and essential requirements. I have always been ambitious and my approach to satisfy my ambitions has been "Seek change of job if its profile is of a routine type and is not challenging." I had always been happy if there was no scope for idling away in office hours. Rather, 9.30-5.30 jobs were not my choice. Honesty of purpose and unflinching commitment to the assignments has always been a source of true satisfaction for me. I have been reasoning with myself thus, "you are in service because you do not possess capital to invest in a business or industry. The only capital you have is brains and capability to perform well. Remember, for anyone in service it is hard work beyond the employer's expectations that matters. If you care for growth and want to fulfil your dreams, be sincere to the job and the organization who have given you means to earn your livelihood. Have patience; rewards will follow, even if late sometime. Don't grumble and do not let your frustration overtake or spoil your performance. Don't forget to enjoy/celebrate the satisfaction of having done a fine job." In this, I was inspired by my mother who never felt tired or conveyed her un-happiness about her fate. Losing the bread-earner of the family at young age with family business in shambles, no regular stream of income and seven kids to look after, she was a perfect picture of endurance. She often used to say, "Nobody loves your skin. It is your hard work that is loved by all." I am proud I imbibed this gem of principle in my life. I believe; it was my good luck to be the son of an illustrious woman like her who faced life' odds and difficulties with solemn determination and courage.

The compliment that I cherished for long

My deft handling of Electro-logging tender in EBG, Bombay, resulted in its happy conclusion and award of work to M/S Schlumberger. The Head (Finance) of Schlumberger travelled to Mumbai at the time of signing of the final agreement and joined in the formal dinner in an exclusive club in Hotel Taj. I was surprised beyond imagination when I was told "The Head (Finance) is keen to meet you." A bit confused, I went to him. I couldn't believe, when he complimented me saying, "I have been closely monitoring the issues brought out by you during negotiations and was delighted to observe the depth of your analysis and comments. That somebody in 3rd world can do it was a surprise to me."

The Benign Gift; my request for transfer to Dehra Dun accepted

Mrs. Aneja had not shifted to Mumbai being busy with her Primary School Project at Dehra Dun. She was alone there since November, 1988, when Ashish went to Lucknow to join KGMC for his MBBS program. Sandeep had already gone to Jamalpur in Feb. for his mechanical engineering under-graduate program of Railways called SCRA. Mrs. Aneja was happily busy with her Project at Dun since 1986. By implication, there was no chance of her leaving Dehra Dun and joining me at Mumbai though both of us were suffering being alone. The only way out for us to be together was my posting at Dehra Dun. And this didn't appear feasible under any circumstances. But, the optimist that I am, I continued to entertain a hope that, sooner than later, a miracle may happen and I get transferred to HQs.

And a miracle did happen. In due course, the Member (Finance) realized our desperate need and agreed to send me back to Dehra Dun. Thus I landed in Dehra Dun in July, 1989.

Bye, Bombay!

Chapter 28
Back to Dehra Dun HQs

The posting at Dehra Dun, was nothing but a dream come-true by all means and was a rich culmination of aspirations; a whiff of sweet breeze filling the nostrils with the prospects of happy family life, once again. It didn't matter that the charge given to me was neither exciting nor challenging.

As has been usual with me in my work-life, I got going about my assignment seriously keeping aside the feeling that the posting in IA is normally considered to be a resort for the non-performers, a sort of dumping ground for low-profile individuals. It took me some time in studying the existing set up and realized that the environment in IA section at HQ lacked the dynamism necessary for effective performance as an agency of consequence. The attitude of many of my juniors reflected a sense of despair. They believed and conveyed to me, "Nobody in higher echelons wants IA to work effectively." I told them my mind, "It doesn't matter to me what others feel about IA. Better, be ready for a new beginning. We must remember, IA is neither perfunctory nor an un-necessary function as many would tell you so. In my opinion, no job is inferior or repugnant. It is the individual who adds to the aura, and enhances the depth of the assignment by enriching it with his high class performance and by showing highly commendable results."

Boss's expectations; shake up & rejuvenate IA

And luckily for me, the Member (Finance) in his first meeting with me outlined his vision of the role he expected IA to play in ONGC. He conveyed his concerns about virtual non-functioning of IA in ONGC and asked me to prepare a blue-print of the action plan for making IA an effective control instrument. His personal focus was on two matters, (i) IA in ONGC should pay more attention to Management Audit for helping the top Management and the Board to be aware of the real situation, find out weaknesses in the system, suggest corrective measures and help introduce policies of checks and balances and (ii) I should travel to Regions/Projects to meet the regional and project heads, apprise them of the support the IA teams were capable of providing to them for effective monitoring of operations and seek their support for meaningful functioning of IA teams there. The need of the hour was to strengthen the teams, boost their morale, discuss and create a reliable structure. Let them be aware of Management's concerns, apprise the teams of the thrust and identify functional areas for deeper scrutiny.

Member (F) also desired that IA at HQs should concentrate on identifying areas of concern in the organization, bring up new ideas/suggestions for functional improvements and devote more attention to scrutiny of high-value contracts, their actual implementation and put forth ideas for mid-course corrections, where felt necessary. What more a person of my commitment could ask for? All my apprehensions had been eliminated and I was happy and ready to give a big push. I made consistent efforts to streamline the set-up in IA but in few months' time it was obvious that concerted and sincere efforts notwithstanding, IA didn't enthuse me. It became clear that there wasn't much of challenge in the job and I conveyed this feeling appropriately to Member (F) and conveyed innocently, "Sir, you can think of adding to my responsibility."

I am moved out of IA and given huge responsibility

If I remember correctly, I held charge of IA for about eight months. Suddenly, Member (F) called me one day and asked, "Are you ready for handling higher and challenging assignments?" And, as could be expected, my reply was enthusiastically affirmative. He briefed me about the charge he had thought of assigning to me and advised me to wait for written formal orders. Listening to details he gave, I was dumb-struck. The proposed charge was not only very heavy and challenging indeed but also a unique combination requiring guts and patience to deal with situations most common in the proposed charge. Well; nothing could be done now. It was the reward of my bold initiative I had taken some time back. Showing brave face and thanking him profusely for having acceded to my request, I left his Chamber. I realized, once again, being ambitious was fine but the discomfort I was facing now was of my own doing. It was obvious that from now onwards, I shall be jumping from one challenge/problem to another. I argued and re-assured myself "Of-course, I am ready to face the challenges. I am not nervous and will do justice to the job. Handling difficult assignments can-not deter me. That challenges remain challenge till a person like me comes to grips with them. Face them with confidence and determination and see these become routine matters."

Courtesy my new job assignment; I become focus of envy

My new job portfolio comprised of two sections, (i) HQ Finance and (ii) Corporate Budget which, on the face, would mean just two sections only. The reality was that each one of these sections concealed in their fold umpteen functions of critical importance and the names concealed more than what they revealed. Till now each of these sections was headed by a senior officer holding independent charge. For argument's sake, one could be under the illusion that M (F) was hard-pressed to take such a decision due to un-availability of sufficient number of senior officers at Dehra Dun. But the facts were otherwise. There were officers either senior to me or of the same rank who were not adequately loaded. Therefore, his decision to give me such a heavy and important responsibility was baffling for me, until his Staff Officer told me, "M(F) is pretty sure you will do justice to the job and will come up to his expectations. Hope, you are happy now. In any case, you invited all this for yourself. Our best wishes for a successful stint. Good luck!" He further suggested, "Now was not the time to make attempts to allay the feelings of jealousy or ill-will in others' minds. Just ignore it and get going hard in your job. Wait and let the dust settle down."

The Corporate Budget section

Broadly speaking, the main functions of Corporate Budget section were (i) compile and consolidate the Capital and Revenue budgets of the Co. after discussions with the regional teams, (ii) hold discussions with RDs and Project Heads, where necessary, (iii) obtain, in principle, broad approval of M(F) and CMD after finalizing the Budget as above, (iv) present the Budgets to the Board of Directors with the help of slides etc. and obtain their approval (v) forward the approved budgets to various agencies in the Govt. Having done this, the next most important step would be to attend meetings/conferences and holding discussions with different agencies of the Govt. of India, namely; Planning Commission, Ministry of Petroleum and NG and Ministry of Finance in New Delhi for seeking approval of Co.'s Capital Expenditure Annual Plan. Unless the Capital Budget is approved and included in G.O.I's Annual Plan, no expenditure could be incurred on Capital Schemes.

As is normal in any big corporate set-up, the two sections in my charge, viz. the Corporate Budget and HQ Finance Sections were the most important and crucial entities, rather backbone, of Finance wing of Corporate HQs of the Co. In fact, these two sections were the hub of activity at corporate level and were always under focus and in lime-light. And the heavy work-load and extensive travelling kept me awfully busy but happy for it satisfied my ego. No wonder, I never had time and inclination to listen to whispers in the corridors, whether about my so-called envious position or some other issue ripe for discussions in the clusters of the idlers.

The first immediate focus of attention in Budget section

After few days' interaction with my staff in Budget Section, it became clear that the computerized system already available wasn't good enough to meet the requirement of proper analysis and generating various reports required at the time of meetings in Co.' Board of Directors and also the Govt. agencies; Planning Commission, Ministry of P & NG, Ministry of Economic Affairs & Ministry of Finance. I brought it to the notice of M (F) and informed that a new integrated computerized system will need to be put in place. However, the budgetary exercise was scheduled to start soon and we will have to live with it in the current year's exercise.

To cut short the long story, we faced a lot of embarrassment in the Board's meeting as also at the time of meetings in the Govt. agencies for the approval of ONGC's Annual Plan for the coming year.

After being free with the exercises as above, we got busy in finalizing a new computerized system. Thanks to support provided by officers/ programmers working on scientific applications in Co.'s Super Computer Wing, a new streamlined system was got ready. In this effort, the zeal with which the Programmers of GEOPIC and officers of Budget Section, VP Shaw, AK Arora, and two junior accountants worked together as a team deserves high appreciation. These worthies worked as a team day and night with the GEOPIC team and made sure that the new system was well on track after regular trial runs for few months. It was not surprising that the new system was not only streamlined but also took away the drudgery of preparing of voluminous statements of budgetary demands manually by the Regions, Projects and Institutes of the Co. The system's integrated facility of on-line processing enabled now the various units to enter the data on CDs only for further processing at HQ.

Not only the team re-wrote the programs, they also developed programs for direct access to the Super Computer in GEOPIC our desk-top in Budget section. Cables were laid from GEOPIC to Budget Section's desk-top and this desk-top now served as a terminal hooked to main-frame Super Computer in GEOPIC. This was a first of its kind in ONGC. It was possible now to feed the inputs, make changes, do analysis and give instructions for generating reports etc. The only constraint was availability of time on the main-frame freely for us but this too was overcome. We were allotted a slot in the evenings and we could access the system after obtaining a confirmation on phone from the Operations in charge there. Lo and behold we were on-line now. This was a glorious achievement of the team of my officers and the programmers of GEOPIC. Well, the team was rewarded for this feat but not as well as I had expected.

The new computerised system; a 'Green' initiative

The new system was a game-changer since the outstation teams need not spend time in GEOPIC for data entry. The final budget lay-out as agreed during discussions would be available soon after the changes in data are incorporated in the file in main-frame and CDs with final data ready without delay. Thus the position had altered now. The teams from regions need not carry voluminous manually prepared budget statements. Just a CD was enough now. In today's parlance, this was a major green initiative. Hundreds of thousands of statements need neither be printed nor carried along. An added advantage was that the RDs and Project Manager could know the agreed outlays for them and press for additions/deletions, if any, well before their regions outlay was going to be incorporated in ONGC's Annual Plan for approval by Govt.

Really difficult job accomplished well; Bravo HQs team!!

In any case, we the HQs budget team, were happy to have successfully installed the new system in time for next year's budgetary exercise. I was happy that Budget section was now on a smooth trajectory capable of providing and seeking information without hassles. The shameful helplessness I had faced in CMD's Review Meeting last year was now a thing of the past and in fact, it was the trigger for all the hectic work that we did with the help of GEOPIC programmers.

One name which occurs to mind for such a wonderful achievement is VP Shaw, a fully committed silent performer. Tell him the job and see it is done. He could obtain full co-operation of not only his own team of Budget section but also the Programmers of GEOPIC. But for his dedicated silent efforts, all this may not have been possible. Bravo!! I am happy; he is now holding the position of GM. I am sure; he must be busy, as usual, making difference in his own style, to the responsibility he is holding. My best wishes for his still higher growth!

The new look Budget section

Budget section now didn't require much of a close attention and it was no more a burden for me except that I had to get involved in meetings at senior levels in ONGC or in various wings and Ministries of the Govt. The young officers' team was capable of handling section's internal operations conveniently on their own. In fact, I got into the habit of inter-acting with this group of officers and staff only for any information that was required. These boys were real gem and a back-bone of Budget section.

All is well that ends well

I was really happy; the team spirit and dedicated work by Programmers and Finance professionals in our Budget section had made budgetary exercise much simpler and easier now for all the stake-holders; the drudgery associated with it was gone. The new system provided a lee-way to senior Managers to make budget an effective tool of enforcing budgetary control and monitoring the implementation of major schemes and the approved work plan. It also made the life of Budget section Executives much easier now. They were now in a position to do quick analysis on the spot, when required, provide the desired information whether in the Board's meeting, or to CMD and other Members or to outside agencies like Planning Commission or Ministries of the Govt. without hassles.

HQ FINANCE; A CONGLOMERATE
OF DIVERSE FUNCTIONS

The nomenclature HQ Finance hides more than what it reveals. Varied functions of F&A wing in Corporate Office were under this umbrella set-up. Broadly these comprised of:--

Play the role of associate Financial Advisor to Member (P) and provide support to him in all matters/policies relating to staff compensation, benefits, perks and facilities etc.,

Examine all proposals of Personnel Dept. either for introduction of new policies/rules or amendments to the existing ones relating to staff benefits, examine the reasonableness of the proposal and its genesis, find out underlying reasons for proposal's origin, bring out details of proposal's impact on Co.'s finances; immediate and long-term both, look at justification/merit cited in the proposal for its introduction, bring out repercussions, if any, of the proposal on other related issues, examine the proposal's conformity or otherwise with Govt.'s instructions on the subject, offer detailed comments on the proposal as a whole, make specific recommendations for either endorsing it, amending it or opposing it, as may be appropriate in Finance's assessment, supported by facts and logic,

Participate and play an active role along with Member (P) in all staff meetings with Unions and Officers' Association, and join in parleys/negotiations with them,

Join in CMD's meetings with Staff Unions, Officers' Association along with Member (P) and Member (F) and render help by bringing out facts, past practices, provision in the rules/instructions, highlight on the spot the inconsistencies or unreasonableness of the demands, actively participate in deliberations and be ready to face odd questions and belligerent comments of Unions/ Association in the meetings,

Similarly, examine the proposals (original and amendments to the existing ones) for staff welfare, medical facilities, post-retirement benefits like Group-Annuity scheme and other similar schemes, awards, sports, grant-in-aid to NGOs as per Govt. policies, social-welfare schemes under CSR policies, office infrastructure and equipment, furniture and furnishings, and other similar proposals emanating from Administration Dept., Civil Engineering Dept. and Electrical and Electronics Engineering Sections etc.

All the above matters/functions were commonly known as 'Financial concurrence' which meant that the powers of the Executive Depts. to incur or commit expenditure were not un-fettered and the proposals had to be referred to associate Finance at appropriate level as laid down in

'Book of Delegated Powers'. In practical terms, it meant that the officers of Executive Depts. at different levels had their own associate Finance group and all expenditure proposals within their competence as per BDP need not be referred to senior officers.

The awe and aura associated with the name 'HQ Finance'

I often heard people talking on our face, HQ Finance what a high pedestal it is seated on? But, in reality, however, this show of platitudes was deceptive. In fact, it was nothing more than a symptom of professional jealousy. The bottom-line was that this show of apparent goodwill towards Finance was nothing but a necessity. People in Executive wing knew that keeping Finance in good humour meant making their own work-life easy. However, the hard fact is that the relationship between other departments and Finance has always been that of love and hatred. Frankly speaking, notwithstanding all the cribbing by Executive depts., I always felt Finance had a crucial role to play in upholding the financial rules of the Organization and to caution the Management against tendency to splurge. Some Finance people might call it a thankless job. My approach towards my job as a Finance Executive, all along my career has been, "You would be letting down the sanctity of your job if you did not do an in-depth scrutiny, raise issues of relevance, point out deficiencies in the proposal, if any, and seek justification for the proposed activity, outlay and project under scrutiny." Granted that sharp, penetrating but relevant comments of Finance are enigma for many and seriously offending to some others who argue Finance is a stumbling block and a bottleneck in progress and growth. It doesn't matter if others feel hurt and offended in the process as long as the comments are not biased or personalized.

Finance; a necessary evil in the eyes of many

Most Executives think Finance to be a necessary evil, at best. Those with sharp-skills and bloated egos would often rake up an issue out of Finance's comments and forcefully project their own counter-views. Such situations always demand skilful handling by those at helm including the Finance executives. Instead of making an attempt to blast the other's ego I believed in giving due attention to the other view-point and accept it openly, if found to be o.k. and reasonable. If not, I would try to bring up my own fresh view-point rather in an amiable tone. Entering into the web of demonstrating one's counter-ego would mean frittering away of the force and logic of valid comments. Granted, the situation is difficult in such circumstances but we must remember that organization's interest would be better served if the logical and correct interpretation prevails and that would be possible only in an environment of understanding on both sides. Getting down to personal acrimony in such matters comes to mind easily but, surely, it is always counter-productive. In my opinion, controversies must be avoided to sustain the benefit of the force/weight of one's legitimate view-point and interpretation of rules. It is equally important in organization's interest to accept other party's views if it becomes clear that the views of other party are equally valid.

Finance better know thy limits; Organization's interest is sacrosanct

The foregoing views guided me throughout my journey in this august section. The cardinal and guiding principle for me has always been, "Organization's interest is supreme and it must prevail. This must override other considerations." I never practiced what was not legitimate in my opinion. To be fair and open to others views has always been my cornerstone. I am convinced this approach of being reasonable pays dividends. People pay due attention to Finance's views when the Finance Executive is known and seen to be not unduly rigid and dogmatic. Bringing up routine queries by Finance doesn't serve Organization's interest, rather it leads to bitterness. Overlook routine procedural issues, be pragmatic and pay due attention to matters pointing to deeper implications and hidden agendas, if any. Persevere and try to concentrate on clauses which have potential to be misinterpreted. After all, what matters and is sacrosanct is not settling some personal scores but speedy and quick clearance of proposals in a fair, transparent and objective manner to help expedite the process of execution and implementation of projects. Be fearless in articulating and bringing up critical issues even if it leads to heated discussions provided there is force of strong evidence in support thereof or the proposal is ultra-vires of the rule book.

I lived by this dictum and gave my views/comments freely and without fear whether in case files or in meetings/conferences. Practical wisdom demands, "Know thy job, beware it would have limitations, remember them and perform within the limitations prescribed." In sacred Ramayana, Lakshman draws a line (Rekha) while leaving Sita alone in the cottage in the jungle and asks her not to cross it and tells her she would be safe and will not be put to any harm while being within the limits of this Rekha. Sita crosses the Rekha, though for valid reasons, and lands herself into serious trouble. Therefore, remaining within limits whether in work place or in personal life is sacrosanct for security, peace of mind and happiness. This principle guided my journey and generally speaking, I was spared of the troubles.

Finance not in Vigilance's role

I never bothered that the others may have some personal agenda. Let them face the consequences of their wrong-doings, if any. Soofi sant Kabir, well known for his couplets containing gems of wisdom, wrote in one of his many pieces, "Kabira teri jhonpri gal kateyan ke pass, karange so bharange, tu kyon bhaiyo udas." Literally, it means why should you worry about ill-deeds of others? They will face the consequences themselves. I was firm that it was not Finance's function to try to meddle in and try to stall any such move. Preaching and attempting to stand on high moral grounds didn't appeal to me. I believed, as long as Finance's comments have their origin in due interpretation of rules and compliance of laid-down procedures/regulations, there is nothing to get disturbed. Award of work, placement of supply orders and monitoring the execution of projects or procurements in conformity with the provisions of the contract/supply order is the responsibility of seniors in the respective departments. Let them and vigilance groups do their jobs diligently. Finance behaving like a super cop is extremely dangerous.

Essence of my role as Head of Finance wing at HQ

It was expected my comments would be like an Executive Summary of what is under consideration, the status/position of relevant rules as applicable including their proper interpretation and a final summary containing Finance's final comments. Normally, this last noting would form the basis for further comments/discussions by Board Members and CMD for taking a final view. Therefore, my assessment, interpretation and comments were expected to be wholesome but brief and concise, touching on and highlighting the financial implications including repercussions, if any, on other similar issues.

One can conclude; the last stage commentary by HQ Finance would be reflective of a definite direction for further confabulations and decision making. For me, it was a judicious responsibility akin to and bordering on arbitration between the demand/proposal on the one side and its feasibility and justification for acceptance taking into account the propriety, reasonableness of the proposal, its financial viability and conformity to rules.

The quantum of work-load handled by me would be better appreciated by the dictation and transcription load handled by my PS and a Stenographer. It kept them fully occupied for the whole day or postponing some of it to the next day after being busy with me in taking dictation for about four to five hours a day. For still better appreciation of the load, let me explain that my average dictation speed was about 120/130 words/minute which was thought to be ideal and very well appreciated by my personal staff. In our times, there were no PCs or Laptops and the only electronic help available was electronic type-writer which had the facility of memory.

Over a period of time, I acquired the reputation of a 'no non-sense man'. The labour leaders acknowledged it unhesitatingly. My detractors in the meetings would privately convey their appreciation for the balanced analysis and a firm stand taken by me and also simultaneously express their regrets for the strident criticism and opposition voiced by them, sometimes violent and very aggressive even. The summary of their refrains used to be, "Sir, we have to cater to our lobby and make attempts to squeeze from Management as much concessions/benefits as possible and justify our position as strong labour leaders. The hard-bargaining that we do is normal for staff representatives like us and what you do is also normal for any one in your position. We both are quits in this game of Snakes and ladders, plays and counter-plays."

Saddled with additional responsibility

As if, Budget Section and HQ Finance were not enough a load for me, I was gifted (loaded with) yet another very important section, PIB, in the year 1993, when the incumbent M (F) was sacked for some alleged malpractices and in his place, my senior who was holding charge of PIB section was elevated as M (F). I don't think it was recognition of my competence or a reward for me. Simply put, there was no other senior officer of GM or higher rank available at HQs and the new M (F) thought I could take this extra load. In hind-sight, I believe this additional responsibility made me learn quite a lot about this vital function and, in due course, I started enjoying this onerous responsibility.

Broad contours of job in PIB section

Literally, PIB stands for Public Investment Board in Ministry of Finance, Dept. of Expenditure, Govt. of India, and name 'PIB' section in ONGC was modelled on that. The prime responsibility of PIB section in ONGC was:-

to co-ordinate with Construction Engineering Sections in ONGC for securing approval of proposals from Govt, where required,

Determine financial and economic viability of the project with the help of IRR and ERR analysis etc. and send it back to concerned Engineering section for review if it is seen to be unviable,

prepare Feasibility Reports of the projects seen to be viable as per IRR and ERR analysis and after due diligence,

scout for and identify the likely source of financing the FE component of the project, if not already committed under a line of credit,

As a next step, initiate action for approval of the Project/Expenditure proposal by the Board of Directors, which entailed lot of preparatory work in association with the concerned Engineering section,

Simultaneously, prepare a case for securing the commitment for requisite amount of Foreign Exchange (FE) from multilateral international agencies like World Bank, Asian Development Bank or an Exim Bank etc.

Having successfully gone through this rig-morale, approach the parent Ministry of P&NG and Planning Commission by submitting a detailed proposal for initiating the process of securing approval of Public Investment Board for the project.

It should be clear from the broad details of the job content, as narrated above, that my new additional responsibility, PIB, was full load by itself. Pity me for being gifted with such a strenuous and heavy responsibility, in addition to my beloved Budget and HQ Finance.

PIB section; a seriously critical responsibility

The projects requiring PIB's approvals were of high value i.e. those beyond the powers of Board of Directors and were continuously under focus of the top Management being the most critical segment for Co.'s growth. Securing approval of PIB as quickly as possible and as envisaged in the Annual Plan was critical for meeting the targets of construction/ production. It was apparent that any delay in approvals would impact the project's completion time schedule and consequently result in delay in meeting the production targets. All this easier said than possible. Each of the various stages/channels/agencies through which the proposal had to steer itself and which were part of long drawn process for entering the last but one stage of PIB meeting was a test of nerves. The worthies at each stage, whether in-house or in the Govt. were a difficult lot; always easily ready with multiple questionnaires and verbal queries. And the poor PIB I/C, though well-supported by in-house financial analysts and technical team, would have sleepless nights worried about project's fate in the meeting. By nature, each one on the other side of the table, thought him/herself to be invincible and a hard nut to crack. We were aware that whatever logical and rational explanation supported by facts and data the ONGC team may bring forth during the meetings, the worthies on the other side would spring a surprise with yet another set of questionnaires and put us back to square one. Whether we liked it or not, it was happening as a routine forcing us to accept it as inevitable and a regular feature of the interaction. Broadly speaking and depending upon the size of proposed outlay, a period of about 2 years was thought to be reasonable for pushing the proposal through various agencies in Govt. and securing final approval.

PIB section; a gratifying and novel experience for me

I acknowledge, the PIB was a great experience for me. The preparation of Feasibility reports called for a high degree of professional competence both of the Engineering group and the Finance officers. These reports were broadly a combination of (i) detailed justification for the proposed investment, and necessity for the project, including S.W.O.T analysis for the project (ii) its physical parameters containing details of engineering, technology and equipment necessary for the project, (iii) financial lay-out for various segments, (iv) financial and economic analysis thereof, (v) sales and marketing, (vi) important features and justification in support of the outputs expected after the completion of the project and (vii) foreign exchange component required for the project and likely source(s) for availability of the same. While the Engineering groups were responsible for providing these details supported by annexures, drawings etc., the PIB section had to handle the chapters on economic and financial viability of the project justifying the proposed investment. It was an assignment that was always demanding and kept me on tenterhooks. It made me run between HQ and Delhi and Mumbai on short notice or no notice at all, mocking on my desire for some respite some time. As if on a cue from destiny, it always made me feel helpless before the penetrating eyes and sound-bites of worthy interlocutors in the Planning Commission and the Ministries of P&NG and Finance who believed, in their wisdom, that they were always impeccably correct and had inherited a right to be intolerant of divergent views.

In addition, the need for urgency in getting clearances expeditiously kept me always under pressure of time squeeze and always worried about 'what next' for each project. Though securing clearances was a joint team work of Project Engineers and Finance, the lead role was that of PIB section for coordination with Govt. agencies. The projects needing PIB's approval were always under focus of the top Management, concerned RDs and also the important torch-bearers of the project in Mumbai (because most of the projects requiring PIB approval were in Bombay High off-shore). Each project being part of the approved Annual Plan was time-bound requiring constant inter-action with others in the loop. Sure enough, any slippage would be analysed thoroughly and difficult to explain because of its serious bearing on production and financials of the Co. The awkward situation and thankless job of explaining the reasons for delay was primarily the function of PIB section of Finance Dept.

Chapter 29
Last four years of work-life in ONGC

To be sure, my last 4 years in ONGC from March, 1990, as I/C of Budget section, HQ Finance and later also PIB section for about a year were a real challenge for me. This spell of four years just before my superannuation in May, 1994, can be said to be a grand finale of a chequered career of over four decades. These four years proved to be a bulwark of stamina, grit and gumption demanding professional competence of high calibre, enduring patience and skilful handling of huge work-load full of challenges and anxious moments. It called for:-

Multitude skills to face high volt pressures within ONGC and the Govt. for securing expeditious clearances and approvals for major projects, defying normal approach to decision making,

Salvaging the wreck of existing computer system and building up and installing new computerized systems of great significance for budgetary exercise,

a test of my skills, patience and fortitude for handling with calmness and adroitly the multiple high-profile responsibilities simultaneously,

successfully lead the team of competent professionals of different disciplines in an endeavour to deliver and ensure success in acceptance of the proposals in different forums,

examine objectively and offer comments on the multiple proposals of Personnel dept., Administration and Welfare section, relating to compensation packages, benefits and welfare schemes for employees and proposals for grant-in-aid and expenditure on CSR schemes,

Be objective and play skilfully a leading role in staff unions and officers association's meetings with the management, respond to demands on the spot tactfully, avoid confrontations despite provocations and face pressures but not agreeing to or conceding the multiple unwieldy demands. In such meetings, the focus of criticism would be the Finance Rep. who was thought to be a spoilsport. Union leaders would often test our patience by taking recourse to bullying in their anxiety to justify their demands but I would just smile and ward off the heat.

To conclude, I would say, the last four years of my work life were an opportunity for me to justify the confidence the Management had reposed in me by giving me onerous responsibility of handling key functions in the corporate set-up of the Company. Though a challenge by itself; considering the enormity of its weight and size of these responsibilities, I took it as an opportunity to do full justice to the position I was holding and justify the confidence Company's top management had reposed in me and thus be my own-self; happy, satisfied and grateful. I never bothered about what nay-Sayers had up in their sleeves. I loved my job and enjoyed the accomplishments.

In fact, this period was a saga of fulfilment, satisfaction and contentment arising out of really credible performance.

Dignified conduct; my approach in work-life

My approach of not hankering for and seeking any credit for good performance on a given occasion has been my real strength. I believed; the appreciation has charm and dignity only if it is spontaneous and is of others' own volition. It helped to place me in a unique position and recognition in the organization. Hankering around seniors and in corridors of power in an endeavour to seek favours or being noticed appeared ridiculous to me. My track record would speak and get me what is my due was my counsel to myself; if not, let me not bother. Simply put,

"I do my job, let others do theirs." I am aware, I could have gone to USA for a fully paid training of four weeks duration had I cared to put a request before my boss. That I missed it was no regret to me.

This psych of mine got built up over a period of time, thanks to my mother. She would repeatedly tell us, 'seeking favours from others is below human dignity. Never stretch your hands before others except the Gods and that too only when you feel you deserve it.' Her pieces of practical wisdom served as a nectar for peace of mind and for getting a meaningful answer when at cross-roads. I am proud I tried to follow her teachings. It enabled me to keep my head high notwithstanding some naysayers, off and on. Her blessings and my resolve to follow her golden advices have been my strength.

Dispassionately speaking, being new in ONGC and little sceptical about the environment in the organization was a sort of disadvantage for me. Not many people, who mattered, really knew me in person; reason being my habit of not visiting seniors unless called for some discussion or in a meeting/conference etc. I knew; it did matter in office culture and was necessary to remain in focus, particularly at senior level but diffident that I was, I was shirking it. My chamber and being busy in my assignments has been my comfort zone all through. Therefore, it is in fitness of things to recall that my interview in 1991for elevation as GM (E-7 level), a senior management position, lasted for just about 2 ½ minutes. Unbelievable it appears to be but this is what happened. And the proverbial icing on the cake was CMD's concluding remarks in the Selection Board which still reverberate in my mind. He had said after exchange of 2/3 questions/answers with one of the Members, "Do we not know him well? Let's let him go." And I came out happy and smiling. A most satisfying and credible recognition it was. The selection panel comprised of entire Board of Directors and only about 3 % of the candidates were expected to be selected.

To be fair, let it not be concluded that I worked hard with zeal or delivered much more than expected with the sole object of advancement of my career or as a quid-pro-quo for the hard labour. No, it (the hard work) happened throughout in my work-life as a routine and without any design. I kept on

315

doing my part as a habit and growth came my way, thanks His Blessings. The growth was not the goal I was working for though it did come up as an expectation, as would be normal for any conscientious employee. In my sub-conscious, though, there lay a feeling that my growth would make my family a happier lot in society. My promotion as a GM did make me proud of my achievement. I took it as a reward; well-earned. And why not, within nine years of my stint in ONGC, starting at E-4 level in 1982, I reached E-7 level in 1991; an honest achievement considering the archaic systems of appraisals in Govt. sector. The word General Manager was soothing, charming not only to me but is well-sought after by many. It conveyed quite a lot to me, to my loving wife and children and to my near and dear ones. It was a sort of symbol of show-off and society at large also regarded it as a sign of high class recognition. My heart-felt gratitude is due to all my immediate seniors who made it possible on their own without letting me know any time and without any requests/ pleadings by me, whatever.

__Bye ONGC, 31ˢᵗ May, 1994.__

PART - III

෨ൠ

WE; the 5 (Me, my better-half and children)

Chapter 1
Essence of our happy family life

It being the tale of my journey, the focus in the preceding pages is on me though, depending upon the context, due and careful coverage came by itself at relevant intervals for my dear wife and children. Yet, in my opinion, the entire effort would be incomplete, colourless and void if it doesn't bring up in its toe, the glimpses of our family life. The truth is that happy family life made my work life happier and successful which in turn enriched our family life as a whole, so to say a reciprocal intuitional arrangement. A balanced and healthy family life provides strength, boosts confidence level and builds up capacity to be truly focused. In turn, it enables us to enjoy and celebrate life and do our assigned jobs with comfort and ease. Mutual help, free and open environment in home serve as a launching pad of immense significance for all its members especially the children who absorb innocuously what they see and come across in the house-hold. Therefore, a glimpse of our happy, vibrant and meaningful family life as a concluding chapter is a befitting finale because, I am sure, this was a great contributor to whatever the family and its members achieved collectively and individually in its sojourn.

It is fanciful to assume that one can push ahead in life even if the environment back home is not congenial and supportive. A happy home is a nursery/cradle where new innovative plans/ideas germinate and take roots. The accommodative and helpful attitude of family members is a silent but forceful impetus for pushing ahead and pursuing what is thought to be a vision of great significance. The peaceful environment builds up satisfaction followed by confidence and generates waves of positive energy. Sometimes, innocent looking ideas thrown up by family members, especially the better-half, during discussions on a vexed issue turn out to be a way out of great significance. No individual, howsoever successful in his/her work-life, can think that he/she achieved it on his/her own alone. Take away the healthy support system a happy family provides and there would be lack of clarity, imaginary obstacles will mount and decision making faculties of the individual will suffer. Therefore, it is of paramount importance for successful business leaders, managers and persons at helm of affairs to be sensitive to the sensitive matter of cordial and happy environment not only in the work place but also in the family. In fact, such persons are expected to be as careful at home, if not more, as in the work place. Happy environment of trust and love makes life easy and reduces the stress and pressures faced in the work place. Well, this can't be one way affair. The family has also to be appreciative of lack of time for the family and pressures the individual is facing in work place and be supportive and sensitive to his/her compulsions/sensibilities.

'Switch on', 'Switch off'; the practical approach

I do not know where to begin for describing how this approach evolved in my mind. But one thing is clear; it did help immensely in the interest of relatively peaceful and healthy environment. While leaving home in the morning for work, I would switch off home and get busy (switch on) with office. Exactly the reverse would happen in the evening while leaving my work-place. What does this really mean? It is very simple. Leave the respective anxieties at home and in the office in the morning and in the evening. Do not mix-up the two diverse situations was my logic/rationale. That is not to say that I would forget soon after leaving my house in the morning all that was required or wanted at home or vice-versa in the evening. The difference would be the focus; utmost priority would be what was ahead then and it would get full attention. In hind sight, I believe, it helped sustain equilibrium in pressures between home and office and also avoided confusion. Being worried about home in the office is a sure recipe for poor performance in office. Similarly, bringing office to home in the evening is sure to lead to conflict at home. The sight of files etc. at home is repulsive and obnoxious to the family members. Therefore, as a well-thought-out strategy, I never brought office files at home. It was ridiculous to expect the family to view it generously. Better inform beforehand and be late than creating a ruckus at home. It happened like that throughout my work-life and it was instrumental in removing, to a large extent, a feeling of intentional neglect of the household affairs. I believe; it worked for me well and gave lesser chances for complaints which normally do exist quite usually in each service class family.

Thanks to technology and changed work-culture, the picture is different now; working from home is quite common now-a-days but it too has its limitations. You need the same amount of concentration while working from home and therefore the home remains cut-off even if you are physically present there. You are not available to family members easily. I saw Sandeep locking himself up in his Study while working from home and not responding to any overtures of his mother for some food etc. This is the essence of a successful work-life. Place of work doesn't matter. What is of concern is performance.

My Better-half; Krishna

My beautiful companion-in-arms in thick and thin of life, a crusader imbued with a unique sense of courage and dashing spirit who sprinkled love in abundance all around in the family. Compassionate and helpful for the needy, worldly-wise yet 'nat-khat' and full of innocent pranks like a child, she always contributed sincerely for the welfare of poor. A crazy mother that she is has always been zealous and keen to protect family's turf of honour. She is different, extraordinary and an achiever of substance. By all means, she occupies a warm privileged place in my heart. A great lady whom all of us love, enjoy her company and are indebted to her for her selfless services, great positive contributions and sacrifices for the family.

Her sterling qualities of head and heart endear her with whom-so-ever she comes into contact. She is God fearing, religious minded, strong-willed, bold and fearless and resolute in her determination to excel. Adversities and lack of resources can never stop her from achieving what she sets her mind on. A visionary in her own way, she is capable of visualizing and anticipating the future. Standing tall shoulder to shoulder with male members, down to earth practical, worldly wise and on top of it, a great relationship and rapport builder that she is, she loves to put in her best always. Put her in a situation of conflict and she would handle it with ease and tact and resolve the differences smoothly as if nothing had happened. Her knack of delivering meaningfully relevant and appropriately coined messages at the closing stage in a conversation would sum up the essence of the matter and win acceptance/gratitude of the receiver. This unique combination of balanced EQ and IQ traits places her in the lead role in situations of conflict.

A happy 'Mamma' and home-maker

A loving mother that she is, she would not mind slogging and sweating in the kitchen for long hours to make sure that the food she makes is full of variety, is healthy and nourishing but tastes very well. By temperament, she cannot compromise on quality whether it is food articles or other household goods. She is always meticulous about the quality of durables, choice of furniture, furnishings, gadgets and interiors for the house. Maintaining every article in good shape and in a presentable manner has been a routine for her. Help or no help, the house and interiors must always be spick and span and if it means slogging let it be so.

Thrift has always been her forte. Go for an item only if the family budget permits it. 'Cut your coat according to your cloth' was the dictum that the family always followed. Be within the available means; credit purchases must be avoided. She must make sure that the price being demanded is reasonable, quality is assured, product is of a reliable standard make/ brand, no better and economical option or a substitute is available and above all, go for it only when essential and unavoidable. She wouldn't jump in haste to buy an item unless sure about its utility and its need for the house. As far as provisions, grocery items, fruits, vegetables and other food products are concerned; she would not compromise or economize. The family must have high quality stuff and in plenty. It would appear to be a tall order to satisfy considering that family's income didn't permit all this. Let me put all this in perspective. But for the habit of thrift and not going in for credit purchases, the family would have been in difficulty. In fact, no pressing demands were ever made by her with the result that I never thought of going in for illegal gratifications or so called 'extra income'.

Mamma, a successful entrepreneur

All what is written above gives an impression as if she possesses high qualities of a home-maker or a charming mother or a lovable life-partner only or a strong voter of the policy of thrift only. No this is far off from being true. The story of her endeavours to make a significant contribution and add to family's resources is worth mentioning in golden letters.

Soon after my transfer to Jammu in 1985, she realized in her wisdom that she had a window of 3, 4 hours free time in the mornings. Sandeep and Ashish would leave for school early morning and come back around 2.30 pm. A brilliant idea crossed her mind; let me start a primary school in our house and she got going with it earnestly. During one of visits from Jammu, I was surprised to see a toddlers' class going on in one of our room which was meant to be used as guests' room. Though she had mentioned this to me earlier also but I just ignored it knowing that we had neither the resources nor infrastructure for it. But she was determined and did it single handedly. She had spent a few hundred rupees for buying the class room furniture, other gadgets and display charts and the room really looked like a well-organized class-room.

In due course, thanks to her rigorous efforts in providing high quality education, emphasis on co-curricular activities, hard push through personal contacts in the nearby residential colonies and sundry publicity efforts bore fruits and the school kept on growing. 'Happy

Hours School' in Green Park became a well-known entity not only in the neighbourhood but also in far-off places. 'Madam', as she came to be known now, commanded a lot of respect. By gradually adding additional rooms on first floor of the house, the physical infrastructural needs of the school were met. Her single-minded devotion and glorious efforts kept on pushing up the number of students every year and at one stage, she had about 125 students.

This venture proved beyond doubt that she is a woman of not only vision but also of substance, action and determination. Starting with one teacher in the beginning in April, 1986, the school ultimately had five teachers, a help and functioned gloriously for 20 years till 2006 when it was decided to wind it up reluctantly/grudgingly due to her inability to continue with it anymore because of pressing needs of her presence in USA frequently with our sons' families.

Her perseverance and hard work earned for her in abundance the respect of parents for the fine quality of education imparted in the school along with lessons of morals.

In fact, Mrs. Aneja never spared efforts to supplement family income even earlier. She had taken up the job of a nursery teacher for few years at a very small salary in a school run by a philanthropic organization in BS City. Considering the quantum of salary on offer I thought the offer was not worthwhile but she insisted saying this would fetch for the family two litters of fresh milk per day. This disarmed me and I nodded my head in affirmation.

Our early family life

Our daily household routine was seriously strenuous no doubt till the last child (Ashish) started going to school but optimist that we were; we always pinned our hopes on 'better days ahead' and thus tried to ward off the tensions. We were conscious that all this was unavoidable for our economic condition didn't permit us to hire some help on regular basis except a part-time maid for daily chorus of utensil cleaning and sweeping and dusting etc. The gadgets like washing machines or cooking gas weren't in vogue much then. In any case, we couldn't afford them. The refrigerator entered our house sometimes in 1973-74. Not going into details and with no intention to express any regrets for ourselves, I only wish to highlight here the drudgery associated with lack of resources in middle-class house-holds. To be honest, our difficulties were further compounded by our attitude; the family especially the kids must not feel let down. Apart from providing what was needed for their education, their other needs must also be met appropriately. Parents' needs were secondary. That in my bachelor period I used to be care-free and accumulate for myself a lot of accessories besides latest clothing was immaterial now.

Enjoy present and look forward to future with hope

I must say that this was the most satisfying and a happy phase in our life. We were very happy in what we had. Expectations were not wild and we were busy making optimum use of what was within our reach. Nobody in the family ever cribbed/complained about the non-availability of facilities with us which others had. We didn't have a scooter till 1974; reason being quota and centralized registration system. One had no option but to wait for an allotment from Delhi. Though all of us felt bad but never let it spoil the household environment. We never felt we were marginalized or denied what was our due. On the contrary, we were happy because we didn't believe in chasing wild dreams. Enjoy what is available, is within your reach and look forward to future with bright expectations. After all, environment of plenty doesn't necessarily bring in its wake true happiness. What really matters is satisfaction, peace of mind and an attitude of self-confidence and capability to look beyond present. Know your strengths; visualize what lies ahead, what is within the realms of possibility, what is in your reach and what the future prospects are. Don't gloat over the progress you have made in life so far. If you do, you will stop growing.

Happiness is not dependent upon miscellaneous facilities, gadgets of comfort and entertainment or convenience of travel in a car. Can it be said that our ancestors had a miserable life due to lack of all this?

The well -known proverb 'cut your coat according to your cloth' and saint Kabir's famous couplet 'rukhi sookhi khaye ke, thanda pani pi, na dekh prayi chopri te na tarsave ji' are a great lesson for those who value peace of mind rather than chasing a mirage of dis-satisfaction.

Our approach; take good care of children and see happiness is around

Our daily routine turned for better somewhat after Ashish started going to school in April/May, 1973 but the burden was still quite heavy. In fact, there was hardly any relief except that nature and type of strain was less rigorous now. Sunita and Sandeep could handle some of their morning (pre-school going) activities themselves. This process continued with children's growth enabling us to be less strained in the mornings.

Well, all of them have been a nice lot; co-operative, very well-behaved, very good at studies, not demanding by nature and no cribbing if sometimes their reasonable need too couldn't be fulfilled. They loved to be together, enjoyed each other's company, helping each other mutually in completing the home-task and happily sharing between themselves the goodies/general reading books and magazines/sweets etc. that were brought in the house. God forbid, they have been a happy lot and a source of genuine pleasure for us. Watching them grow so happily before our eyes has indeed been a matter of great satisfaction and pride for us. Colloquially speaking, it is said in our male-dominated society, 'watching your son grow before your own eyes is a great charming satisfaction and exalted happiness.' I do not know but may be; we too were impelled by it and never spared any efforts to fetch the best possible items of daily consumption. Our attempt used to be to give them tasty, nutritious, healthy and hygienic and variety of delectable food at home. Going out for eating was not a routine in our family.

We also took care to let them have opportunities for development of their skills for balanced growth apart from education in high-end public schools. Praise be to them that they responded to all these efforts very well and brought laurels for themselves and the parents by securing high grades/positions, recognitions and lot of merit certificates in co-curricular activities and games and sports. There was never any need to hire for them tutors during school days or sending them to coaching classes for entrance exams for entry into professional courses. Mrs. Aneja did spend time with them while they were in primary classes. After that, it was all their personal efforts which pushed them through. They proved themselves to be worthy of appreciation by successfully competing and entering into professional courses on merit.

Chapter 2
Our expanded family Children's glorious success stories

While Sunita was successful in getting admission in BSC (Home Science) program on merit in the prestigious Lady Irwin College in Delhi, Sandeep was successful in SCRA (Special Class Railway Apprentice) competition conducted by UPSC on all India basis in which about 25000 candidates compete for a limited number of openings, about 15 to 20 in all. This is a premier in-house program of Indian Railways for training in Mechanical Engineering and is one of the most difficult and sought after open competitive exam for budding +12 students. Competing successfully and being a member of this prestigious service in IR is a dream come-true. Once in it, you are sure of growth, and a distinct place of pride in society. Granted that joining Railways as SCRA was a major achievement but right from school days, Sandeep had set his mind on going to the land of plenty, USA. He had worked hard for it, got admission in undergraduate programs in prestigious colleges/universities in USA by successfully competing in SAT (Scholastic Aptitude Test) but couldn't join due to our inability to support him financially. He did successfully complete his training program in Railways but couldn't continue in the job for long. Simultaneously, he was preparing for GRE and TOEFL tests, secured admission in a university with scholarship of $ 1200/pm and lo and behold, he was gone without bothering for his bond etc. with Railways. The rest is history; he qualified in MS program, got a job, served for about two years and not happy with prospects of rapid growth in engineering profession, decided to go in for MBA program. In GMAT, his scores were 99.4 percentile which entitled him to aspire for admission in top most Business Schools of USA. He set his mind on Stanford University and was successful in getting admission in Business School in MBA program of this prestigious university. Again, he did all this on his own with the help of a bouquet of loans from University/Govt./Banks and other institutions. An ambitious boy with determination to excel and make rapid/meteoric growth in life had achieved what he had so meticulously planned and worked hard for. Such a glorious saga of accomplishment was possible due to his unrelenting efforts of many years and Blessings of Lord Almighty.

Sandeep's journey of struggles to fulfil his ambitions

After being in USA for about 12 years of which the last 5 years were in VCF industry, Sandeep started exploring possibilities of setting up a venture-capital fund of his own in India. He made numerous exploratory trips here starting from June, 2005 to understand the business environment in India and also to build up contacts with local senior professionals since he had not known any influential and successful business magnates before. This meant starting from a scratch but he persisted with his efforts till he was successful in cobbling up a team of two very senior Managers (CEO and President to be precise) of two leading business houses. Encouraged by it, he redoubled his efforts in USA to build up a support base there and succeeded in receiving positive response from a leading Fund House of NY who agreed to be the sponsors and also agreed to infuse substantial amount as the seed capital for the proposed venture. This was a break-through of great significance but there was a serious setback when in January, 2007 one of his potential partner ditched him at the last moment and refused to severe his existing position. Sandeep was betrayed and was crest-fallen as his efforts of about eighteen months had been washed off. He had been deceived and a bright future in the horizon for him had vanished all of a sudden. He had quit his job in USA and now he was face to face with dark clouds. He recovered from this shock of intense severity soon and re-started on his mission more vigorously and was able once again, after prolonged parleys, confabulations and detailed presentations to get a firm assurance from top management of a leading public sector utility company to join him and invest in the proposed venture. Finally, the family landed in India in July, 2007 with dreams in their eyes for a great future. Aneja family's streak of ambitions and entrepreneurship in him had culminated in pushing him to this stage of expectations. As the ill-luck would have it, he again faced deception and the company's management was non-committal. Imagine, what could be the mental state of the entire family. There was no hope but the destiny had a pleasant surprise for the family; he was successful in entering into a VCF based in Mumbai as its COO and a promise of partnership in due course.

Sterling support provided by Sim to Sandeep in his endeavors

In this entire phase of struggles and tribulations, Sim, his life-partner, our daughter-in-law, stood with him resolutely, co-operated with him thoroughly and happily supported him in all his moves but for which nothing could have been possible. With great pleasure and a sense of deep satisfaction, we the parents admire her for her stellar role in Sandeep's journey of ups and downs in pursuit of his, nay theirs, ambitious pursuits. Ultimately, their concerted joint efforts have catapulted them into a position of envy for many. With God' Grace and Kindness, Sandeep is lucky to be the Promoter and CEO of a PE Fund in Mumbai. Under his leadership the Fund is making great strides and is pushing ahead successfully, of-course with full support of Sim, who herself is a Business Graduate from a leading Business School of Europe.

Ashish's saga of struggles to fulfil his dreams

Now, let me briefly talk of brilliant success of Ashish. Right from school days, he was clear he would go in for medicine. He was aware that his parents didn't have the money to pay for capitation fee etc. and the only way it could be possible was to qualify in the open admission tests after his 10+2. Even here, there were numerous hurdles; seats were limited, there were reservations for different categories to the extent of fifty %, number of candidates in general category was very large and therefore only the best performance in the entry test could help. Very high grades in Senior Secondary exam (10+2) had no relevance. Therefore, the task was up-hill and called for extra-ordinary hard work in preparations. This scenario was applicable both in the State's and Central competitive exams. He was too sure about himself and his capability to clear the entry tests on his own and therefore refused to undertake any coaching facility. "I am sure, I will be successful" was always his reply. And he proved he was right. He took up tests of 5 prestigious Medical colleges and was on high merit in 4 of them i.e. he could aspire to secure admission against the limited number of seats open to general category candidates. He was successful in AFMC, Pune, KGMC, Lucknow against state and central exams both and in BHU, Varanasi. His success in so many colleges put us into dilemma; which college should he join since all these colleges were considered to be in the top list. After hectic discussions and consultations with seniors in the profession, it was decided that he should join KGMC. In hind-sight, one can say this was the correct decision by all means. KGMC, Lukhnow, is one of the top most medical colleges in India and is well-known for very high standard of education. In fact, it is a dream destination for many an aspirants.

Ashish did his MBBS with Honours and secured Gold Medal. Admission in PG program too proved to be too easy for him thanks to his position in the merit list and he joined his previous college, KGMC, in MD (Medicine) program. He completed this program in 1997. He was in two minds whether to take up a job in India or opt for going to USA. As a matter of fact, he too was stung by USA virus but also entertained ideas to stay back. Our daughter-in-law, Jyoti, was not keen on going to USA and kept on persuading him to drop his plans. But not being happy with the work environment in different hospitals in Delhi/NCR, he redoubled his efforts, qualified in USMLE & TOEFL exams and migrated to USA in 2001. Now, after lot of struggles he has ultimately achieved his dream;

Fellowship in Cardiology and a super-specialty program of monitoring heart's health with MRI etc.

Jyoti's silent and sound support for Ashish & her own journey of success.

Jyoti, his life-partner, a medico herself, not only supported Ashish in all his endeavours in USA but also worked hard to fulfil her own ambitions too. She was MBBS when they landed in USA but set her mind on doing the Residency Program there. Thanks to rigorous efforts, she successfully qualified in the prestigious qualifying exams, USMLE & TOEFL, apart from part-time assignments in research projects. She successfully completed her Residency Program in Human Psychiatry from a leading hospital in Cleveland (Ohio) and is now very well-known and respected for her competence in the profession. Her tale of struggles for first securing admission in Residency Program and thereafter pursuing it along with her responsibility towards children and house-hold is itself an achievement par excellence. Her determination in pursuing her aims against odds and difficult situations is no less than Ashis's. We are proud that under her able guidance, close supervision and perseverance, both our grand-children, Anushree and Arihant, are doing exceedingly well in their studies. Lord Almighty's Blessings be with them always!!

Our sons' children; our pride

Our grand-children, Shardul and Munn (Sandeep's sons) are a class by themselves; naughty, care-free, good at studies and of-course, very loving. They provide a wonderful company when we are in Mumbai. It is real pleasure watching them grow so well and happily. A lot of credit goes to Sim for this because Sandeep is mostly hard-pressed for time.

Aarushi, Sandeep's eldest daughter from his first wife, has cleared her High School successfully in USA and shall be joining the Under-graduate Program in August this year. God's Grace; she has grown up too well and is blessed with an impressive joyful persona.

Ashish Jyoti's siblings, Anushree and Arihant in Cleveland (USA) too are a happy lot; enjoying each other's company, doing extremely well in studies and co-operating very well with parents considering the difficult schedules that Ashish and Jyoti have to work on in their hospitals. Anushree is a gem; she is not only at top in her class in critical subjects like Maths and English but has also secured awards/medals in open competitions like Science Olympiad at state level in Ohio in last year. And now she has achieved what is the dream of thousands of students in US; winning Science Olympiad at National level. No compromises are acceptable to her in life; she is always focused on top position and spares no efforts to reach the top even if it means neglecting her personal routines and comforts. Arihant too is doing very fine in school and I am sure, he too would match his performance with that of Anushree.

All our grand-children, individually and collectively, have done proud to the family.

Sunita, our darling daughter; an embodiment of what is thought to be noble

My apologies to Sunita, our darling daughter, for having not talked about her so far in these discussions. The reason is the context. In our society, the daughters are expected to be more devoted to their own families after marriage. Their prime responsibility is towards their own family and their in-laws. Physically also, they are in their own places, even if residing in the same town/village. It is commonly said, "We are happy if our daughter is happy in her own family." In our society, this is thought to be necessary for a meaningful happy family life for daughters. Notwithstanding all this logical and practical exposition, it is well known that daughters are more attached to parents even after marriage. It is believed, the emotional bond of daughters with their parents is very strong. I must confess that Sunita, forced by her divine nature, is always concerned about our welfare. She is such a simple and innocent creature of which there can hardly be any example. Since childhood, she has not known what is being smart and diplomatic with any one. She talks innocently plain language, cannot follow if the conversation is not in straight manner, will not talk ill or listen any derogatory language, has neither told any lie in her life nor expects others to do so and gets quickly hurt if somebody uses foul language in her presence. She has not known why people whisper and complain in hushed voice when the obvious method, in her opinion, is 'talk straight, plain and clear the air'. Dishonesty, cheating or ill-will for others is alien to her. She gets hurt when somebody thinks/talks ill but any talk of revenge for a wrong done to her or her family is meaningless to her. Surely, she is a different person; different from what is normally considered to be normal now-a-days. Love for poor, down-trodden and compassion in general are her real forte. A genuine philanthropist that she is keeps herself regularly engaged in activities of social help. To be honest, to us she is like a 'Devi'. This rare God Gift for her is a source of inspiration for us as also for those who care about honest and clean values in life. Sunita, our darling daughter, is a Blessed child! Amin!

Rajesh, our darling son-in-law; a highly successful entrepreneur

Sunita's life-partner, Rajesh, is highly supportive of her; stands by her in all her endeavours of help to the needy persons as also running their house-hold in a dignified manner. God has blessed them with wisdom to handle their responsibilities of married life harmoniously together with due care and love. Their children, Swati (27 now) and Dhruv (25) are very charming, well-behaved and thoroughly well-versed in making a mark in whatever they do.

Rajesh, in his own right, is a gem of a person; a very loving husband besides being mature, worldly wise and blessed with powerful acumen and big vision for managing successfully the affairs of his industry. His life story resembles the stories of success achieved after long struggle by highly successful businessmen. Starting with a retail outlet of timber/plywood/adhesives in a small town, he along with his younger brother, Sanjay, decided to enter the manufacturing business. Starting on a modest

334

scale in the beginning, they have built up a vast industrial complex for manufacturing plywood and other related products. Their products are well-known for high quality, good finish and durability and are therefore highly in demand.

Swati is happily married to Sakun Aggarwal in Pathankot. Their daughter Adania, our great grand-daughter, is very sweet, charming and blessed with pleasant personality and is full of witty enjoyable responses. Adania is shaping very well under the love and care of her parents & grand-parents. And see; now we are proud great grand-parents.

Dhruv, our grand-son has successfully completed his BBA program from a prestigious university and has completed a business-oriented MBA program of a prestigious college in Mumbai. He is busy helping his Dad, Rajesh, in day-to-day affairs of their big Ply-wood manufacturing unit at Yamuna Nagar in Haryana. A very happy family, indeed!

Family on visit to Mussoorie on 8th May 2015

Sandeep, Sim, Shardul & Munn

Sandeep & Aarushi

Ashish with his family – Jyoti, Anushree & Arihant

Sakun, Swati & Adania   Rajesh, Sunita & Dhruv

PART - IV

৯০ ০১

My Influencers

Eldest Brother-in-law Shri Ganesh Dass Sachdeva

Eldest Brother Manohar Lal Aneja & Bhabhijee

Father and Mother-in-law Shri N. D. Chawla

Observation skills; a significant prelude to getting influenced

Getting influenced by others is a normal phenomenon in human beings. But it happens only if one is inclined to observe, open to listening and ready to follow the substance. For those who watch but do not observe, who listen but do not pay any attention, this behavioural attribute is difficult to come by. Keen attitude to observe carefully what is happening around therefore takes a central place for us.

My mother, a master of practical wisdom, used to tell, "Keep your eyes and ears open, see and listen attentively to what happens around you. Be careful to understand the meaning behind by all what you see, hear and watch. This is how you can learn how to observe meaningfully. Careful observation helps you to discard what you find to be un-appealing or un-convincing or just an act of pretension. In day to day dealings, try to pick up what is nice and good, ask questions when and where in doubt. Take the guidance of elders whom you like and feel they have the answer to your queries or doubts. Do not follow blindly even if it is me. This helps you to retain/absorb what appeals to you. Be-ware; this learning gets embedded in your thought process and shall always be with you. You shall not have to make any attempts to rekindle it. It helps you on its own without any conscious effort by you."

Thanks to mother's rustic style of delivery and wise counsel of other elders, such fundamental gems of practical wisdom were easy to follow. I felt at ease in observing attentively and started drawing my own conclusions in a simple plain manner. Most of the times, I didn't see any hidden agenda in what transpired in front of me. 'Take it on face value and go ahead,' was my approach. The result was that the process of keen observation developed and helped me in my day to day routines. Thus, picking up good values and making use of them in time helped my learning faculties to be unbiased and healthy. As a consequence, I realized to my advantage that the real test lies in what we practice and actually do in real life.

The highly motivated/committed influencers

The tendency to do the preaching assuming it is enough by itself is quite common in most of us. We assume it is the exclusive prerogative of intelligent people and others must follow what is told to them. Being blessed with knowledge and ability to deliver the message eloquently may be a praiseworthy trait but its impact would be temporary if not accompanied by real time demonstration of its adoption by the deliverer in his own life. People may dub it mere hypocrisy and ignore it even though the text and context may be laudable. Preaching and sermons are rendered shallow and lose meaning if they do not demonstrate the deliverer's conviction about their veracity.

On the other hand, there are those who are inspired to do public good, do not preach nor sermonize but influence others by doing and demonstrating in real life what is practical, praiseworthy and laudable, is within the realms of equity and justice, conforms to the norms of 'sarv jan hitai, sarv jan sukhai', meaning what serves the best interests of all i.e. society at large. All this would appear to be a tall order for common folks who, it is believed, are not blessed with such price-less qualities. It is often argued that such nice people are few and far off and majority of the human beings being poor and pressed with hardships are busy struggling for survival and making both ends to meet. This may be true to a large extent but not wholly true.

Lord Almighty does not gift benign and open mind only to select few or only to those who are economically well-off. It is against Nature's Law of equity and justice. It is wrong to suggest that poor people being pre-occupied with anxieties of sustenance, have no chance of acquiring finer attributes in life. The task may look uphill and difficult but is not insurmountable nevertheless.

Mankind's history is replete with examples of persons of so-called low origin making sterling contribution to society; *Angulimal,* the dreaded

342

dacoit, renouncing his deadly and sinful life, becoming a 'Bhikshu and Preacher and embracing celibacy after he came into contact with Budhha; Balmiki, the dacoit, writing 'Ramayana' and becoming a learned scholar after he met a group of saints in his hide-out, come to mind easily.

Basically, the Lord doesn't differentiate and blesses all human beings with the ability to determine what is good and what is not. HE blesses each sincere effort irrespective of its origin. The difference lies in one's own perception, environment and sometimes circumstances.

My mother was an illuminating example of achieving success on both the fronts i.e. building up values alongside the struggle/hunt for arranging resources for giving two square meals a day to us. Of course, it meant a lot of sacrifice; spend day time in discharging her domestic house-hold responsibilities and try to connect with Him early morning around 4 am which she used to call 'santon ki bela', which she explained as the time when saintly and holy persons get up and pray to Him. The world would be enjoying the blissful morning sleep when this lady would be up and singing devotional songs (Bhajan) in serene peaceful environs. In the process, probably she was also attempting to bare her heart to Him while doing some house-hold score like spinning on her wheel or grinding wheat Atta on the hand-operated stone mill.

Who, I believe, were great influencers in my life?

1. MY MOTHER

Probably, I was the naughtiest of all her children and perhaps that is why she had a little softer corner for me. Her life story is a treasure full of practical lessons and it has always continued to impact me in my journey. Turn to relevant page of her story and you will find an answer to the question you are facing. That is the beauty of her journey. Each mile-stone in her journey is an inspiration. You have to know how to decipher it and adopt it.

What left impeccable imprints on my mind were:-

she was full of courage, was always determined to protect and secure a better future for her children, was un-relenting, like a male member, in her efforts in meeting her obligations to the family and had the vision to pursue her goals with vigour,

knew how to manage her time diligently,

was always seen to be alert and vigilant lest some odd happening destabilize her,

was practical and consistent in her approach,

was resolute and firm about protecting family's 'izzat',

was a living repository of intelligent colloquial phrases full of wit and humour of which she made full use in appropriate situations,

was always demanding before Him as though it was her right,

would open up her heart to Him only and seek solace in His Mercy and Generosity,

a 'Karm-yogini' in true sense though she had not read the 'Gita'.

The source of her indomitable spirit and energy was her mind. The great philosopher and thinker, Aristotle said, "The energy of the mind is the essence of life."

She hated her children being called orphans saying 'I am there. He had told me to do his (our father's) duty as well. I am sure, I am doing it well.'

2. MY ELDEST BROTHER-IN-LAW, SHRI GD SACHDEVA

His persona was that of an angel. The most striking qualities of his character were sacrifice, compassion and generosity.

He was a patient and attentive listener, was full of practical wisdom, always calm and composed while dealing with others and also while taking decisions; be it his patients or taking a view on some important question before him. I never heard him shouting at others. He never faltered in his judgment/assessment given his emphasis on fair and straightforward approach. What is humane, noble and praiseworthy was his legacy worthy of emulation.

His noble qualities of head and heart greatly impressed me. I always get over-awed with gratitude while recalling his services rendered to our family of his own volition. The best tribute to him is his elder son, Madan, who appears to be his carbon copy; action-wise and looks-wise both.

I am sure, but for his physical presence by our side and an un-remitting support, we would have faced a very dark future and probably the family would have been ruined. What more can one expect to get inspired and feel obliged?

To recall his services with sober gratitude and respects is a true tribute to the legend, Mr. GD Sachdeva.

3. MY ELDEST BROTHER, SHRI MANOHAR LAL ANEJA

What to say of a person who was just an adolescent and was the eldest male member in a family of seven when the calamity of his father's untimely death after prolonged illness struck the family. The life turned dark for him suddenly. The boy of thirteen was required to leave his school and step into the shoes of his late father. The only hope for a hapless widow and mother of six was her eldest son. It was in these circumstances that a decision was taken to send him to our uncle in Ferozepur to work as a helper in his Army Canteen. He struggled all his life for survival and remained busy in trying to meet one obligation or the other for his family.

His story is nothing but a tale of heroic struggle for survival. Leisure or relaxation was alien to him. Be busy in your assignments is what he always did as a honey bee would do in extracting nectar from flowers. There was only one priority before him; how to augment resources for family's needs. His thoughts and actions never bordered on self alone.

He believed and let it be known to us all that valuing, caring for and properly utilizing the available time effectively was the only way out for us, the under-privileged. He would often say, "Time is a treasure trove. Make sure, you do not waste it. Consume it judiciously and diligently to reap the most out of it." His famous and oft-repeated lines were, "time and tide wait for no man," and "Gaya waqt phir haath aata nahin." Being punctual, disciplined and stead-fast in action rather than theory was close to his heart. The burden of necessity and his long stint in army canteen had deeply impacted his approach to life.

4. MY BROTHER-IN-LAW, SHRI DC KALRA

A true saintly person; an embodiment of sterling qualities like truthful behaviour, honest to the core, pure and transparent conduct, simple by nature, God-fearing and helpful, thousands of miles away from deceit and cheating and last but not the least non-corruptible in his official dealings is how one could think of him. I was lucky to be under the tutelage of such a noble person for three years during the most critical impressionable age group of 14 to 16 years from 1949 to 1952.

He was very strict and expected me to be a top performer in studies. He felt he was fully accountable to my family for my performance during my stay with him.

He was a very religious person; would get up very early in the morning, take bath and go to neighbourhood temple for performing 'puja' and listening to discourses and participating in 'Kirtan'. I used to accompany him to temple almost every day partly out of fear and partly in the hope that this would keep him in good humour. Of-course, in due-course, I got influenced and am happy that this opportunity came my way.

I believe; thanks to his strictness and close supervision, I emulated him in many ways and picked up unconsciously some of his nice habits. Gradually, while I continued to stick to most of his positive traits, the fear complex that I developed then impinged on my personality. Not indulging in corrupt practices in official duties was his benign gift for me. I feel indebted to him for this pure legacy.

5. MY BOSS, MR. JR PASRICHA IN AG'S OFFICE AT SHIMLA.

I concede that my coming to Shimla in 1959 was a stroke of good luck but the bigger bounty was my association there with Mr. Pasricha. This association turned out to be the cradle of a great learning for me; of nuances of a genuinely happening, meaningful and satisfying work-life. His mannerism was charming and betrayed his unique knack of attracting people around him. Delivering his best in office was a passion, and a craze for him. A compassionate approach was the mantra he loved. He would often say, "While dealing with people's claims, be objective, considerate and reasonable without compromising the basics and fundamental provisions in the rule book. Coming from an audit professional, this approach was liberal, to say the least. And, surely, it was in sharp contrast to the approach of most of his colleagues. Just similar was his disposition to his staff. As for seniors, he knew their pulse, would happily accept challenging assignments and having done that, would spare no efforts to deliver.

I believe; his IQ and EQ levels balanced each other. And what can I talk of his AFQ (Adversity Facing Quotient)? He had a unique caliber for facing adversities head on.

I am sure, he knew himself well which according to great philosopher, Aristotle, is the beginning of wisdom.

He was my role model not only in office work but also in personal life. I loved to imitate him and tried hard to imbibe his virtuous qualities of head and heart. Our relationship was like that of a Guru and chela. His actions genuine, true and transparent as they were always inspired me. My close association with him was a turning point in my life; he shaped my destiny and inspired me through his personal examples to believe in self, integrity and honesty of purpose. The direction my life took from then on was his benign gift to me. I owe it to him in whatever I achieved in my life.

6. MY MOTHER-IN-LAW and FATHER-IN-LAW

Both my parents-in-law were blessed with high qualities of head and heart. They possessed unique similarities of sound ethical disposition and open hearts like their other compatriots of those days. I wonder sometimes, how come, personal values, social relationships and mutual inter-actions have changed so drastically just in the last few decades and the era gone by is a history now.

My mother-in-law, though physically rather weak and frail, was very robust at heart and head; was highly emotional but without any show-off, was an oasis of pure love for the family. Very thoughtful, vigilant and alert, worldly wise and circumspect in dealings, always busy in one chorus or other, she would handle the house-hold responsibilities smilingly. Eagerly willing to satisfy even irrational demands of family members, a marvellous cook capable of dishing out variety of delectable food, home-made sweets and tongue-twisting 'pakoras' endeared her to all. She wouldn't take her food until every-one in the family had taken it and, if in the process, very little food is left for her, she wouldn't let anybody else know it.

She was terribly affectionate, possessed very simple nature, and was honest and plain to the core. And what to talk of her attitude towards her grand-children (our progeny) for whom she was always crazy in love. She would happily meet even their idiosyncratic demands believing her refusal would alienate them from her. Her love and blind emotions for them would stop her from saying no. Mrs. Aneja being her first child was very close and dear to her. The mother and daughter enjoyed a very cosy relationship of great depth sharing secrets of great significance.

Alas, she was snatched away by cruel hands of destiny at the young age of about 60 after brief illness.

I was greatly impressed by her countless noble qualities and this generated a lot of respect for her in my mind.

My father-in-law was the true epitome of what is fearlessness and courage. He hailed from a region known for the indomitable spirit of liberty and freedom of its habitants; Pathans of Frontier. He wouldn't succumb to any pressure, would vigorously fight for his due, pursue his goals relentlessly and rest only after he had accomplished on what he had set his mind. Outspoken, dashing and vigorous in chasing his dreams, he wouldn't mind picking up a duel, here and there, or wield a gun along with his brothers, when they felt it was necessary to secure their due. In today's parlance, he was a 'Dabang'.

He was in security establishment of Govt. of India and courageously escorted all members of his expanded family to safety in India after partition of the country.

I admired him for his courage and determined resolve in protecting his terrain but I never thought of following him in all these activities. Mrs. Aneja was his favourite child and it is no surprise that she too imbibed his qualities of fearlessness and courage. In fact, I am told, he used to depend more on her conviction rather than anybody else's in the family. Why not, after all both of them shared a common vision in matters relating to protecting their rights.

7. MY ETERNAL FRIENDS

The wonderful, memorable, unbelievably cherishing moments and nice time spent together with the collegium of my 'true' friends in Shimla is simply un-paralleled. Its memories are scintillating and I frequently recall these ten years when I need a dose of heavenly bliss. I travel backwards; ignite the flames of passion with which we enjoyed our togetherness and enriched our lives. Such a talisman didn't happen thereafter though I continued to survive on the rare tonic, 'true friendship.' Then there were my colleagues in BSL whose friendship made life comfortable and enjoyable in the forlorn place called BS City. And my old school buddies in Dehra Dun whom I met after a gap of 30 long years in 1982 welcomed us all with open heart and gave us love in abundance. They and their families are a true source of support for us.

True friendship has no substitute; expectations of reciprocity have no place here. Go ahead whole-heartedly; welcome this benign gift if you are indeed lucky to have been afflicted with it. Be cool, it is a life-long affair. Rest assured; it will do you good always. It is a very delicate substance that needs to be nurtured with genuine desire of giving rather than receiving supported by passionate care.

PART - V

౷౦౦౯

Vanprastha; the Creative Post Retirement Phase

Chapter 1
The Four Stages of Life

As per Holy Scriptures, there are four stages in a human being's life; 'Brahmcharya (1 to 25 yrs.), 'Grihastha' (26-50 yrs.), 'Vanprastha' (51-75 yrs.) and 'Sanyas (76-100yrs.). This distribution of assumed spell of 100 years of life is deeply significant. The four stages as envisioned in scriptures are essentially a guide for organizing one's life in a well-considered manner so that transition from one phase to the other is smooth. Our 'Rishis' visualized that these guidelines would go a long way in providing comfort and satisfaction to human beings in their endeavour to live a tangible life free of illusions about self and the world at large.

An eminent scholar of world's religions in his exposition states that it is appropriate that attachment to wants should eventually decline, for it would be unnatural for life to end while action and desire are at their zenith. A time comes when sex and the delight of senses (pleasure) as well as achievements in the game of life (success) no longer yield novel and surprising turns; when even the discharge of a human vocation (duty) begins to fall, having grown repetitious and stale. When this season arrives, it is time for the individual to move on to the third 3rd stage in life's sequence (Vanprastha). He further says that people, who cannot bring themselves to relinquish key positions when a younger generation with more energy and new ideas should be stepping into them, ultimately suffer ignominy.

Krishan Aneja

The third stage of life in present context

Granted; that as per ancient scriptures, 'Vanprastha' starts at the end of fifty years of age. However in the present context of longevity, when service class is in large numbers and such persons superannuate in sixties, the third stage of life (Vanprastha) can be said to begin long after superannuation. One need not be bogged down by the age factor for it only means that the third stage of life begins when one is deemed to have crossed the era of serious hard-hitting work-life. Therefore, simply put, 'Vanprastha' does not mean an end of work-life altogether. Further, the third stage can be said to be a transitory phase for an onward journey; a prelude to the ultimate phase when one is expected to get ready to gradually relinquish the worldly responsibilities and give up big personal ambitions. Mythology lays down that in grown-up age when one's desires for sensual pleasures and worldly attachments start on a down-hill journey, one should let them take a back seat, start exploring and seek to devote more attention to sublime attributes of life.

Pass on the baton to the next generation but continue to lead and provide guidance till the next generation gets well-versed and equipped to handle the responsibilities themselves. In other words, the elder member should get relieved of the day to day nitty-gritty but be available for support, guidance and mid-course corrections when necessitated. Gradual detachment is the answer to the dilemma which surfaces before all of us.

Post-retirement phase

For service-group people, the post-retirement phase is an opportunity of great significance; give a definite shape to ideas/plans for satisfying urges and accomplishing what possibly could not be done during active work-life for whatever reasons. Forget the past; make full use of the window of opportunity available now and do what you wish to do. Thanks to rich experience and mature wisdom available now, one can divide time between hobbies and finer urge(s) of choice, if any, like painting, music, arts, book-writing, social-service etc. etc. in addition to a vocation, business or a consultancy to meet family's fiscal needs. For,

354

age is no bar for pursuing and devoting keen attention to more than one option of choice.

For those who seek to pursue sublime activities of soul, this phase is a serious opportunity for introspection, making an inward journey, communicating meaningfully with self to make attempts to understand various inner urges and thus reaching the stage of taking a calibrated view about the next step. As a result of such a soul-searching exercise, one can come to the conclusion that I shall be happy to tread on this path. If necessary, do seek the company and guidance of a holy-man, a spiritual Guru to satisfy your inner urges and to pursue the ultimate goal of blissful contentment. But being unsure about future plans at this ripe stage of life is not pardonable. Whatever be one's disposition, one need not be at cross-roads. Be sure and push ahead with zeal failing which, there may be regrets and unhappiness converting this golden phase into misery. Find out options of choice, analyse them and decide which one is closer to your style and thinking, which one really looks feasible now and where you can make a difference and feel happy.

A word of caution though

However, it is also a fact that one is more cautious and circumspect by nature in this age-bracket. Therefore, for variety of reasons, one has to dispassionately analyse the pros and cons of the chosen option and do sort of s.w.o.t analysis (financial and societal both) to try to seek answers like feasibility, viability, desirability and relative strength of the inner response for it. By now, one is well aware of the constraints and one's shrinking capacity of taking risks. 'Hurry makes the curry' is deeply ingrained in one's psych. Another very important and seriously valid factor is the views of one's life-partner, whose opinion plays an equally important role in decision making. Yet, for many, another influencing factor could be the strong opinion of grown up members of the family, who need to be taken into confidence before zeroing in on a final choice.

Krishan Aneja

My Achilles Heel; unable to decide 'how to get busy.'

It happens with most of us during work-life; remain busy in meeting normal responsibilities of work-life; be it a struggle for earning proper and decent livelihood, or meeting other responsibilities towards oneself, family, friends, elders and society at large. The prime concern in work-life for employees like us is to give our best to the job. For sincerely committed people, nothing else matters except to meet obligations associated with the position one is holding. However, when one gets closer to the age of retirement, the question, 'What next' looms large and this, in fact, is a serious poser.

I was no exception to this universal truth. Having remained single-mindedly and awfully busy whole-time in discharging my responsibilities of job, I had not given attention to post-retirement plans. I hadn't picked up any hobby, had spared no time for playing games and didn't pursue any creative activity along with my job. In fact, to be honest, nothing else except job mattered then; of-course for valid reasons; growth in career. Post-retirement, the realization of total neglect of hobbies etc. was painful but to no effect. The only choice before me now was either a stint of a new job, if possible, or to start some venture of my own. Well, I was not quite young but, Thanks to My Lord, I was quite healthy; physically as well as mentally and capable of working hard and planning for my future patiently in a calm manner. I believed, having to remain idle would be suicidal for me; a sure recipe for illness, mental as well as physical. Therefore, it was essential that I keep myself engaged in a venture of my choice and liking.

My dilemma

Having lived a clean work-life all through my career, I had no comfort of some accumulated wealth when I laid office on 31st May, 1994. The retirement benefits like gratuity and Provident Fund were just marginal. There was no comfort of pension from my employer either. Therefore, the compelling reason for me was to keep working and get busy in some meaningful pecuniary activity. Also, the option I choose should be appropriate to my competence and in tandem with the respectable positions I held during my work-life. This could be a job in a senior

356

position in some Co. but nothing seemed to be feasible in a small town like Dehra Dun. The other option could be my own venture but here again, there was a big constraint; non-availability of seed capital. Hence, I was in a serious dilemma and not able to move ahead in any direction. In fact, this was a most disturbing phase in my life. Nothing seemed to be working and nothing was visible on the horizon. There was no answer to 'what to do?' As the time passed, my worries kept on multiplying.

The first quick option that surfaced

Mrs. Aneja was running a Primary school since 1986 in our own house and it was a good show. Even before that also she had worked as a head teacher in a Primary school for ten years in BS City. Therefore, she was well-experienced by now in teaching and running a school. We thought her rich experience of about two decades and my involvement as a real support could be an answer to the dilemma. Encouraged by it, we both started toying with the idea of opening a proper school. But how to find resources required for it and where to do it was the moot question. The only possible solution appeared to be 'sell the house and move to Bareilly where we believed there was good potential for growth in education sector.' It was an encouraging workable idea and we gave serious thought to it. The prospects of making it a success in Bareilly seemed bright considering that a large number of new residential localities were coming up in the outskirts of the town. However, winding up our establishment at Dehra Dun was easier said than done. The hurdle of packing up and moving was serious enough which we thought, we won't be able to ignore. And we were back to square one; mulling and trying to find some other option. I wished and prayed; some solution may emerge out of the blue and relieve me of the pain/sufferings. Mrs. Aneja would often console me saying, "Don't lose heart. God willing some good option will surface soon or may be; we shall firm up the plan and go ahead with opening of a school in Bareilly.

Luckily, an apparently workable option comes up

By now, my friends and well-wishers too had become aware of my dilemma. It is in these circumstances that one of my respected close acquaintances, whom I regarded to be like my elder brother, came up with a suggestion which I felt was worth considering. The suggestion was to open, on franchise basis, a Learning Centre at Dehra Dun of NIS (National Institute of Sales), an upcoming subsidary of NIIT, a reputed leading IT training Co. of the country. The very mention of the idea of opening an educational centre enthused and attracted us both. I believed; getting associated with the subsidiary of a prestigious and highly acclaimed training Co. NIIT was indeed an excellent opportunity. As a first step, I set down to meet the head of NIIT, Dehra Dun Mr. Tandon, to know some broad details about NIS if he had. He wasn't aware about NIS but he was highly positive about NIIT with which he was associated for the last about five years and he was extremely happy with the business model offered by NIIT. He was categorical that NIS like its parent Co., NIIT, should also do well. I came to know more about NIIT from him and it encouraged me to explore the option.

Having thus satisfied myself, I sat down to understand the nitty-gritty of the business proposal my friend had in his mind. His motive was to find a reasonable business opportunity for his son-in-law at Dehra Dun so that he could be persuaded to stay on in Dehra Dun. This gentleman was without any business activity at Dehra Dun for some time now and had decided to go back to Delhi to re-start his old business of cloth merchant, whereas due to emotional attachment with his daughter and grand-children, my friend was keen that the family stays on in Dehra Dun. My friend believed that the proposal to open NIS's centre in Dehra Dun would meet the twin objective of finding a reasonable business option for me as well as his son-in-law. He suggested; we could join as partners in the venture with responsibility to run the centre resting on me and him being just a financer.

The final decision; open an NIS Centre

The spade work done by this family had revealed that considering my qualifications, my communication skills, my experience and the position I held in ONGC, there would be no difficulty for me to secure the consent from NIS. I too had similar expectations as far as getting a positive nod from NIS was concerned but I was not comfortable with the idea of him being the financer and I being responsible for running the show. For me, this relationship of owner and employee was hard to digest. Having lived an honourableand clean life at senior management level, I was certain that the business relationship should be between equals and not as an owner and an employee. Further, I had genuine apprehensions about partnerships as such and more so when the arrangement is not between equals. Be careful and build up sound legal safe-guards before you go ahead was the refrain of some reliable friends.

I conveyed my mind to the other party accordingly and after few sessions of discussions, my suggestion was accepted; each one of us would invest equal amount as share capital in the proposed Co and pending sanction of loan by the bank, he would lend additional funds to the CO at market rates of interest. This agreement (verbal at the moment) between us set the ball rolling.

NIS agrees for franchise arrangement for me

I paid two, three visits to NIS office in Delhi and succeeded in getting their consent for grant of a Franchise to me. The crucial stipulation was that the franchise arrangement would be between NIS and me in my capacity as majority stake holder in a legal business entity in the form of a Private Limited Co. duly registered with the concerned Registrar of Cos. After this a period of very hectic activities started simultaneously on various fronts; setting up a Private Ltd. Co., a formal partnership agreement between me and my partner for the interim period, arranging accommodation required for the Centre, short-listing two banks after contacting their local Managers, putting in formal request for loan with one of them considering better chances of acceptances of the request by Bank's Regional Office, attending to officers of NIS on visit to Dehra Dun, fixing up communication and publicity agency, fixing up the agency for creating physical infrastructure, furniture and furnishings, paint and polishing to set up the centre as per the standards and specifications of NIS, starting the process of selection of Faculty, Sales and Publicity Manager, Counsellors and other staff members, firming up strategy for field publicity, building up contacts with select principals, teachers of leading local colleges and schools and other leading opinion makers of the town and all this to be accomplished with fantastic speed and alacrity in about two months' time. The stipulation from NIS was to hold the inaugural function with pomp and show in a befitting and graceful manner where apart from local media barons, the galaxy of the town to be invited. Director, NIS was to hold the press meet followed by question-answer session to be handled jointly by him and me. In short, it was to be a big publicity blitzkrieg.

NIS Centre's launch function; a great success

It is indeed difficult now to describe as to how did I manage to meet the challenges; complete the tasks in the stipulated time-frame and got the infrastructure ready to my own satisfaction and to the entire satisfaction of penetrating eyes and attitude of NIS Manager, Mr. Rana, who was a hard task master and was very specific about details. He had conveyed clearly in the beginning itself that the final product ought to be a master show-peace Centre like what they had at Delhi. At the end of the day, he was all praise for the excellent get-up, finish and high quality infrastructure created by our team.

The inaugural function was held on 5th July, 1995, at the centre itself which was attended by large number of invitees. It was a thunderous success considering the appreciative comments showered by all; the dignitaries, the select invitees from schools, colleges, media, business professionals, and my erstwhile senior colleagues of ONGC, our friends, relatives and political heavy-weights of the town. The press meet in the evening followed by question-answer session was organized in a high-end hotel of the town. Praise be to Lord Almighty, it too went off very well and it received full publicity in local news-papers as well as some national dailies of Delhi!!

Chapter 2
I get going with the project, 'NIS', despite some inhibitions

Getting involved in the business of running a professional training institute after superannuation when you don't have adequate comfort of seed capital of your own was a great risk alright but my enthusiasm to make it big helped. I was firm, "notwithstanding some inhibitions, I will do it and not let go this unique opportunity." I felt, NIS (National Institute of Sales) had the potential to alter the equation for the good for me and would also keep me productively and happily busy; a critical factor for me then. The hang-over of some inhibitions couldn't stop me from pushing ahead with the project I liked.

Being associated with NIS, a subsidiary of premier training co., NIIT, was a great feeling. I believed; the Diploma/Certificate Programs designed by senior experienced professionals of NIS after research and inter-action with Industry Professionals were well placed to equip young college going students with training as competent Sales Professionals. I was informed in meetings at NIS, Delhi, that the studies done by their research teams had established that the Industry was looking forward enthusiastically to this initiative of NIIT/NIS and Delhi, Chandigarh Centres' passed out students were well-received by the Industry. Encouraged by positive news, I felt, we at Dehra Dun would also do well and spare no efforts to train the students well. I was assured that placements were no problem. Industry Managers were open to the idea of qualified professionals exclusively managing the sales assignments rather than MBAs. Ironically, no Organization or a University till then had come forward to fill in this gap. In any case, churning out MBAs in large numbers was not an answer to Industry's needs for Sales Professionals.

The nagging anxiety, however, for me was that NIS was still in its infancy with 6/7 centres country-wide and, in a way, it had yet to establish its credentials as a competent agency of meeting student community's aspirations. An additional concern was that all along my work-life I was in accounts discipline which in corporate parlance was a back office job only. This new responsibility was totally different, rather reversal of role. The business set-up as a franchisee of a professional Co. was alien to me and it called for understanding its operations rather minutely. Realizing that my anxieties were genuine, I was asked to visit NIS Delhi office to get introduced to the senior Managers and spend 2, 3 days with the Regional Head I/C to get familiar with the operations and be aware of the support I could get from NIS in professional matters like training in NIS of my staff, visits by Faculty/Managers from head office and marketing/ publicity support available from head office etc. This visit and meeting with President and other seniors in head office helped me to appreciate better the relationship between us.

Back home, it was clear that I was expected to handle the entire load by myself without looking towards Head Office for a big push. Prepare Dehra Dun centre's business plan, work plan, induct suitable persons for different roles, guide, supervise and monitor their progress on regular basis, meet personally the influencers in the town, prepare and work on publicity campaign, look after finances and pursue with Bank the request for a loan, deposit the cash/checks of fee in NIS's account in the bank daily, prepare monthly accounts, submit the work-sheets as per the requirements of Auditor, get the audit satisfactorily completed on due date every month, receive the check of our part of the fee from NIS's Auditor and handle all matters relating to operations in the centre. My partner was a 'sleeping partner' which meant the entire responsibility to keep the business going rested on my shoulders all alone and it could mean disaster if I failed to deliver. For this reason and also for my own satisfaction, it was necessary that the team comprising of Counsellor,

Marketing Head and Faculty co-ordinate well and spare no efforts to achieve the targets set by NIS HQs for us.

NIS, Dehra Dun, gets huge response from town's youth

On the very first day, huge number of youngsters (enquiries in our parlance) lined up in the centre to know about the institute, programs offered and prospects of employment after a successful stint at NIS. In fact, the presence of large number of girls in the crowd was a testimony to maturity of mind, excitement to know and explore more in Dehra Dun's student population of both sexes. Of course, it also spoke well of our publicity campaign. NIS was in its infancy as it existed at that time in few places like Delhi, Mumbai, and Kolkata and Chandigarh only and wasn't getting any significant exposure in national Media. We handled more than 500 enquiries on the first day itself and about 350 on the next day. This was very exciting and gave us hopes that with proper follow up, we may make a really good start. Mr. Rana of NIS head office was a great help during this tumultuous phase. He stayed on with us for about a week after the launch of the centre and paid regular visits thereafter. He inspired us all with his eloquent professional skills and mentored the staff about efforts and skills to be employed for converting an enquiry into registration. It helped the centre to launch the first batch within one month followed by the 2nd batch in the next month. It was momentous and great morale booster for the team. It was a good show in terms of absolute numbers of registrations but not satisfying considering the very large number of foot-falls we had.

Made serious efforts to improve Institute's
success (conversion) ratio

The poor success (conversion) ratio was a matter of concern. Therefore, we stepped up our follow-up and marketing efforts to create better awareness about NIS as a lead agency of training, the programs offered by it and prospects of a decent job after completion of the program by a student. We put in more ads, full of meaningful contents, in the local media, increased the number of hoardings and banners in the town, and launched publicity campaign in nearby towns like Hardwar, Rishikesh and Saharanpur. Also started building up personal contacts with influential teachers/ principles in colleges and schools, holding seminars in the centre and local colleges/schools for spreading awareness about NIS, what courses it offers, why should I join NIS, prospects of getting a decent job after finishing the course and placement support provided by NIS.

Dehra Dun has a very large number of research Institutes of G.O.I with number of employees running into thousands. We conducted awareness programs in some of the leading Institutes and their attached residential colonies. Finding out innovative ways to create awareness about NIS was a regular feature of our campaigns. Holding fun parties and bashes with band in attendance for students at the centre itself served twin objectives; entertainment and fun for students to motivate them to share their happy experience with their friends, (a promotion technique called 'spreading business through word of mouth') and building up satisfaction amongst the staff and motivating them to put in coordinated efforts in business promotion.

NIS's concept of training through part-time courses for a professional career was new in the education space. It enabled students after 12th standard to continue their UG studies in colleges and also pursue the professional program at NIS. This was known as dual-qualification opportunity; by the time, the students finished their college studies they were eligible for a job having already completed their professional training program/diploma at NIS. Our continuous efforts yielded good results for us.

During six years of its functioning, Dehra Dun centre imparted training to about 450 students in Sales and Marketing programs of different durations and supported them in getting jobs, besides short duration courses like personality development, communication skills and training in spoken English.

In NIS family of about 45 centres, we were rated as one of the top ten.

Commendable performance of staff members

One name that props up gloriously in NIS, Dehra Dun's success story is Kalyan Sen. He came up on the scene, without any efforts by me and who offered his services enthusiastically of his own volition, right from beginning and stayed behind me as a reliable support. I was alone and badly needed the help of some young reliable hand to build up the tempo of numerous activities for meeting the dead-line of launch of the Centre. His first major contribution was helping us in selection of a Counsellor, who was expected to play a stellar role in motivating the foot-falls to join the Institute. And thanks to him again, we were lucky to secure the services of a very competent candidate, Ms. Sandhya Panwar. Her performance happened to be excellent and full credit is due to her in the quick launch of 2 batches within the first two months. Not only this, Kalyan continued to help me in various important activities like building up contacts, identifying some important service providers and also running around for seeking appointments for me to meet principals and teachers in schools and colleges. His gratuitous support without any offer of pecuniary benefit from my side was really gratifying. It is another matter that subsequently, he was appointed as a Faculty after successfully competing with others. He continued to serve NIS, Dehra Dun, diligently for more than 5 years when he was selected by a leading Insurance Co. as their Training Manager.

Another name that is worthy of mention and great appreciation is Lipakshi Arora, my partner, Mr. Baldev Raj's daughter. This young lady would be in the centre regularly and provide critical support to the Counsellor in motivating the footfalls in joining the institute. Her contribution in conceiving and professionally organizing Institute's first Annual Day function and making it a big success is worthy of being recalled with pride. Her creative faculties surprised us all. I am grateful still for her contribution.

The Project, NIS, delivers good financial results

Summing up, despite constraints, hurdles and unhelpful attitude of my partner, we were able to achieve great success in generating good amount of revenue to the delight of head office and also ourselves. I repaid the entire bank loan of rupees thirteen lakhs along with very heavy amount of interest (approximately fifteen lakhs) within the stipulated time-frame. Our centre's track record; generating handsome business and maintaining high standards of education earned us the pleasure of being rated among the top ten centres of NIS country-wide. The ultimate yard-stick of measuring success of a professional training institute is measured in terms of its track-record of placements secured for its pass-out students. Here too, our performance was excellent. We were the first small-town centre which had the honour of getting recognition from the high profile MNC, Coca-Cola who picked up five of our students after rigorous process of selection. Till then, Coca-Cola had been focusing on NIS's metro centres only. Barring some students who joined our programs for enhancing professional skills and shoring up their confidence level to handle confidently their family's business, we provided full support to our students for placement either through our own efforts or with the support provided by head office. Our track record in this vital support to students was excellent, almost 100 %. Some of our female students whose prime objective was personality development and grooming too were deeply satisfied and confessed, "The program at NIS has helped us immensely in meeting our objective; enhancing prospects of success in matrimony in high-end families."

Shift in focus by NIS; a disaster for Franchisees like us

Unfortunately, NIS shifted its focus from career education to corporate training in early 2000 and this turned out to be a real tragedy; rather a betrayal of serious magnitude for franchisees like us. The hard work we had done to build up brand 'NIS', the huge investments we had made and the expectations of great future evaporated. The tragedy was callous considering that by the time brand 'NIS' became a known and reliable source of pool of trained Sales Professionals, NIS, HO, called it a day as far as career education segment was concerned. This decision came at a time when the stake-holders of the venture; franchisees like us, students and Industry, all were happy for their own reasons. The franchisees were happy for the venture was at a take-off stage now, the Captains of the Industry were happy for they had found a reliable source of trained Sales Professionals now and the students were happy for finding a great career opportunity as Sales Professionals. In fact, NIS Brand was at a final take-off stage now. An opportunity of great significance was lost due to ill-considered decision of NIS. And the biggest tragedy and deception was that we the most important stake-holders were not taken into confidence before taking such a crucial and drastically negative (for us) business decision. I realized to my dismay and chagrin the precarious position we, the franchisees, had vis-à-vis our principal. The franchise agreement we had signed was 100 % one-sided and in any case, it was no use putting in more money now in fighting it out in the court of law. Practical wisdom demanded that we got busy in winding up and settling the final accounts with NIS. After lot of struggle and with help from the Auditor and an officer from NIS, who was aware of the process of winding up, I succeeded in receiving the final dues from NIS pretty soon. A good riddance considering the situation we were faced with.

Terminated the arrangement with my partner

The final settlement with NIS happened sometimes in 2002, where after the issues related to distribution of residue assets of the venture and settlement with my partner had to be handled. Believe me, the experience with him turned out to be nerve-wrecking and extremely painful. Very soon, it was obvious, that any just and reasonable settlement shouldn't be expected. Surely, I was in for a heavy financial loss but not inclined to fight for it. I surrendered mentally and got prepared for any loss in a settlement. Frankly, I found myself to be under grave mental pressure considering the over-all position. After-all he was introduced to me for the tie-up by a person whom I thought to be like my elder brother and who, I believed, would be hurt if the matter resulted in big controversy. Having lived an honest clean life as a proud govt. employee I had not known that majority of businessmen have different approach in relationship. That

367

Goddess Lakshmi (Money) is the only mantra that matters the most in life was revealed to me during the course of this association. Ultimately, I gave up and relieved myself of the continuously agonizing pain. Thank God, that was a good riddance!! After all, it gave me the most precious gift; peace of mind.

Chapter 3
A Big Poser; What Next After NIS?

The old ghost phrase, "What Next and what to do?" started haunting me once again after I completed the process of settlement with NIS, wound up operations and arrived at an understanding with my partner for termination of the arrangement. I was about 67 then and could jolly well think of calling it a day and retire from active work-life but no, it was not to be. Why? I realized; it was beyond me to start looking for some other passion now other than work. And financially also I was not comfortable yet. A single track person that I have always been had focused on job only. Everything else was secondary. Little did it ever occur to me that besides hard-work in office, I had a responsibility towards myself also? Literally, yes I was taking care of my own and my family's economic needs but in the hustle and bustle of all this, I didn't realize that I was ignoring some equally important need; leisure, introspection or a hobby for enriching life. In the process of burgeoning and hectic work life, the finer urges of mind and soul got side-lined. The rat race to excel continued unabated till it was too late to think of other constructive diversions seriously. Any way it was no use now to stoke the flames of dis-satisfaction. What was best suited and appropriate in those circumstances was well-accomplished, I argued with myself. After all, satisfaction of basic needs is always the first priority for any responsible individual.

Krishan Aneja

What is a complete life?

Clarity of thought, creative thinking and determining in time the correct priorities helps to push ahead, clears the cob-web of doubts and phobia, helps in developing a long term vision, generates positive energy which in turn provides impetus to the urge for putting in one's best efforts for striving to seek a balance between work-life and other diversions for a meaningful complete life. The end-result of such an approach in life would lead to steady performance on both counts which in turn would lead to the stage where one feels happy and fully satisfied. And, well, this is the ultimate goal which a seeker of fulfilment can aspire for in life. It is God's Grace that He equipped human beings with brains to learn to strive and know what is good, what is just, what is appropriate in a given situation, what is meaningful, equitable and worthy of being pursued for total freedom. Satisfying own and family's personal needs is no big achievement. This routine is taken care even by animals and birds that the Lord Almighty has not blessed with brains.

"Did I measure up to all this?" keeps haunting me. I acknowledge, I did succeed in generating resources just enough to take care of family's pecuniary needs of running the house-hold and other current expenses but not enough to generate surpluses leading to the comfort of capital formation or big investments. God's Grace, that our spending on children's higher professional education was minimal. They did us proud and entered into professional courses on their own through their successful performance in competitive entry tests.

On the whole, I have the comfort of reiterating that I devoted my maximum to job only to achieve what really matters in job; satisfaction, growth and well-earned recognition. That in the process, I neglected my urge for hobbies etc. didn't matter then and rightly so. The phrase in urdu, "Sab ko mukammal jahan nahin milta" is reason enough for my satisfaction. The sum-total: though I was awfully occupied with my vocation and busy in discharging sincerely my responsibilities as head of the family, yet I was carefree and happy, am like this only even now and God willing shall be happy like this only till my last!! O, My Lord, help me!!

Workaholic life schedule; my privilege

Let me confess; throughout my life, I never felt any time I was free. Being free meant a vacuum. Before I finished an assignment, I always found the next one was in queue. You have not yet finished the next one and the third raises its head seeking attention. Hence, there was no time for any thought other than completing the tasks one after the other, whether in office or at home.

I do not know why but I always overlooked or postponed or cut short my personal daily routine to be able to rush in time to my work-place. Spending lot of time in getting ready has been an anathema to me. With everything having been properly arranged and kept in its designated place before-hand, there was no reason for personal daily morning routine to take a lot of time. Probably, it has something to do with my approach to life; single track and focused on first priority of the moment. Big attention to personal care didn't figure anywhere. Hurry up and get ready quick was all that I knew. I never cared to use various items of cosmetics. Good quality bathing soap, some shampoo and some oil sometime was all that I needed. Take proper care of personal hygiene and cleanliness, dress-up properly in a tidy, clean and ironed dress and that is all. Of-course, I have been particular about choice of colours, dress, its stitching and foot-wear etc.

I was not alone in believing like this. The fact was that both of us always thought that while our personal needs could be postponed, curtailed or ignored, but not the other jobs/responsibilities before us. A belief existed somewhere in our psyche that making sacrifices and ignoring personal needs is a virtue, especially when it results in some satisfaction for those whom we love. I may not have been unduly rigid in this matter but making a sacrifice for the sake of kids has been almost a matter of faith for Mrs. Aneja.

Happy side-effects of a workaholic life

We did have part-time helping hand for daily chorus at home but engaging some-body on whole-time basis was beyond us. The resultant scenario was wonderful; enjoy finishing the tasks in the evenings and enjoy care-free sound sleep during night. In fact, both of us would fall asleep as soon as we reach the bed and enjoy the bliss of happy good morning. As a result, neither of us knew what was bed-time gossiping. Considering the present scenario of rampant maladies like hyper-tension, stresses and insomnia etc., I feel we were/are lucky to be gifted with the bliss of sound sleep and a happy 'Good-morning'. The same routine, more or less, happened every day, sometimes irritating of-course. Healthy breaks used to be the occasional visits/social calls to a friend's place or a party or a visit to a movie theatre/club in week-ends. Holiday/vacation/break etc. were not so common, as it is now. However, the family did go to a number of towns like Kolkatta, Varanasi, New Delhi, Chandigarh and some other important historical sites. In addition, attending some marriages in the family, a social function or some pilgrimage was thought to be a happy relief and an enjoyable diversion/change.

The compelling next consideration;
get busy to ensure financial security for the family

Having remained happily busy in work and seeking satisfaction there from was alright but financially we were still not secure. It was alright that both of us worked hard throughout but it was also a fact that the resources generated by Mrs. Aneja in her school and me in NIS after retirement mostly went to meet family's current needs of running expenses, house building's upgrade, daughter's marriage, a better car and other expenses of capital nature like acquisition of gadgets etc. for the house-hold. Why, because financially, the hard-earned money was adequate enough to make us comfortable at managing current needs but not comfortable enough with savings/capital for our future and old age. We were a typical middle-class family, 'Safed-Posh' in common parlance. Satisfying the ever increasing aspirations in the family in tune with the changing environment too was in the horizon. Therefore, I started looking for an option; part-time, of my liking, enabler of generating some revenue and not calling for any big-ticket investment.

An offer came my way from a local Management Institute to work as a part-time Faculty for MBA students and I was delighted at the idea but the terms offered were in no way commensurate with the efforts and labour I was expected to put in for the job. Therefore, I declined it and started looking for some other option.

Finally short-listed call; go for stock market operations

Finally, I chose stock-trading and investment in equities as a part-time option to keep myself busy and put in efforts to make some money. This option met, more or less, the parameters I had in mind for remaining busy for few hours in the morning. Go in the morning after break-fast and come back in time for lunch, stay at home and make some moves, when conveniently possible. I wasn't crazy about creating a huge wealth out of this activity considering the limited funds available for this activity coupled with the thought of avoiding being rash. Since it was my first exposure and I wasn't aware much about tricks of intra-day trading, I concentrated on deliveries. The focus was short-term and long-term investment both. Luckily for me, the market started looking up soon, thanks to positive policy announcements by the Govt. It was a good beginning for me. The market boom lasted for about 2, 3 years and I was happy.

The market and stocks' movements are un-predictable, novices like me do get swayed by hypes created by media, make wrong moves, land up in trouble and suffer losses. I was no exception but over-all it was a mixed bag situation for me. India's economy was on growth track, policies of Govt. were focused on reforms and the corporate houses were dishing out attractive results. I continued to be reasonably active but not rash. Functioning within reasonable limits was my prime attitude. Therefore, the gains and losses were modest but I continued with this activity to keep my-self busy. Trying to track the markets through media (electronic and print both), doing analysis of the results and being in touch with over-all economic scene was an interesting effort. This exercise used to keep me posted with the trend and enabled me to think seriously and make reasonably informed moves.

Disillusioned, I dilute my involvement in stock market operations

The un-predictable ups and downs and the swings in stock market indices were irritating. The more I tried to find the logic, the more I got confused. The old-timers and die-hard fellows would console me saying, "Market swings are related to news-flow and sentiments; genuine and fabricated both." Catch-up, be in touch with analysts and you will be happy. I would make efforts to update myself with the news and tried to anticipate moves by Cos. based on such news, worked hard to understand and follow the hints behind analysis dished out by experts on the TV channels, did my own analysis of news and tried to look at logic and rationale but was disillusioned. Most of the times, the result would be a wrong move and in frustration, I would give up and suffer a loss. This happened mostly in secondary market deals. The moves in IPOs turned out to be gainful. On the whole, it has been a mixed bag. In due-course, due to pre-occupation with other important responsibilities, my involvement in stock markets came to stop though I have been making moves in MF schemes of equities and debt both.

A paradigm shift makes us happily busy

Both our sons, Sandeep and Ashish were in USA. The urge to meet them as frequently as possible and also the need to render support to them at the time of new arrivals in their families necessitated frequent visits to USA. The period of stay there was mostly of longer durations for obvious reasons. These visits being of longer durations (5 to 6 months at a time) meant that we reduce our engagements in India. Hence, in these circumstances, Mrs. Aneja shut down her school in 2006 with a very heavy heart consoling herself with the satisfaction of being able to provide help and support to our sons and their families in their hours of need. It goes without saying that to close the school after 20 years of glorious performance was the most difficult decision. I will try to explain later in details the real and vibrant happiness and satisfaction that the school had provided to her for over twenty years and how she helped the poor parents in her desire to support the needy section of society.

A new phase begins in our life

Now began a new phase in our life. Responsibility towards children was over, school had been closed down and I had decided to wind up my stock-market engagements. We were free, no doubt, but unsure about how to remain purposefully engaged in some sublime activity. In other words, there came to an end the last vibrant chapter in our life. We were no more formally busy in any routine. Suddenly we were free but direction-less. We had no agenda before us. Free time was not a pleasure as it should be. A workaholic all his/her life suddenly realizing that he/she has nothing substantive to do now, starts believing that life has stopped, a dead end has arrived. For us, the situation was more perilous. That we may have to visit USA again was a reality but when was uncertain. True, the visits to USA were a necessity and also an obligation to our children but a game-changer for us at the same time. Whatever plans we might think of for ourselves appeared to be tentative only. Just for record sake, our last visit to USA to provide support to our younger son's family happened in 2008-2009 and we came back in March, 2009 and that was it.

Realities of life prevailed over a period of time and we got reconciled to this new phase in our life but not without quiet rumblings within.

In retrospect; closing down school, a hasty decision?

Frankly speaking, Mrs. Aneja found it difficult to reconcile to this sudden vacuum. Twenty long years of her most satisfying days in school were difficult to forget. She yearned to go back to her past glorious life; rendering yeoman's service (education and knowledge) to the needy and poor students of the neighbourhood like a charitable missionary work. The present phase was really agonizing to her. She felt rootless, rued the emptiness she faced now. In retrospect, I also feel the decision to close down the school was a gross ignorance of its fateful impact later in her life; because it proved to be too difficult for her to think of another option now. Adjust with the circumstances and try to find out ways to be happily busy was the answer.

Krishan Aneja

Braced happily the change

What worked for us? "Take note of the changed circumstances, happily adjust with the emerging scene, keep your cool and find out newer options appropriate to ground realities, and the age factor."

Perceptions and priorities are a dynamic phenomenon. They throw up alternatives in tune with one's position influenced by the overshadowing past, the existing scene and coming future. And we were no exception. Now that Mrs. Aneja didn't have a regular work-routine like looking after her school, she started trying to find satisfaction in different ways one of which was; sit down for prayers and sing devotional songs in her sweet melodious voice. I know she is very enthusiastic about it and whenever an occasion presents itself, she indulges in this act whole-heartedly and with full sincere devotion. In our family and circle of friends she is well-known for an exquisite charm in rendering the devotional songs with sweet grace. This is her Divine strength and gives her blissful satisfaction in abundance. Apart from singing the 'Bhajans' herself, she loves to listen to devotional music on Radio/TV. I wonder why she didn't make it an inseparable daily routine in her early life or adopted it as a hobby or profession. Most likely, it was due to her preference to help her own family in difficult times. Now that she does have free time, she tries to remain busy by doing knitting, embroidery, stitching and other similar activities making some articles of need for the family or making some innovative gift articles for her grand-children. Hats off to this woman, my life-partner, who never complains about the change and finds out some creative house-hold activity to remain busy.

In comparison to her, I am lucky a bit. I have to frequently visit market for grocery, provisions, fruits and vegetables and other articles of needs, go to Bank/Post office, go to hospital for consultation and picking up medicines etc., visit state govt. offices for making payments of utility bills and many other similar chores to attend to. More or less, such activities keep me engaged till afternoon followed by lunch and mid-day nap. In the afternoons, I get busy in reading newspapers, magazines/books etc., go for a long walk or some other activity. Evenings keep us busy

376

in watching some TV programs etc. And see, the day gets over for me without much hassles.

For the last more than four years, i.e. commencing from July, 2010, I am busy writing my memoirs and now there is no question 'how to remain happily busy' before me. A real big change it is; satisfying to the core enabling me to delve into past and giving me an opportunity to understand myself, derive comfort that I am baring myself by narrating my own story in my own way and make attempts to present my achievements, my failings and capability to face life as it presented itself.

Let posterity judge whether we succeeded in adjusting to the changed circumstances and came out successful. However, my answer is yes and no both. Yes, because we rose and delivered best what was expected of us at different intervals in our life and no because we didn't foresee/ anticipate comprehensively the change that was in the horizon for us in the middle age. We also ignored what was apparent and our due i.e. sparing time for ourselves in leisure, developing some hobbies of substance or indulge in pastime/games and sports as a routine. That is not to say that we are not comfortable now or harbour some regrets. On the contrary, we both are satisfied that, Thanks to His Krupa, we are able to manage ourselves our house-hold chorus and also attend to our health-care needs. Touch-wood, it is deeply satisfying that with His Grace there have been very few occasions when our children had to rush to our aid in an emergency. We do try to keep ourselves physically fit and mentally alert. 'Healthy mind in healthy body' is what we believe in and also make efforts to live it.

PART - VI

෨෨

Some reflections

What sustains human beings?

'Contentment' when nothing more remains to aspire for in life. Contentment generates the solemn energy of clean thoughts. Its foundation is built on sound moral aptitude and values of ethics. Life journey becomes very smooth for a contented person. He/she is satisfied and happy in a world of his/her own. Thinking ill of others is alien to him/her. It makes him/her understand the meaning of true love and compassion. It builds bridges of tolerance and mutual understanding, regards and adjustment. It also helps in developing creative faculties being free of mundane thoughts for survival. Contentment may appear to be elusive but surely it is achievable.

Gautama Buddha said, "Health is the greatest Gift; Contentment is the greatest wealth and faith and trust make for the best relationship."

I believe; the gift of blessings of contentment is available for all but only those who deserve it get it. 'He is Kind and Generous for all but not for those who are egoists, greedy and blindly self-centred. To them, He leaves un-touched of civility, compassion and open heart. First deserve, be worthy of His Krupa, have unwavering faith in His System of rewards and punishment, then desire and make your request most humbly. Do not complain if your request is not heard any time. Who knows you didn't deserve it this time or it was not your due. Persist and pray with an open heart.

Request Him to grant you the strength to be able to discharge satisfactorily all your worldly day to day responsibilities, be able to look after yourself and be blessed with calmness and grace when His Messengers come calling at the end of your itinerary on earth. Remember, death is not the end of life. You enter a new glorious phase if your track-record has been absolutely clean and worthy of His Kind and Benevolent Largesse. Agreed; it is not so easy to reach this level of satisfaction and contentment but is not difficult either. As a first step, gradually keep reducing your needs and expectations, try to control your senses particularly taste buds and your tongue for it has propensity to invite trouble by indulging in loose talk, avoid outbursts of rage on slightest provocation, stop hankering after variety, look the other way when being chased by an un-healthy temptation, happily adjust to what comes your way and be thankful to Him for giving you the instinct to seek satisfaction through positive acts. Needs, choices, preferences and tendency to fall prey to ill acts ought to reduce in direct proportion to growing age. Equanimity and peace of mind are two happy twins. Make attempts to be their friend and a companion to make a deep lasting imprint of happiness in life. This would appear to be a very serious and difficult code of conduct in life. But actually it is not so. It is an ideal way of life that one need not impose suddenly. One surely can aspire to build it up gradually sequentially. Thank Him day in and day out for all that you have. This is what sustains life and gives it colour. It is my concept of 'Karma' theory of doing one's best and leaving the result in His Hands. 'Moksha' I do not know.

What really matters in life?

My work-life can be summed up as a long phase of sincere hard work with honesty of purpose. Acquit yourself responsibly well, be determined to excel and relax not until the goal is achieved. Yes, it did mean struggles, pulls and pressures but the will to deliver, come what may, was always dominant. The determination to out-perform did not permit me to relax. The guiding principles throughout my journey have been, "Be focused on the target, keep pushing until satisfied with the outcome, overlook pin-pricks, and do not get way-laid by assorted temptations." The underlying message throughout has been, "Let not the obstacles and detractions undermine your enthusiastic approach to the task. Innovate and simplify the process. Push away the thought of lack of ability, if any, to accomplish the job successfully." The born optimist that I have been didn't let the negatives creep into my psych. Building up expectations and looking for a bright future, seeing silver lining on the horizon in tandem with performance, aspiring for a healthy outcome, never losing hope even when facing overwhelming odds has been my main-stay in life.

In all these endeavours, the catalyst that built up dreams was my self-confidence to accomplish, come what may. Never gave up in desperation, thought of viable alternatives when in two minds and didn't feel shy to take the advice of seniors and consult pals when necessary. Overlooking personal comforts and ignoring the destabilizing emotions was a regular routine when face to face with challenges at hand.

The learning process

It is true that all what I have mentioned above is not only ideal, high-sounding and appears difficult to imbibe in real life. It is also improbable that a lay and just a little literate person like me could gather all this wisdom. True, but it is not my case that I learnt it all at once or was born gifted with this wisdom. No, it has been an evolutionary process. It was a process of self-learning and I gathered the bits of wisdom as I moved along the path of struggles and kept my eyes and ears open. Remaining awake and sensitive and being attentive to what elders and other senior visionaries say has been my routine.

The work life took its course and moved on happily forward opening up avenues and vistas of growth. And the end result is what reflects in my growth chart.

It is indeed creditworthy and marvellous that a very long spell of work-life passed off peacefully; no enquiries for any misdemeanour or under cloud for any misdeeds and I laid office with dignity and respect. I am conscious and humbly grateful that it all happened due to His Benign subtle Guidance throughout this long spell. I can vouchsafe, an unknown inner call took charge of the situation and guided me to make the right move whenever I found myself at cross roads or in two minds for taking a final decision.

Fulfilment in life; a sure possibility for all

I believe, to be able to keep in focus long-term vision and attain fulfilment is possible only:-

If one's mind is open and thought process is clean, when one's focus is on Dharma,

when there is no ill-will/malice towards others,

when one is able to listen to tweets from within,

when one is at peace within,

when one has the capability to see a dazzling bright future on the horizon,

when one possesses the determination to move ahead on the right path without caring for the results and,

when the inputs are squeaky clean and boisterous, the reward of success follows.

One has to be honest in what one believes in, perform and let the matter rest there. During my days in Dehra Dun (1949-52) when going to a nearby temple every morning was a daily routine for me, I often heard the key exponent there, Pandit Gopal Krishna, telling the audience, "That keeping one-self engaged in assigned job without boasting that I am the 'Doer' is the essence for a happy life. Human beings are at best 'Karta' only. Your role ends when you do your duty most sincerely. He used to make it light saying, "Leave the burden of accomplishment on His Shoulders; He is always available. He watches and listens to what we say. He surely Blesses the efforts that merit fulfilment."

Most likely, this simple exposition took roots in my psych and innocuously guided me in my journey.

My vibrant destiny; a dream come true

My thanks are due to Destiny for guiding me throughout my journey;

helping me identify and spot opportunities when at cross-roads,

not letting my ambitions to go wild, keeping under check the illegal temptations and possible slide-down,

opening up path-breaking avenues of growth for me,

never letting me have a feeling of being alone,

saving me of awkward and embarrassing situations in work-life,

bestowing peace of mind and enabling me to see merit in what was really meritorious and shun what was un-ethical,

kept me engrossed and happily busy in my job and assignments thus denying me time to indulge in idle gossiping, conspiracies or thoughts of revenge etc.,

be free of pettiness and jealousies in my psych,

let me believe in honesty, integrity in dealings,

introduced in me the concept of being open and free in welcoming new ideas of virtue,

prevented me from adopting hostile, petty minded and aggressive attitude,

bestowed me with the cardinal principle of believing that the person I am going to deal with in life is honest and open until his conduct reveals the opposite,

made me approach difficult issues with an open mind and conviction and,

last but not the least, showering His Blessings to let me be free and happily ready to absorb some good values in life.

That it was a smooth sailing always and I didn't face problems or faced no awkward and embarrassingly difficult situations or there were no temptations to lure me and destabilize me or there were no threats and challenges, would be an understatement. I did face them all from time to time but all this didn't deter me and couldn't stop me from going ahead on the right path.

In all this process, I don't know if I offended somebody un-intentionally. My sincere apologies if someone felt hurt because of me.

Some praise-worthy quotes

"Prayer is my secret."

"On all occasions of trial He has saved me. I know that the phrase 'God saved me' has a deeper meaning for me today and still I feel that I have not yet grasped its entire meaning. Only richer experience can help me to a fuller understanding.

But in all my trials, of a spiritual nature, as a lawyer, in conducting institutions, and in politics, I can say that God saved me. When every hope is gone, 'when helpers fail and comforts flee', I experience that help arrives somehow, from I know not where. Prayer has been the saving of my life. Without it I should have been a lunatic long ago. In spite of despair staring at me in the face on the political horizon, I have never lost my peace. That peace, I tell you, comes from prayer.'

Mahatma Gandhi

"Nearly all men can stand adversity but if you want to test a man's character, give him power."

Abraham Lincoln

"Farming looks easy when your plough is a pencil."

Dwight D Eisenhower

There is no need for temples, no need for complicated philosophies. My brain and my heart are my temples, my philosophy is kindness."

The XIV Dalai Lama

"If the mind becomes balanced and detached and comes to dwell in its own true home, imbued with love of God, then it enjoys the essence of supreme spiritual wisdom; it shall never feel hunger again."

Sri Guru Granth Sahib.

"We need to be aware of our own-selves, our body, our breadth, our mind, how the mind works. Become confident of who you are."

Sri Sri Ravi Shankar

"Life has been compared with a battle and rightly so, as each day comes up with a new set of challenges which we must meet. One cannot just shy away from problems if one has to survive. One has to meet the challenges with courage."

Sam Veda

"Life is a journey of experiences and every set-back is indeed a new experience for greater learning and growth. As we create positive beliefs around our set-backs, we feel more empowered and experience greater equanimity."

Anonymous

"The energy of the mind is the essence of life."

Aristotle

"Life is a balance between rest and movement."

Osho

"In school, you are taught a lesson and then given a test. In life, you are given a test that teaches you a lesson."

Tom Bodett

"I know by my own pot how others boil."

French Proverb

Value the present.

"Yesterday is but a dream; tomorrow is only a vision. But today well-lived makes every yesterday a dream of happiness and every tomorrow a vision of hope."

Kalidasa

Do not dwell in the past, do not dream of the future; concentrate the mind on the present moment.

Gautama Budha

"Life has been compared with a battle and rightly so, as each day comes up with a new set of challenges which we must meet. One cannot just shy away from problems if he has to survive. He has to meet the challenges with courage."

Sam Veda.

Annexure
My Heritage, My Background.
My ancestors

To know and collect authentic information about one's origin and ancestors is stimulating and many healthy minds face such an urge. It gets stronger as we progress in life and age. It is similar to what we, the social animals, feel in the form of a collective desire in society to chronicle its history and culture that helped shape society's present.

I always had a feeling that my ancestors were educated, enjoyed respectable status/position in society and were economically and financially well off. Although, no clear supporting details were known, but few anecdotes narrated on different occasions by my mother fed my curiosity to learn more about my ancestors.

An important bit of information given by my mother was that our father migrated from his native village 'Khanglanwala to Isa Khel, the sub-divisional headquarters on the banks of river Indus to be able to pursue his studies unhindered. I also learnt that my father's cousin brother was the Headmaster of the Primary school in Isa Khel and our father's uncle (our grand-father's brother) was a senior teacher in Kundian, another sub-divisional town in Mian-wali district. These important clues surely pointed to our elders' penchant for education which was rare in a backward region like ours in those ancient times.

Our native place, Khaglan Wala, was a prosperous village near Isa Khel where our grand-parents lived. Our family had large land holdings and our grand-father was a big stockiest and trader of herbs and was also a medical practitioner of repute. My father was the only son of his parents but had large number of cousin brothers.

My urge to gather more information about my ancestors

A lingering feeling always goaded me to do something more to know more about my ancestors. A sudden idea, one day, showed me the way out. I told myself; go to Hardwar, meet the family chronicler Pundit ji there, have a look at the old record books available with him and try to dig out information about forefathers available in these books.

During my visit along with my elder brother on June 12, 1989 when we had gone to Hardwar for immersion of mortal remains of our mother, we were successful in locating our family's Pundit ji and had recorded our visit in our family's chronicle maintained by him.

What are these Chronicles?

These books are unique valuable pool of information about visits to Hardwar by elders since times immemorial. They date back to $18^{th}/19^{th}$ century AD or even earlier, contain live notes mentioning the date and purpose of visit recorded by family elders in their own hand-writing. Seeing these notes in elders' own hand-writing is a unique mesmerizing experience. It is a wonderful nostalgic dose, enough to transport oneself, in a way, to the date and age of elders' visit.

In ancient times, maintaining diaries by individuals was not so common. Therefore, there was no reliable source of information for knowing about one's predecessors. It is here that these chronicles served a very useful purpose; enabling the seekers to satisfy their urge to know about their past and elders.

I visit Hardwar to scan our family's chronicles

The urge to know more about my ancestors took me to Hardwar on 15/11/2012 and met our family's Pundit. The moment I mentioned Isa Khel and Aneja and told him of my last visit in June, 1989, he immediately brought the relevant chronicle. And then he started un-rolling one book after another containing record of visits by our elders earlier. With his help, I collected the following information about my elders:-

Grand-father's name—Sahib Ram,

Great grand –father's name—Fateh Chand. His brothers' names were Ghanna Ram, Uttam Chand and Punnu Ram,

Great great grand-father's name---Ballu Ram,

Next senior's name---Asa Nand,

Our father came to Hardwar along with family on 19/10/1923 for a dip in holy Ganges, a pilgrimage-cum-family vacation,

Our father again visited Hardwar on 18/3/1924. This time it was for immersion of our grand-father Sahib Ram's ashes in holy river Ganga,

Our grand-father's brother, Tharu Ram, breathed his last at Rohtak, Haryana, on 21/4/1965 which suggests that our grand-father, Sahib Ram, had died at a very young age in comparison to his brother, Tharu Ram.

Our father's next visit to Hardwar was on 17/7/38 for a dip in holy Ganges along with his sister-in-law, the widow of Balak Ram.

It became obvious that these visits were undertaken either as a pilgrimage or for immersion of ashes of a deceased family member in holy Ganga. It was believed that the immersion of ashes in holy Ganga leads to salvation for the departed soul and it is the moral duty of the family to do it as a mark of respect and regards for the deceased family member.

A very interesting noting seen by me in the chronicle was that one of our fore-fathers came to Hardwar in 1878 and travelled to Gaya, a distance of about a thousand KMs; the obvious purpose being to perform some rituals there in the memory of someone who died a sort of un-natural death.

This denotes two important things; (i) our elders were highly religious minded and simple folks, had full faith in Holy Scriptures and (ii) ignoring severe hardships and risk to life, travelled long distances for following the scriptures even though no reliable means of transport were available.

It is said that most of these worthies especially those in ripe age bracket, were given a celebratory final send-off by family members, relatives, friends and village folk thinking they may not be able to come back considering the poor medical facilities available, long distances involved and problems associated with safety and security of life while travelling unescorted through insecure habitations and jungles when the animal-drawn carts were the only means of transport. It would take them months to complete the pilgrimage and there would be community celebrations when, if at all, these worthies returned back.

I found the book to be a wonderful read. It provides the reader a lot of insight into what it was like to be a part of the family and growing up facing several challenges in those times of the struggle during pre-partition & partition and re-establishing oneself post partition. It portrays very vividly, what a committed individual like you has gone through to get where you reached since you  *were a child. I have high respect for you and sharing these details of life was a brave thing to do.*

I am hopeful that everyone will take time to read this book.

Dinesh K. Sarraf
Chairman & Managing Director, ONGC Ltd.

Written with erudition, this autobiography of K. L. Aneja covering a wide area of his life is engrossing in substance, tone, and tenor. Lucid and engaging in style and laced with interesting facts and anecdotes, I am sure, this remarkable and inspiring book which bridges the gap between vision and action will evoke a thoughtful  *response in the mind of readers for their personal excellence.*

S.J.S. Ahluwalia
IA&AS
Retd. Accountant General, Punjab,
Chandigarh.

Printed in the United States
By Bookmasters